TRANSCENDING
POST-INFIDELITY
STRESS DISORDER

PISD

TRANSCENDING
POST-INFIDELITY
STRESS DISORDER

THE SIX STAGES OF HEALING

DENNIS ORTMAN, PhD

CELESTIAL ARTS
www.tenspeed.com

Celestial Arts
an imprint of Ten Speed Press
PO Box 7123
Berkeley, California 94707
www.tenspeed.com

Distributed in Australia by Simon and Schuster Australia, in Canada by Ten Speed Press
Canada, in New Zealand by Southern Publishers Group, in South Africa by Real Books,
and in the United Kingdom and Europe by Publishers Group UK.

Cover and text design by *the*BookDesigners

Poem on page 28 reprinted by permission of the publishers and the Trustees of Amherst
College from THE POEMS OF EMILY DICKINSON, Thomas H. Johnson, ed., Cambridge,
Mass.: The Belknap Press of Harvard University Press, Copyright © 1951, 1955, 1979, 1983
by the President and Fellows of Harvard College.

Excerpt on page 216 copyright © Watkins Publishers. Used by permission.
The Tao Te Ching (trans: Ralph Alan Dale) (Watkins Publishers, London, 2005).

Library of Congress Cataloging-in-Publication Data

Ortman, Dennis C.
Transcending post-infidelity stress disorder (PISD) : the six stages of healing / by Dennis
Ortman.
p. cm.
Includes bibliographical references and index.
Summary: "A psychologist uses post-traumatic stress disorder as a model for the partner
wounded by infidelity to explore rage and emotional pain and to learn the secrets of
recovery"—Provided by publisher.
ISBN 978-1-58761-334-0
1. Adultery. 2. Self-help techniques. I. Title.

HQ806.O78 2009
248.8′44—dc22

2008033607

Printed in the United States of America
First printing, 2009

1 2 3 4 5 6 7 8 9 10 — 13 12 11 10 09

In memory of Winifred Ennis, mother and friend,
and Rob Ortman, brother and Great Soul.

CONTENTS

ACKNOWLEDGMENTS

No one stands alone. We are all related, interconnected. Our lives are shaped in many ways, known and unknown, by everyone we encounter, up close and from afar. I want to acknowledge those who helped shape this work. I am grateful to my family who endured my absences and obsessing about the book yet still loved and supported me through the process. They continue to teach me the way of love. I am especially grateful to my wife, Francesca, who persistently offered encouragement, insight, and wise criticism. I am indebted to my supervisors, Paul Kaye and Bernard Mikol, who helped me understand human nature and the ways of healing. I am grateful to Ray Sayers and Mark Ortman for our discussions on religion and the ways of the Spirit. I want to thank Doug Childers who contributed immensely to making the manuscript a readable book. I also owe a debt of gratitude to the editorial staff of Celestial Arts, and especially to Lisa Westmoreland, who offered expert guidance throughout the publishing process. Finally, I want to thank my patients who shared their lives and trusted me enough to accompany them on their healing journeys.

PREFACE

Nothing cures like time and love.

—LAURA NYRO

I have firsthand experience with infidelity. I was unfaithful and have struggled for years with a heavy burden of guilt. Let me tell you my story. With admiration for my parish priests and encouragement from my family, I entered high school seminary at age thirteen. My heart was filled with love and devotion for the Catholic Church and the priesthood. I wanted nothing more than to serve the Church and her people as a priest for the rest of my life. Through my years in the seminary and theological studies in Rome, my devotion deepened, and I embraced celibacy as a way to be more available for the service of God's people. However, as the years passed and I served in various parishes in the Detroit area, I felt a deep loneliness that could not be remedied by my spiritual exercises or friendships. I became friends with a woman. As our friendship deepened, I felt longings to spend the rest of my life with her. But such a choice would involve giving up the priesthood I loved and breaking a promise I had made to the Church.

I struggled with that decision for three years in weekly therapy, prayer, and spiritual direction. I was torn between two loves, and I saw myself as being unfaithful to my commitment to the Church. In the discerning process, I faced my guilt for not keeping my word and my anxiety about beginning a new life at age forty, after living in the refuge of the Church for twenty-seven years as a seminarian and priest. Each day I prayed fervently for the gifts of the Holy Spirit: for wisdom and counsel to make the right decision, for knowledge of God's will for me, for apprehension of the veil of self-deception, and for fortitude (courage) to live out my decision. After three agonizing, yet liberating years, I decided to leave the active ministry and get married.

After leaving the priesthood, the crisis did not end but deepened. I encountered new challenges in being married with three stepchildren and starting a new career as a psychologist. I also grappled with feelings of profound grief for the loss of my former life, with all its joys, sorrows, and familiarities. The guilt was a constant companion, and I was wracked with anxiety about whether I would succeed in my new life, with all the financial pressures. I was also angry with the Church for all its rules and at myself for failing at my lifelong dream. Each day I prayed with a full heart for guidance and forgiveness. I also continued to pray for the gifts of the Holy Spirit, especially for wisdom and patience with myself and my family and generosity and faithfulness in my new life.

My personal soul-searching was paralleled in my new career as a psychologist. I graduated from the doctoral program in clinical psychology at the University of Detroit-Mercy. There is an interesting irony in my educational pursuit. While the University was a Catholic, Jesuit-run institution, the clinical psychology program was psychoanalytic. The program followed the tenets of Freud, sharing his suspicion of religion as a neurotic escape from reality. The personal irony for me was that I spent most of my life embracing religion and studying theology yet was being trained as a psychologist to dismiss them. In my subsequent professional work as a psychologist in private practice, I felt deeply the lack of soul (psyche). I felt alienated from the Catholic Church, like an outcast. That sense of alienation propelled me to search for wisdom from the Eastern, non–Judeo-Christian approaches to spiritual living, particularly Buddhism, which Buddha said was "about suffering and its relief." That approach mirrors what I am trying to achieve in therapy. To my amazement, I discovered a large common ground between Christianity and Buddhism, particularly in spiritual practices, ethics, and the belief in the sacredness of all creation in general, and human beings in particular. My explorations led me further to study other religious traditions, such as Sufi, Taoist, and Native American. In the process, I have come to appreciate the rootedness of these many religious traditions in the universal human spirit. With renewed enthusiasm in my work, I have attempted to integrate psychology and spirituality in my therapy. My firm conviction is that God's grace builds on and perfects human nature. However, I now think of God, less in denominational terms, but as the Great Mystery and Source of Life, beyond any conceptualizations. Our talk about the Supreme Being is really a feeble attempt to articulate a profound experience of the Divine, just "a finger pointing at the moon."

I see myself as a "wounded healer" in my therapeutic work. That is my current vocation. I am a companion with my patients, who are fellow sufferers and seekers of the truth about their lives. I encourage them to trust in their inner wisdom and competency to pursue their own life goals. Every day and before each session, I pray for my patients, often with the traditional Buddhist prayer of loving-kindness, wishing that they find happiness, peace, relief from suffering, and the deepest truth about themselves. I also pray for the gifts of the Spirit in my work, especially for wisdom, understanding, and a compassionate heart.

Numerous couples I see in therapy and several family and friends have shared with me their distress at being victims of infidelity. They expressed rage at being betrayed and reported sleepless nights, flashbacks, nightmares, numbness, and crippling anxiety. Through our discussions, we both realized that they were traumatized, which helped them accept with more patience their long journey toward recovery. Furthermore, I shared with them the insights I gained through my personal journey, particularly the possibility of healing and growth through spiritual understanding. Repeatedly, they told me how helpful it had been to view their trauma from a larger, spiritual perspective that does not dismiss the pain and sees it as an opportunity for growth. At their urging, I decided to write this book, with the hope of offering relief to many others who are suffering.

INTRODUCTION

The question haunts all of us, for me previously as a priest and now as a married man: "How can we make love last? How can we preserve love's passion and excitement without succumbing to the boredom of a lifelong commitment?" In the not too distant past, an *Ozzie and Harriet* ideal of family life reigned, at least in appearance. It seemed that relationships flowed with some ripples, but no disrupting tidal waves. Couples stayed together, somehow worked out differences, and accepted their commitments to lifelong marriages. Couples accepted their roles and were not too demanding of passion, adventure, romance, and excitement.

FRAGILE RELATIONSHIPS

But a tidal wave has hit, and we are left floating on a sea of change we cannot control or grasp. Often we feel like we are just treading water in our relationships. We now take our longings for passion, romance, and intimacy more seriously. We are more willing to leave a marriage if we do not enjoy the romance and passion we expect. Many of us have come to believe that the ideal of marriage for life is now unrealistic, impossible with today's longevity, or too restrictive of freedom.

A marriage without emotional closeness becomes a prison that needs to be escaped. The statistics about marriage reflect its instability: over half end in divorce.

THE TRAUMA OF BETRAYAL

Some marriages end with a whimper, and the couples simply grow apart. However, many others end with a bang. All too often, couples separate because one partner has been betrayed when the other has sought a fulfilling love elsewhere. While the numbers vary in the studies, some recent researchers have estimated that 37 percent of men and 20 percent of women have had sexual affairs sometime during their marriage.[1] More tellingly, 40 percent of divorced women and 44 percent of divorced men reported more than one sexual contact outside their marriage.[2] These are not just impersonal numbers; they represent persons who have experienced untold pain and confusion with disrupted lives. If you have been abandoned by a lifelong partner, you know how overwhelming and unspeakable the hurt and outrage can be.

In my fourteen years as a Catholic priest and seventeen years as a clinical psychologist in private practice, I have met many who have suffered the trauma of a discovered affair. I call it a trauma because of my observations that many of those who have discovered their partner's infidelity have been traumatized. They feel overwhelmed, enraged, and unable to cope with life. They are preoccupied with the betrayal, have nightmares about it, and suffer flashbacks. At times, they feel emotionally numb, then at other times, crazy. Their reaction can last for years and interferes with their capacity to enjoy their lives and trust others. I call their reaction "post-infidelity stress disorder," with the acronym PISD, which expresses the rage that is the primary symptom and the intensity of the feelings. I use this term not to suggest a new diagnostic category but to suggest a parallel with post-traumatic stress disorder, which has been well documented and researched. Those who have been wounded by their partner's infidelity are often filled with rage, directing their anger, obviously, toward their partner, but also against themselves in self-blame. They also project their anger onto the world of relationships, which becomes dangerous and evokes mistrust.

Some clients in my practice ask me, "Why can't I just get over the affair and move on with my life?" I find it is helpful to explain the nature of the trauma they experienced and how their reaction is a predictable response to an extraordinary event. I tell them their reaction is in many ways similar to those who have suffered life-threatening events, such as war, violent crimes, or auto accidents. In reality, their psychic lives have been threatened and their assumptions about their marriage shattered. These clients often breathe a sigh of relief and tell me, "I thought I was going crazy." In understanding their painful experience and reactions in the broader context of a traumatic response, they become more patient with themselves and the recovery process. They are enlightened by the parallel of their experience with others who have suffered post-traumatic stress disorder, which has received so much publicity lately. They feel more confident they will survive the journey on the road to recovery traversed by many others who have experienced life-threatening events.

HEALING THROUGH THE GIFTS
OF THE SPIRIT AND POWER OF FORGIVENESS

I have written this book for those who have been traumatized by the discovery of their partner's affair. I refer not just to the married, but to all in any committed relationship who have felt the sting of betrayal. I have written this book to offer hope to those who may feel lost and hopeless. Those who have been or are considering involvement in an affair may also benefit from this book, to appreciate the impact of their unfaithful behavior. Those who have been unfaithful also feel pain and need to be involved in their own recovery, a recovery that is similar in many respects to those who have been traumatized by infidelity. This book is a practical guide offering some insights, exercises, and advice to aid those with deep interpersonal wounds on their journey of recovery. Make no mistake that inner healing requires a journey with many turns and setbacks, a journey that takes time and effort but ends at a surprising place of peace, contentment, and wholeness.

I will reveal in advance the secret of recovery. But take heed that my recommendation may initially seem repulsive, unrealistic, or even impossible. That reaction is understandable in light of the terrible wound of unfaithfulness. Ultimately, you will recover from the trauma of infidelity to the extent that you forgive your offending partner and yourself. Forgiveness is the key to inner and lasting healing. Unless you release your anger and desire for revenge, replacing it with an attitude of kindness, you will not feel contentment. That is a strong, uncompromising statement. Nevertheless, my personal experience and clinical work confirm its truth. You forgive for your own sake, so you can mend your broken heart and find peace. Arriving at that place of forgiveness requires an extensive preparation of the emotions, mind, will, and heart. A forgiving attitude is the fruit of purposeful effort, a cultivation of virtues, and the healing of inner wounds.

In this book I will describe the journey toward forgiveness, which involves an unconditional acceptance of yourself and your unfaithful partner. I have delineated six stages in the process of forgiveness, which engage the emotions, mind, will, and heart. Each of these stages, or steps, represents a season of change on the journey toward wholeness and peace. Healing unfolds in stages from the ground up: from the body/feelings, to the mind, to the will (soul), to the spirit.

1. The first stage is to calm the emotional storm unleashed by the discovery of the affair. Like many who have been traumatized, your initial reaction may be one of shock, disbelief, and emotional numbness. You may shut down to survive. But soon you likely feel overwhelming anger, sadness, fear, shame, and maybe even guilt. The anger, in particular, protects you from being overwhelmed with pain. Working through the emotional storm, you can learn temperance (self-control), equanimity, patience, and fortitude (courage).

2. The second stage entails understanding why the affair happened. An affair is a way of disconnecting in the relationship. You will likely be disillusioned with your partner and obsessed with why the affair occurred. Understanding will bring you some relief and prepare you to make important decisions to rebuild your life.

3. The third stage involves coming to understand yourself, your interactions with your partner, and your personal struggles with intimacy. You may feel stuck imagining your partner as the powerful, guilty persecutor and yourself as the powerless, innocent victim. Such a one-sided misrepresentation will only set you up to repeat the tragic drama of betrayal. I tell my patients, "Unless you understand your part in the relationship, you will repeat the same dance with a different partner." Through the honest confrontation of your doubts and uncertainty, you begin to nurture the spiritual gifts of understanding, knowledge, and truthfulness.

4. The fourth stage involves making a wise decision about the relationship. Logically, there are only two options: to continue the relationship or end it. In either case, it will be important to understand yourself, your partner, and what went wrong in the relationship in order to make a wise decision. You will need to look deeply into yourself and discover what you really want and what is in your best interest. Grappling with this decision, you are nourished by and cultivate the Spirit's gifts of wisdom, counsel (right judgment), and fortitude.

5. The fifth stage, resulting from working through the previous stages, is discovering self-forgiveness, which is letting go of anger and embracing kindness. The primary symptom of PISD is rage, against your partner, yourself, and the world. You may well blame your partner for the affair but may also come to blame yourself for your blindness or not being an adequate partner. Forgiveness begins with accepting yourself and rebuilding your own self-esteem.

6. The final, and longest, stage of healing leads you to forgive your unfaithful partner. You recognize how your resentment saps your strength, peace, and contentment. You heal inwardly as the poison of anger is transformed into the medicine of compassion. Through recovery, your broken heart is opened up to love in a deeper way. You may also develop the virtues of generosity, gentleness, patience, and loving-kindness.

The stages of recovery through forgiveness are similar to the stages of grief described by Dr. Elizabeth Kübler-Ross in her classic work, *On Death and Dying*. She observed in her dying patients five overlapping stages in their facing the reality of death, the ultimate loss: (1) denial, (2) anger, (3) bargaining, (4) depression, and (5) acceptance. Before finally accepting death, patients typically deny they are dying, become angry and depressed, and bargain with God to spare them.[3] In a similar fashion, those who have been traumatized by the discovery of their partner's affair experience grief, which is a process that proceeds through identifiable stages:

1. Denial: shutting down, not wanting to believe the affair occurred

2. Anger: closing off behind a wall of rage

3. Bargaining: hanging on to old behaviors without acknowledging the need to change

4. Depression: pulling back from life

5. Acceptance: letting go of anger and opening up to a new life

These stages present emotional challenges that need to be negotiated for the advancement of inner healing. The reactions of denial, anger, bargaining, and depression are gradually transformed into openness and compassion. A heart broken and torn apart by betrayal becomes an open, tender heart that can reach out to others in love.

From my clinical work and personal conversations with friends, I have observed that those traumatized by the discovery of their partner's infidelity suffer both a personal and a spiritual crisis. They suffer a profound loss of faith, hope, and love. They experience a loss of faith because their assumptions about themselves, their partner, their relationship, and the meaning of their lives have been shattered, leaving them plagued by doubt and despair. Because their dreams of a happy future with their partner are destroyed, they experience a loss of hope. Because they are so filled with rage, their love and ability to trust again have disappeared.

The remedy for this spiritual crisis comes from the gifts and fruits of the Spirit, which are prayed for and nurtured through recovery.

While the gifts of the Spirit are beyond counting, the Hebrew scriptures list them as wisdom, understanding, counsel (right judgment), fortitude (courage), knowledge, piety (reverence), and fear of the Lord (wonder and awe) (Isaiah 11:2).[4] The fruits of the Spirit are presented in the Christian scriptures as love, joy, peace, patience, kindness, generosity, gentleness, faithfulness, and self-control (Galatians 5:22). There is an obvious parallel, which joins Eastern and Western spirituality, in the ten *paramitas* of Buddhism. These *paramitas* are perfections, qualities of being, that need to be nurtured in order to reach enlightenment. The *paramitas* are generosity, proper conduct, renunciation, wisdom, energy, patience, truthfulness, determination, loving-kindness, and equanimity.

A third parallel can be found in the traditional symbol of the Sacred Tree in Native American folklore.[5] The Sacred Tree is the rallying point for the tribe and possesses healing power. Its roots extend down to Mother Earth, and its branches reach up to Father Sky. The fruits of the tree are the gifts of the Great Spirit that bring the people nourishment and show them the path of wisdom, love, compassion, patience, generosity, humility, courage, and countless other blessings. These fruits grow under the right conditions, in their own time and season, bringing health and wholeness to the tribe.

While sharing common roots in the universal human spirit, these traditions view the virtuous qualities somewhat differently. From the Judeo-Christian perspective, the gifts and fruits of the Holy Spirit are freely given by God and are nurtured through disciplined effort into virtues. God's grace builds on and perfects our flawed human nature. In the Buddhist tradition, the *paramitas* are natural human qualities that we cultivate by mindful practice. They are the expression of our true nature, which has been obscured by ignorance, greed, and hatred. For the Native American tradition, all creation is spirit filled and bounteous with the blessings of the Great Spirit. The rhythms of nature, the seasonal changes, and particularly animals, reveal the path to wholeness. All these traditions teach that adversity is the fertile ground for the growth of these life-enhancing virtues. Virtuous living is ultimately the only remedy for suffering and the path to joy. In the end, what unites these traditions far surpasses what divides them because they possess a common spirit. As the Sufi mystic and poet Rumi expressed it, "Christian, Jew, Muslim, shaman, Zoroastrian, stone, ground, mountain, river, each has a secret way of being with the mystery, unique and not to be judged."[6]

The genuine recovery from the trauma of betrayal requires the release of the gifts of the Spirit, which are then nurtured through disciplined effort into virtues. The virtues are good habits of living that replace the self-defeating behaviors revealed by the affair. As a crisis, the discovered betrayal can become an opportunity for growth toward a more mature, wiser, and more compassionate love, either with or without the offending partner. The recovery process, though painful, can be the occasion to cultivate life-enhancing virtues that lead to authentic happiness.

The approach I take in this book is holistic, integrating psychological and spiritual insights. For the Eastern and Native American mind, there is no distinction between the psychological and spiritual, between the natural and supernatural, because there is no separate Deity. Human nature itself is sacred. Mindful practices and loving attention lead to wholeness and a sense of connectedness with all reality. For the Western mind, there is both a distinction and a connection between the human and the Divine. God freely bestows His gifts, which are received and nourished in faith. Grace builds on and perfects nature. Consequently, in the healing process, spiritual exercises, such as prayer, contemplation, and meditation, build on and perfect the use of our psychological resources, such as therapy, group support, and journaling.

This book is a spiritual guide through the trauma of betrayal that offers hope for new life. I use many stories from my clinical work to illustrate the struggle to overcome the interpersonal trauma of infidelity and arrive at a place of forgiveness, contentment, and inner peace. Names have been changed, details altered, and examples integrated to maintain confidentiality. Furthermore, I suggest many psychological and spiritual exercises drawn from both Western and Eastern wisdom traditions, particularly the Judeo-Christian and Buddhist. I believe that the naturally confident and awakened heart is a healing heart and that health occurs with the release of the gifts of the Spirit from within. As the Sufi sage Hazrit Ali expressed it, "Your medicine is in you, and you do not observe it. Your ailment is from yourself, and you do not register it."[7] The first four chapters of the book focus on the traumatizing effects of infidelity. I describe the nature and symptoms of post-infidelity stress disorder, the differing responses of men and women, those most vulnerable to being traumatized, and the impact of parental infidelity on the adult children. The next six chapters describe in detail the six-stage recovery process through the gifts of the Spirit toward forgiveness: from calming the emotional storm, to understanding why the affair happened, to understanding your partner and yourself, to making a wise decision, to forgiving yourself and your partner. To refrain from being overjudgmental, I will refer to the one involved in the infidelity as the offending partner and his counterpart as the wounded, offended, or hurt partner. For grammatical simplicity, I will alternate the masculine and feminine pronoun to refer to the unfaithful partner, unless the context indicates otherwise.

PART ONE

INFIDELITY
AS TRAUMA

ONE

SYMPTOMS OF POST-INFIDELITY STRESS DISORDER (PISD)

Imprisoned in Hurt and Rage

The wounds invisible
That love's keen arrows make.
—SHAKESPEARE

JENNIFER'S STORY

Jennifer imagined her marriage a never-ending love story. She and Bruce had been together for seven years and had a daughter. The day the dream ended is indelibly etched in her memory. At first, it seemed like any other day. She and Bruce had breakfast together, and he left for work. Jennifer, a stay-at-home mom, dressed and fed their four-year-old and began her daily chores. Then, her routine was interrupted by a phone call. Her best friend, Jane, called and was uncharacteristically solemn. She said, "I hope you are sitting down. I have something to tell you. Bruce is having an affair with his secretary." Jennifer was stunned. She could not think clearly. A million thoughts raced through her mind. Nevertheless, she settled herself enough to get the details about what Jane knew. Jane told her that for the past several months her husband had been meeting his secretary secretly after work. She had seen them in a bar together being affectionate on several occasions. She followed them one night to a motel. Jane admitted that she agonized for several weeks about whether to tell her and how. Jennifer thanked her, and her nightmare began.

After the call, Jennifer sobbed uncontrollably. She could not stop the tears. Thoughts swirled in her head: "How could this happen? How could it be true?" Her daughter kept asking her what was wrong, but Jennifer could not talk. She just hugged her daughter and began pacing. Her mind was so agitated she could not think about what to do next. Should I call Bruce and confront him? Should I wait until he gets home? Maybe Jane is wrong, and there was some misunderstanding. But Jennifer had sensed that something had been different with Bruce these past few months, although she could not put her finger on it. She had asked him many times if anything was wrong. He just said he was worried about problems at work. Somehow, Jennifer did not quite believe him. Bruce had always been honest with her, at least, she thought. With her mind and emotions whirling, how could she wait to talk with him? She decided to call him to come home immediately because there was an emergency. She said she would tell him about it when he got home.

Bruce rushed home. When he walked in the door, worry on his face, he asked what happened. Jennifer had carefully planned what she was going to say. She said, "I know you are having an affair with your secretary. How long has this been going on?" She could tell by the startled and guilty look on his face that it was true. Her worst fears were confirmed in that instant. The unthinkable had occurred. He denied that anything was going on, became angry, and berated her for not trusting him. But Jennifer knew he was lying and begged him to tell the truth. When he became even more indignant, she told him to leave the house. He immediately turned around and walked out the door.

And so the nightmare began for Jennifer. The life she knew and all her dreams were shattered. For the next few weeks Bruce continued to call and begged to come home. Jennifer was adamant that she would not let him return unless he confessed to the affair and explained what happened. But he refused. Jennifer was left with her tormenting thoughts and imaginings. She became obsessed with the betrayal and filled with rage. Nights were the worst time for her. She had nightmares of her husband and his lover in bed together. Each morning she woke up exhausted and with back and neck pains. She relived the horror of Jane's phone call, her initial shock and disbelief. She was so tense and depressed she could not function at her part-time job. She let everything go at home and only did what needed to be done for her daughter. She didn't want to leave the house. Crying spells often overtook her. She admitted she was traumatized and told Jane, "Something inside me died, and I can't bring it back to life. I don't know what my life means anymore."[1]

POST-TRAUMATIC STRESS

Jennifer's story portrays only the tip of the iceberg of the deep distress you may feel upon discovering your partner's affair. It is a shock from which you may believe you will never recover. Your faith in your partner, yourself, and your relationship has been shattered. What security you felt in your marriage has been stolen. All the past expressions of love and commitment that you relied on have turned out to be lies. You may wonder how you could have been so foolish not to recognize the truth. You ask yourself how your partner could be so cruel to betray you and your children. "Could I have been so wrong about my life partner?" you ask. You are likely filled with confusion and dread about what the future now holds for you. You might feel lost in the whirlwind of conflicting thoughts.

Not only does your mind seem to be playing tricks on you, but your body and emotions may also be wreaking havoc with you. Sometimes the body knows more than the mind. You may feel sick to your stomach and unable eat. Your body may be so tense you believe it will break under any more stress. You may feel pain in new areas and wonder if you have developed some serious illness as a result of the stress. You are restless and cannot sleep, and what little sleep you manage is disturbed. It seems as if your emotions are running wild. At times, you may feel numb and dead inside. At other times, you feel so anxious it's as if you are jumping out of your skin. A paralyzing depression may engulf you so you feel like withdrawing into a cocoon to recover the security that has been lost. The anger, which is closer to a rage, may be so intense you are afraid it will consume you.

Feeling as overwhelmed as you do, you might be thinking you are going crazy. You may be afraid you are falling apart and can never be put back together again. Let me assure you that this is normal for what you have probably been going through. It is a normal reaction to an extraordinary event, the devastating discovery of a partner's infidelity. I think the reaction can best be appreciated by putting it in the context of a traumatic experience. Those who have discovered their partner's infidelity have been traumatized. The word *trauma* means wound, and the offended person has been wounded to the core of her being by her partner's betrayal of trust.

In recent years clinicians and researchers have paid considerable attention to the reaction of people to overwhelming, life-threatening events. In fact, nearly a century and a half ago, observers noted that soldiers who had fought in the Civil War were emotionally disturbed for years afterward. They called it "soldier's heart." Veterans of World War I suffered a similar reaction, which was called "shell shock." It was assumed that their nervous response to battle resulted from being exposed to the percussion of exploding shells. World War II veterans experienced "battle fatigue," which incapacitated them for further combat. After Vietnam, an identifiable and prolonged stress reaction was identified as "post-traumatic stress disorder." We have come to realize that many people who are exposed to life-threatening events suffer a syndrome with predictable symptoms and progression. More recently, we have also realized that individuals who have been exposed to a wide range of catastrophic events besides combat have a similar reaction. People who have experienced serious auto accidents, natural disasters, or physical assaults are often traumatized. Others who feel vulnerable and face serious physical injury as victims of domestic violence, rape, and child abuse can also be traumatized.

Clinicians have described and researchers have catalogued the symptoms of post-traumatic stress disorder. These symptoms are listed and described in the *Diagnostic and Statistical Manual of Mental Disorders*, a book clinicians use for diagnosis.[2] Although you most likely do not experience the intense and extreme reactions of those most traumatized, for example, by war or prolonged physical or sexual abuse, you may hear echoes, however faint, in your experience as you read these symptoms:

1. Exposure to a life-threatening event

2. Intense fear and helplessness

3. Re-experiencing the event

4. Avoidance of reminders of the event

5. Emotional numbing

6. Heightened anxiety

7. Irritability and rage

I have observed in my clinical practice that many individuals whose partners have been unfaithful exhibit many of these symptoms, to a greater or lesser degree, which led me to coin the term "post-infidelity stress disorder." I believe there is a notable parallel in the reaction of many to the discovery of their partner's infidelity and the disorder described as post-traumatic stress disorder.[3] They have been personally and deeply wounded and will need patience for the often long road to recovery. Nevertheless, they can also be hopeful because many victims of trauma have found and continue to find health and healing through the recent insights gained in treating this disorder.

1. Exposure to a life-threatening event

You may ask yourself, "How can you compare the discovery of my partner's affair with being in combat, an auto accident, a physical assault, or being raped? How can you say my life has been threatened?" The discovery of the affair of our chosen life-partner is experienced as a profound betrayal of trust. For a moment, think about what this betrayal means. When we marry or make a lifelong commitment to someone, we intend to be with this person for the rest of our life. We promise, "To love and honor each other until death do us part." When that promise is broken, all our hopes and dreams of a life together die. All that we assumed about the character of our partner, about the enduring quality of love, and about our own strength is often shattered in that moment of revelation. We may not experience the discovery as a threat to our physical life, but as a psychic catastrophe. At the moment of discovery, it may be experienced as the death of our relationship and our psychological well-being. The meaning of our life, constructed around our relationship with our partner, is unalterably changed. That is the traumatizing crisis caused by the discovery of an infidelity.

You may think that I am being too dramatic in talking about the death of the marriage or of your psychic life, but let me explain further. Eric Erikson, a renowned American psychologist, wrote many years ago about human growth and development. His description of the life span is now considered a classic. He contends that individuals progress through several identifiable stages toward maturity. In each stage, the person is presented with an age-appropriate challenge that must be successfully completed before moving on to the next stage of growth. Each challenge requires a psychic risk, which leads to a new perspective on life and a new challenge. Each stage is a building block on which the next building block of growth is constructed. Failure to negotiate the challenge of any stage leads to weaknesses in the foundation of the personality.

Erikson identifies the first stage of human growth as the choice between trust and mistrust, and claims that developing a sense of trust is "the cornerstone of a vital personality."[4] It is the first building block of a stable and mature personality. It is the foundation on which the entire personality develops. Recognizing the trustworthiness of oneself and others opens the person to relationship, love, and growth, whereas mistrust leads to estrangement and withdrawal from others and oneself. Mistrust also destroys the possibility of engaging in any life-giving relationship with others. It shatters the sense of personal security needed to engage in an intimate relationship. In this way, an affair, because it is a betrayal of the trust that is the foundation of the relationship, is often experienced as a fatal psychic wound and a death blow to the relationship.

What is considered a fundamental betrayal of a relationship? I believe that every couple decides this for themselves. Both enter the relationship with certain expectations about being faithful and usually talk openly about it. Some of these expectations are explicit. For example, both undoubtedly agree never to have sexual intercourse with someone else. They may agree that a certain amount of privacy and intimacy should remain exclusive to the relationship. However, many expectations of fidelity are more implicit, in the mind of one or the other, but not so clearly defined. For example, the boundaries of emotional intimacy can become unclear and even vague. Can I be a friend to someone of the opposite sex? At what point does this friendship violate the boundaries of the marriage? How emotionally intimate can I be? How much affection can I show? How revealing can I be of my personal life and especially of my relationship with my spouse? Notoriously, complaining to a friend of the opposite sex often leads to an affair of the heart ("you're the only person who understands me") and then to a sexual liaison. The boundaries of sexual intimacy can also be unclear for some couples. When do playful flirting, affectionate hugging and kissing, or sexual fantasies cross the line? The Internet provides fertile ground for infidelity with intimate or frankly sexual chat room discussions and pornographic websites. The list of intimate and sexual activities on the borderline of infidelity is almost endless. Nevertheless, each person knows, even if one tries to delude the other, that a border has been crossed and a betrayal has occurred.

Jennifer and Bruce were teenage sweethearts. They met in high school and were instantly attracted to each other. Jennifer was a shy girl who had a small group of friends and never dated. She was more involved in her schoolwork and band. She had always admired Bruce from a distance but believed he did not even know she existed. Bruce was a strikingly handsome, outgoing, popular senior, the star of the football team. It seemed all the girls in their class drooled over him. When Bruce began paying attention to her in class, Jennifer was amazed, flattered, and suspicious. But over time, as he sought her out more often, her mistrust melted and she became infatuated with him. She could hardly believe that Bruce cared for her so much because she thought of herself as so homely. As they began dating and their relationship became an item, Jennifer was the envy of her senior class. In their high school yearbook, they were dubbed the "perfect couple" and "most likely to marry." After graduation, they attended nearby colleges and became inseparable. No one was surprised when they announced their engagement in their senior year and were married a year later. Their lives unfolded like a storybook romance. Jennifer and Bruce were completely devoted to each other and were thrilled at the birth of their daughter. Bruce began his career as a stockbroker, and Jennifer cared for their home and new family.

It was a devastating blow beyond words when Jennifer learned of Bruce's affair with his secretary. She thought she had the perfect marriage and the perfect life. She was living her lifelong dream of raising a family with the only man she ever loved or believed she ever would love. Bruce was her soul mate. She believed she could never find another to match her heart's deepest desires. Now her life was over. She didn't know what to do.

2. Intense fear and helplessness

After the initial shock of discovery, you're likely overwhelmed with fear and preoccupied with the question, "What do I do now?" Your sense of personal security may seem shattered in the instant of that dreadful discovery. You may also feel helpless because the one on whom you had relied for your sense of happiness and well-being has betrayed you. You now realize you cannot depend on your partner as you did before. Feeling so devastated and overwhelmed, you may not believe you can survive on your own. When you think about what happened and what it will mean for your life, your heart may be filled with dread and horror. You dread further discoveries of betrayal and feel helpless to prevent more hurt. Sometimes, the sense of helplessness and fear may become so overwhelming that you believe that life is not worth living. You may fall into despair and even entertain suicidal thoughts.

It may seem difficult to appreciate, but your intense reaction of fear serves the purpose of survival. You may have come to believe that your marriage or committed relationship was a safe haven from the world and its dangers. What you have discovered in the moment of betrayal was that your sense of security in the relationship was an illusion. Your fear likely causes you to withdraw in self-protection so that you will never be hurt again in the same way. Fear energizes you to create a shield against further harm. Your fear and recognized helplessness, as painful as it is, is the beginning of something new. By withdrawing within yourself, you can begin to heal and search to find another source of strength and security.

This fearful reaction is similar for a variety of traumatizing events, for example, a serious auto accident. Many drivers who have an accident once felt secure and carefree in their cars, never thinking they could be hurt. They may have had a great love of cars and enjoyed the excitement of speed, but after the accident, all is changed. Images of the crash fill their minds, evoking fear and dread of another crash occurring. Driving now becomes a hazardous activity for them, and they feel out of control behind the wheel of a car. Their fear may paralyze them, or it may make them more cautious and safe drivers, refusing to take the risks they did before.

After discovering the affair, Jennifer initially felt she had gained some control over her life by demanding that Bruce leave their home immediately. However, she became frightened because she had never lived alone before. Every night some noise or creaking sound startled her. She also thought of herself as a violated person, "damaged goods," a woman no one would ever love again. She believed she was condemned to live the rest of her life alone because she could never trust another man again. She had never worked full-time and was terrified thinking about how she would support herself and her daughter. Jennifer felt helpless in confronting her fears and could not stop crying.

When Bruce repeatedly begged to return home, Jennifer eventually acquiesced because of her intense and crippling fear. She insisted they sleep in separate bedrooms until she sorted out her feelings and made some decisions for herself. But her uneasiness never disappeared. She dreaded being victimized again by her husband, although she was unsure she wanted to remain married to him. She kept replaying the betrayal over and over in her head.

3. Re-experiencing the event

What may make you feel most crazy is that you are so preoccupied with the betrayal. You cannot stop thinking about it. That is a natural reaction. You may try to distract yourself, but the horrifying thoughts about how you were violated return, as if you've lost control of your own mind. Furthermore, little things may remind you of the betrayal. You hear a song, see a favorite dating spot, or hear the phone ring and your mind is drawn back to the affair. When this happens, you might relive the horror of the initial discovery. It may be months or even years later, but you re-experience it as if it were yesterday. These are called flashbacks. Awake or sleeping, you may relive the trauma of the affair in nightmares. You may wake up angry and terrified, and have vague recollections about what you dreamed, but know it is related to the affair.

As distressful as these preoccupations, flashbacks, and nightmares are, they also serve a survival purpose. You are reliving the experience in order, unconsciously, to gain a sense of mastery and control over an overwhelming event. You replay it in your mind so that somehow it will turn out differently. Again, you may remain stuck in this perpetual déjà vu, or it may be the prelude to your beginning the process of inner change.

I recall meeting with an elderly gentleman who was a veteran of World War II. He told me about an incident many years ago of playing golf and hearing a plane backfire as it flew above him. He immediately dived to the ground and covered his head in terror. His golf partner, who had never been in combat, laughed and asked him about his unusual behavior. He told his partner that at that moment he had relived the terror of the numerous bombings he had experienced in combat many years before. After relating this incident to me, he also said that he refused to see any movies about the war because their depictions of battle caused him to have flashbacks of his friends dying.

Jennifer became preoccupied with her husband's affair and obsessed about how he could have done that to her and their daughter. For months, she woke up in the middle of the night, having had nightmares of her husband in the embrace of his secretary. She also dreamed of encountering his secretary on the street and being violent with her. Whenever she saw a woman with blond hair, she was reminded of her husband's lover and experienced flashbacks of the betrayal.

Jennifer was filled with indignation and rage, just as she had been on the day Jane told her about the affair. Whenever she saw a couple holding hands, she imagined her husband with his lover and burst into tears. She became panicked and could not breathe. Hearing favorite songs from when she and her husband were dating caused her great sadness and despair about lost love. Jennifer did not seem able to escape painful reminders of the betrayal and of her loneliness.

4. Avoidance of reminders of the event

Feeling so overwhelmed, you may naturally try to avoid thinking about the affair, just to cope. Then, to your dismay, you may begin to realize how many common, everyday experiences remind you of the infidelity. How do you then cope? You begin to withdraw from many activities, to avoid any painful reminders. You may avoid talking with your friends about what happened, just to turn off your mind and try to get off the emotional roller coaster. You hope that the pain will go away if you do not think about it. You might run away from anything that will remind you of what happened and try to put on an optimistic face. "There's no use thinking about it because there's nothing I can do about it now," you rationalize. It is easy to see how avoiding conscious thought about the pain and anything that reminds you of it helps you survive. It provides needed temporary relief that is obviously beneficial, unless such avoidance becomes a way of life. Then your life begins to contract, without your awareness, and you shut down. You avoid the pain but also the joy in life.

Several books have recently been published about the "greatest generation" and their involvement in World War II. Our generation is curious about our fathers and the impact of the war on their lives. One observation is persistent in all the books about war veterans: their silence about their experience, their refusal to talk about the war. One reason for their silence is obvious. They do not want to relive the terror of battle. Another reason may not be so obvious. They feel ashamed because they felt so terrorized in battle and survived. The only heroes in their minds were those who had the courage to die. Their silence is a way to protect themselves from painful reminders of their traumatic experience.

Jennifer had always been a happy person. Although she was shy, she enjoyed the company of a small group of friends. She enjoyed going to the theater and to movies. Jennifer's friends noted how she seemed to "disappear" after learning about her husband's affair. She became more withdrawn and did not frequent her usual places. Jennifer admitted she avoided restaurants and theaters because she had enjoyed going there with her husband. She said, "Going there is too painful now. I feel so sad because I miss the happy times with Bruce. But then I become so angry I can't see straight. Those places won't let me forget what happened. I feel so stupid for not seeing this happening." Jennifer felt lost and began to feel safe only when she was alone.

5. Emotional numbing

While you may consciously avoid thinking about the affair and reminders of it, another more unconscious process is also occurring. The feelings of anxiety, rage, shame, sadness, and helplessness can become so overwhelming that you begin to cope by withdrawing into an emotional cocoon. You might start to detach from life and from your feelings to survive the emotional storm. You begin to feel "dead inside" and might view yourself more as spectator than actor in your own life. While you are aware of shutting down the pain, you also realize that the joy, excitement, and even loving feelings for others are disappearing.

This emotional numbing is an almost involuntary survival tactic. You need a refuge, which you begin to find within yourself, to escape the emotional turmoil. You may be afraid of being swamped by your feelings, of drowning in them, so you find safety in insulating yourself. Again, the numbing provides effective temporary relief while you attempt to rebuild yourself and your world. The danger, of course, is that emotional detachment will become a way of life.

Such emotional numbing is well documented about trauma survivors. For example, many concentration camp survivors have been described as "the living dead" during and after their imprisonment. They learned to cope through resignation and passivity because fighting back led to frustration or even death. They often described their experience as being detached from themselves, watching the beatings as if they were happening to someone else. Trauma survivors frequently numb their feelings by self-medicating with alcohol or drugs, as has been reported by combat veterans in recent wars. Countless veterans returned from Vietnam, the Gulf War, and the Iraq War addicted to drugs. Patients of mine who were molested as children have reported to me occasional experiences of feeling as if they are walking in a fog, detached from their lives.

After discovering her husband's affair, Jennifer became a different person. She had always been full of life in her own quiet way. She enjoyed her small circle of friends and often had lunch with her best friend, Jane. She loved to curl up in bed with a good book for hours. Now she reported feeling dead inside and not enjoying anything. She sat in her backyard and daydreamed for hours to avoid painful thoughts about Bruce's adultery. She knew she wasn't paying as much attention to her daughter, often sending her to her mother's. She felt guilty about it but barely had enough energy to take care of her daughter's and her own physical needs.

In addition, Jennifer began having trouble at her part-time job at the local bookstore because she had trouble sleeping and felt so fatigued on the job. She had always been such a conscientious person but began making mistakes at the cash register and in placing book orders. She was so distracted, "off in another world," as her boss remarked. She had never been a drinker but now found herself needing a drink at night to help her sleep. Jennifer felt too ashamed to talk with her friends about what had happened and began to isolate herself more. Jane almost begged her to talk with her about it, but she refused. Jennifer believed she was losing all hope for the future and could not imagine herself ever being emotionally involved with a man again.

6. Heightened anxiety

After discovering the affair, you may feel like you are living on high alert. A danger you never imagined would exist, your partner's betrayal, is now a reality. "What else can go wrong? What other atrocity can occur?" you ask. You might be thinking that the world is no longer the safe place you imagined. A sense of impending doom may grip you. You may become restless and distracted. It is as if your motor is always running because you need to be ready for a quick escape. Part of the craziness may be that you are not sure what the danger is now, since your worst fear has already occurred. You are just waiting for the other shoe to drop, while not knowing what that shoe might be. Perhaps the worry and preoccupation keep you awake, and when you do sleep, nightmares disturb your rest. During the day, you may be tense and hypervigilant, ready for evasive action. You might believe that your sense of security, which your partner provided, is destroyed.

Anxiety, as uncomfortable as it is, serves a purpose. It is an early warning signal that prepares us for danger. We are hardwired to be prepared to confront dangers. Because we are intelligent, we can anticipate the future and make plans to face obstacles and dangers. If we had no anxiety, or innate early warning system, we would be very vulnerable. Realistically, there are threats to our survival in the world. But what happens when we are traumatized is that we develop a heightened, exaggerated sense of danger and react with constant preparedness for attack. In other words, our natural early warning system has gone haywire and overreacts to situations. We begin to imagine dangers where they may not exist and live with a tense readiness to defend ourselves.

Jennifer complained that she had not had a decent night's sleep since discovering Bruce's affair. At times during the day, she suddenly experienced panic attacks, and she could relate the feelings to her preoccupation about her uncertain future. After she allowed Bruce to move back home while she was deciding about her future, she felt compelled to monitor his activities, telephone calls, and emails. Whenever he was on the phone, suspicion seized her. Whenever he went out, she wondered if it was to meet his lover. Then she loathed herself for being so concerned about him and his activities. She was baffled by her behavior because she was not even sure she wanted to stay married to him.

7. Irritability and rage

After discovering the affair, you may be preoccupied with the injustice of it and how you have been victimized. You may notice that the more you think about what your partner did to you, the angrier you get. You may have thoughts of revenge against your partner and his or her lover. You may also feel frustrated that you are helpless and can do nothing about what happened. Your thoughts may turn to self-blame because you think you were so foolish to marry the person and did not see signs of the affair. "How could I be so stupid?" You may begin to berate yourself, turning the anger against yourself, and suffer plummeting self-esteem. In the process, you may also notice that your mood is affected. There is an underlying sense of irritability and impatience. Even little things seem to annoy you more than before, the loud TV, your child's crying, your neighbor's complaining. To your dismay, you may feel dominated by moods and have temper outbursts you never had before. As time passes, you may be concerned that the anger will consume you and you will disappear.

Some people enjoy being angry because it makes them feel powerful. Anger is energizing. It motivates us to fight for ourselves, to confront obstacles in the way of our goals, and to defend ourselves. Furthermore, anger, and the energy it provides, is essential for survival. Instead of fleeing, we fight for what we need. Healthy anger stimulates us to assert ourselves. However, if the anger is evoked from a frustrated sense of helplessness and does not lead to constructive action, it can consume us. Instead of motivating us to constructive action on our own behalf, we may strike out in rage, expressing this powerful emotion in destructive ways that harm ourselves and others. The angry outburst invites a retaliatory response that continues a cycle of violence.

Those who have been traumatized have a deep sense of being violated and needing revenge to right the wrong and restore the balance of their lives. For example, victims of rape or physical assault frequently entertain revenge fantasies, which compensate for their feelings of helplessness. Children who have been physically or sexually abused often grow up with a reservoir of anger. They become sensitive to being bullied or exploited and may react with an explosive temper. Smoldering rage is characteristic of those who have been victimized. That rage may explode against others with violent or abusive conduct or against themselves with self-destructive or suicidal behavior.

Jennifer had always thought of herself as calm and even-tempered and was surprised that she became an angry person after the affair. At times, she experienced crying spells, but at other times, her anger erupted. She wanted to throw things. She was irritable and particularly impatient with her daughter. She experienced remorse after her outbursts but felt helpless to control them. Jennifer also had disturbing fantasies of becoming violent toward Bruce and his secretary. She began to hate the person she was becoming.

Your reactions, like those of other trauma victims, may seem contradictory but make sense when viewed as a means of self-protection that is appropriate to the extreme seriousness of the threat. Your psychic life and well-being have been threatened by your partner's infidelity. Animals fight, freeze, or flee when threatened; humans react similarly. When a threat is overwhelming, we naturally tend to become paralyzed and withdraw within ourselves to find safety. We separate ourselves from the painful memory, thoughts, and emotions.

Compare this withdrawal to putting the painful memories of the traumatic event into a mental box. The box contains all the memories, thoughts, and feelings associated with the trauma, and we store the box away from our everyday life and thoughts. We work hard to keep the box hidden and secure, because if the box were opened, we would relive the terror of the memories enclosed. We develop strategies to avoid the contents of the box and even alter our daily activities to avoid reminders of the contents. However, despite all our efforts, something knocks the lid off the box, and the horror of its contents pours out. Eventually, we are able to replace the lid on the box and continue our everyday life, but we live in dread of the next unpredictable opening. Recovery is gaining the inner strength to embrace the contents of the box without being overwhelmed by it.

Emily Dickinson perceptively observed and poetically expressed our reaction to traumatizing pain in the following poem.

There is a pain—so utter—
It swallows substance up—
Then covers the Abyss with Trance—
So Memory can step

Around—across—upon it—
As one within a Swoon—
Goes safely—where an open eye—
Would drop Him—Bone by Bone.[5]

When you discover the infidelity of the one you love, your heart is likely broken. Initially, you may be in shock. But soon the emotional numbness gives way to a flood of hurt, sorrow, fear, and rage. You may alternate between periods of deadness and overwhelming pain and unexpectedly relive the horror of the discovery in dreams and flashbacks. You may believe you will never put the pieces of your life and fragile emotions back together again. To cope with the trauma of a broken heart, you may close yourself off, becoming a prisoner of the hurt, rage, and fear. However, if you listen closely, in the midst of the noise of your pain is a quiet voice crying out for healing. Through your brokenness, you experience a deep longing, often ignored in peaceful times, for wholeness.

SOME DOS AND DON'TS FOR RECOVERY

1. Acknowledge, don't hide, the pain about being betrayed. Do you minimize your hurt feelings, considering them a sign of weakness? Do you refuse to talk about them with close friends or family because you do not want to burden them? Are you afraid of being consumed by the feelings if you acknowledge them?

2. Don't be impatient with yourself because of the intensity of your reactions. Do you consider yourself irreparably damaged because of what you have experienced and how you have reacted? Are you afraid you will never get over the infidelity? Do you feel condemned to live in despair and loneliness?

3. Be gentle with yourself as you work on your recovery. Are you a demanding and impatient person, especially with yourself? Are you angry with yourself for allowing yourself to be victimized? Do you express that anger through your impatience with yourself?

4. Don't rush the healing process. Do you tend to look for quick fixes to problems in your life? Are you impatient to get over the pain? Do you believe that hard work alone can overcome any obstacle?

5. Take time for yourself and make your recovery a priority. Do you feel guilty taking time for and indulging yourself? Does it seem selfish to you to make yourself a priority? Do you believe you are neglecting others by caring for yourself?

6. Expect your recovery to take time. Are you impatient about recovery because you underestimate the harm you have experienced at being betrayed? Do you see your reaction as normal in light of the trauma you experienced? Do you consider it a waste of time to work at your own recovery?

7. Allow others to help you. Are you afraid of burdening others with your problems? Do you consider it a sign of weakness to ask for help? Do you really believe you are worth the care and assistance of others? Are you afraid to trust others because your partner showed himself to be untrustworthy?

8. Open your mind and heart to understand yourself and your partner. Do you lack confidence in your ability to understand yourself and others in light of the deception you experienced? Are you afraid to trust yourself, and your perceptions and judgments?

9. Pay attention to your longings for wholeness. Were you satisfied with your life before the affair? Did you take the good things in your life for granted? Did you ignore what was missing in your life?

TWO

DIFFERING RESPONSES
OF MEN AND WOMEN
TO INFIDELITY

The Many Faces of PISD

Spend time every day listening to what
your muse is trying to tell you.

—ST. BARTHOLOMEW

While the discovery of an infidelity causes deep pain, not everyone responds in the same way. Almost everyone will be traumatized to a degree, but the way the hurt is expressed can vary, depending on many factors. Many ask me, "Do men and women respond differently to infidelity?" As has been observed countless times, men and women often behave differently, as if they come from different planets. Biology, cultural expectations, and personality differences between them undoubtedly influence their differing responses to the betrayal and their approach to recovery. However, everyone, whether male or female, is a unique individual, with their own personal history, temperament, and idiosyncrasies. Nevertheless, with caution and some trepidation, I would like to paint with broad strokes a picture of the differing responses of men and women to infidelity, according to my own experience working with countless couples. I offer some generalizations, which I hope are not too stereotypical, to help you appreciate the differing responses. Perhaps you may see a brief glimpse of yourself in the following portrayals.

DIFFERING RESPONSES OF MEN AND WOMEN

In my experience, men and women tend to respond differently to their partner's infidelity and approach recovery in their own ways. The following are some generalizations, taking into account biological, temperamental, and cultural influences. While, of course, many men and women today find themselves caught between cultural ideals and do not subscribe to any gender stereotype, none can escape the profound and subtle influences of the broader culture. Hopefully, these brief portraits will shed some light on the ways you find yourself responding:

1. Vulnerability to trauma

2. Reasons for affairs

3. Reactions to the discovery of an affair

4. Ways of disconnecting

5. Decision making

6. Paths to recovery

Let's examine each of these in more detail.

1. Vulnerability to trauma
*Women are more easily traumatized because
they invest more of themselves in relationships.*

A majority of American adults have experienced some traumatic event in their lives—an accident, assault, natural disaster, sexual or physical abuse. However, only about 8 percent of them experience symptoms of post-traumatic stress disorder. Men and women experience different types of trauma. While women are more vulnerable to physical and sexual abuse in the family setting that causes them to be traumatized, men are involved in serious accidents, physical attacks, and combat that may lead to post-traumatic stress. Overall, studies indicate that women, because of their vulnerability to interpersonal trauma in the home, have twice the lifetime prevalence of post-traumatic stress that men do.[1]

While everyone who discovers a partner's affair is emotionally devastated, some are more traumatized than others. Women tend to be more deeply wounded because they typically invest themselves more in their relationships. Women, more than men, equate their self-worth with being loved. Our culture fosters a romantic view of love that promises happiness and fulfillment through a loving relationship. Women tend to be more easily captivated by this fantasy, while men tend to find their identities in their work and accomplishments. Women learn from the cradle to depend on others and to become nurturers. When their relationships fail, they often feel they have lost their identity and purpose in life. Men, on the other hand, are encouraged to be independent and rely on themselves, which inoculates them to a certain extent against being let down by others.

A second factor influences the heightened vulnerability of women to being traumatized by their partner's infidelity. Women are more at risk of being abused physically and sexually as children. Some researchers suggest that nearly one-fourth of women have been sexually abused before their teens. They are also victims of domestic violence and rape. Their histories of being exploited lead these abused women to form "betrayal bonds" in their significant relationships. The pattern of abuse is continued with their unfaithful partners, and they experience the accumulated pain of their histories of being victimized. Although in smaller numbers, men are also vulnerable to being traumatized by an infidelity because they are not immune to being abused as children and continuing the pattern in their adult relationships.

2. Reasons for affairs
Women seek emotional intimacy, while men want sex.

In general, women tend to find themselves through their loving relationships. When intimacy is lacking in their primary relationship, they feel the loss deeply and are vulnerable to seeking an emotional connection elsewhere. They will seek a friendship with another, someone they can talk and share their life with. If they become friends with a man and their conversations become personal and intimate, an emotional attachment develops. It is a short step before the emotional intimacy develops into a sexual relationship, often initiated by the man. Once such a strong emotional bond is formed with another man, the woman often detaches from her partner. She is then less likely to seek reconciliation after the discovery of the affair.

Men, in contrast, seek sexual partners. It is often sexual chemistry, rather than a desire for friendship, that initiates the affair. Men may love the adventure and excitement of the affair, rather than the romance of it. They are active by nature and often become involved with their lovers through shared activities, such as work or recreation. At times, they justify their affairs because of a lack of sexual intimacy at home. They believe they are entitled to satisfy their sexual needs and may deny any guilt for their straying. Some men see no contradiction between having a wife, who provides care and stability at home, and a mistress, who provides adventure and sexual release. Men often have the ability to compartmentalize their lives and rationalize their behavior. However, the sexual relationship may develop into an emotionally intimate one and turn his world upside down. Then, he is more inclined to leave his wife for his mistress.

Shirley Glass, who has researched and written about affairs for many years, observes a changing pattern in infidelity. She notes that for both men and women "friendships, work relationships, and Internet liaisons have become the latest threats to marriages."[2] Since women have increasingly joined the workforce, they have become friends with their male coworkers and face the risk of emotional and romantic involvements. The workplace has become the new danger zone for both men and women to become romantically involved with others. Dr. Glass's research revealed that 50 percent of wives and 55 percent of husbands who committed adultery had their first affairs with coworkers. Current studies are suggesting that both men and women are increasingly initiating extramarital affairs through Internet contacts, as many as 27 percent of affairs in one study. Instead of the stereotype of women seeking romance while men look for sex, infidelity for both increasingly begins from casual work or Internet encounters. For both men and women, casual friendships become more intimate and slip, sometimes with little deliberation or awareness, into an emotional, romantic, and sexual involvement.

3. Reactions to the discovery of an affair
Women become depressed and shed tears,
while men become angry and withdraw.

Women are twice as likely as men to suffer from depression, according to a national study of mental health in the United States.[3] One
reason for their increased depression is that women tend to direct
their anger and criticism against themselves in self-blame, rather
than outward against others. At an early age, they are taught not
to speak up for themselves. For example, girls are more discouraged
from expressing anger outwardly than boys. While they express
their emotions in tears, they also tend to internalize their feelings.
Their feeling states often become expressed somatically in headaches,
muscle pain, back pain, gastric distress, or other medical problems.
Because they commonly invest themselves so much in their relationships, when their partner is unfaithful they experience a profound
sense of loss. Their world has collapsed, and they feel adrift and
alone. They become obsessed about the betrayal and fearful of their
ability to survive on their own.

Men, on the other hand, are conditioned by the culture to be
strong and withhold their feelings of hurt and pain. To express sadness and hurt is perceived as an unmanly sign of weakness. Instead,
men become angry and direct their rage against their partner or her
lover, rather than themselves. They indulge in other-blame, rather
than self-blame. Their anger gives them a sense of power and being
in control. Men also react by shutting down and suppressing their
feelings. They compartmentalize their painful feelings and distract
themselves with activity, alcohol, drugs, or other addictive behaviors.
To protect themselves from trauma, they withdraw into their caves.

4. Ways of disconnecting
Women cling to love, while men detach emotionally.
Both avoid intimacy by fighting for control in the relationship.

Women tend to learn at an early age to become nurturers and to
value relationships. They learn to define themselves in terms of the

success of their close relationships. They value intimacy and exhibit strong needs for attention, affection, and support. Above all, they seek to love and be loved, attempting to create harmony in their relationships. However, there is a danger in their focus on love of becoming unbalanced to the point that they lose a sense of themselves as separate individuals. Emotionally unhealthy women tend to become dependent personalities who lean on others, fear abandonment, and lack self-confidence. They lack self-esteem and do not believe they can survive on their own. When their security is threatened by their partner's infidelity, they cling more desperately, believing they will fall apart if their partner leaves.

Men, on the other hand, are raised to be independent and assertive in our culture, defining themselves in terms of their work and performance. They value activity, competition, and achievement, especially enjoying personal freedom. They gain a sense of strength and security in their assertiveness and their accomplishments. If the pursuit of independence becomes extreme, however, their relationships suffer. They become detached emotionally and withdraw from intimacy, creating a sense of abandonment in their partners. They may even resent their partner's initiatives for closeness, feel smothered, and withdraw into activities. Emotionally unhealthy men become detached from their own feelings and desires, fleeing from intimacy. When they discover their partner's affair, they withdraw even more into their own world, sometimes pretending not to care.

Both men and women can disconnect from each other by fighting for control in their relationships. In healthy relationships, both partners freely express their desires and needs, and they learn to negotiate differences in a give-and-take process. However, when either feels insecure and becomes obsessed with control, the relationship becomes a battleground. Men and women are both susceptible to this power struggle, which results in a flight from intimacy. Their anger shields them from the vulnerability of a close emotional relationship but also creates a sense of isolation.

5. Decision making

Women try to maintain the relationship, while men leave.

Research indicates that marriages end for almost half of those having affairs.[4] If the wife is unfaithful, the husband tends to seek divorce. However, if the husband is unfaithful, the wife makes efforts to preserve the marriage. An exception is when the wife has developed an emotional relationship with another man because of her dissatisfaction with her marriage. She then tends to leave the marriage for the other man.

Why do women more often choose to stay with their unfaithful partners? As mentioned previously, women typically find their identity and meaning in their close relationships. Consequently, they work harder to maintain and improve the relationship. They may interpret the affair as a sign of a problem that needs to be fixed and work at fixing it. They may even sacrifice themselves because of their fear of being alone. Furthermore, there is more at stake for a woman to leave her husband, if she is at least in part financially dependent on him. She normally takes responsibility for the care of the children and will suffer economically if she needs to work and care for them. One young woman with three children who discovered her husband's infidelity lamented, "I feel stuck. I want to leave him, but I can't afford it. I've decided to enroll in a nursing program so I can eventually support myself. Then I'll feel free to decide whether to stay or leave."

Men, on the other hand, are generally in a more secure position financially. Although they often complain about the cost of divorce and how poor they have become, the reality is that they are often in a financially more favorable position than their spouses. They have the financial independence to leave. Furthermore, men often experience a deep personal insult to their self-esteem when their partner is unfaithful. They feel inadequate as lovers, and their macho image is challenged. In angry retaliation, they may leave their unfaithful partner to save face.

6. Paths to recovery

While women are more traumatized by their partner's affair,
they have more resources for recovery than men; they
focus on feelings, while men focus on problems.

It appears women are more disposed to engage themselves fully in the
recovery process than men. Because women are generally more emotionally invested in their relationships, they feel the pain of loss and
betrayal deeply. They are usually more aware of their feelings and
willing to talk about them. Some men complain about how much their
wives discuss their emotional reactions and analyze them to death.
The disposition and ability to acknowledge, express, and process feelings are essential to healing the wound of betrayal. Women are more
willing to talk with friends about their pain and benefit from social
support. They are also more willing to see a therapist or join a support group to accompany them through their recovery. Seeking help
is less a sign of weakness.

Men pursue recovery in a different way. They tend to compartmentalize their feelings, often ignoring their presence and influence
on their lives. They are less likely to talk about their pain, which to
them is a sign of weakness. Consequently, they do not share with their
friends or family their emotional experience, often isolating themselves in their suffering. They are more reluctant to see a therapist
or join a support group, considering it a stigma to seek psychological
help. They cope with uncomfortable feelings by distracting themselves with work or activities. They may even anesthetize themselves
with alcohol or drugs. In recovering from the trauma of a discovered
affair, men tend to engage themselves in problem solving, and in making adjustments in their schedules and finances for the new situation
caused by the infidelity.

Women and men differ in the ways they become stuck in their
recovery. Women tend to become caught up in their emotional storms
and fail to fully engage their minds to progress through recovery.
I asked one woman, early in recovery, how she would cope with
her husband's affair, and she half-jokingly responded, "Get a gun."
Furthermore, because of their dependency and need for harmony,

they may embrace a quick forgiveness, without expressing to their partner the depth of their hurt and anger. On the other hand, men tend to detach from their feelings, not facing squarely the pain of betrayal in order to work through it. One man, a successful business-man, described how he coped with his wife's affair: "I got to the point that I didn't care. I just buried myself in my work and was never home." Men may also react with anger, refuse forgiveness, and impul-sively end the relationship without gaining self-understanding.

Facing crises in our lives presents us with a unique opportunity to learn about ourselves. How we respond to a crisis, such as a dis-covered infidelity, reveals our personality strengths and weaknesses and presents an opportunity for growth. Typically, men and women, because of biological and cultural differences, respond in differing ways to interpersonal betrayal. They react to the pain, cope with the pain, and pursue recovery in their own ways. If men and women respect each other's individuality, they can learn from each other and develop healthier, more balanced ways of coping with the stress of life and failed relationships. Men can learn to value their feelings and relationships, while women can learn to be more assertive and trust-ing of their insights.

SOME DOS AND DON'TS FOR RECOVERY

1. Do not expect to react like everyone else. Do you imagine that everyone reacts the same way to painful events? Do you compare yourself with others in your reactions? Do you seek their approval?

2. Pursue your own path to recovery. Do you trust your own wisdom to know what is best for you? What helps you to cope with over-whelmingly negative thoughts and feelings?

3. Be open to learning about yourself. Can you see this painful event as a path to self-knowledge and growth? How do you tend to shut down, especially when you feel most vulnerable? What negative quality has become most apparent as you struggle with your partner's infidelity?

4. Appreciate your unique gifts. What do you like most about yourself? Do you see yourself as a resilient person? What is your greatest strength in adversity?

5. Trust in your own potential for growth. Do you lack faith in your ability to cope and to grow through adversity? Have you felt stuck in your life? How do you imagine your future, as bright or bleak?

6. Do not be afraid to learn from others. What qualities do you admire in others? Whom do you admire most, and what can you learn from that person? Are you afraid to share your pain with others and ask for their advice?

7. Do not give up on the work of recovery. Are you easily discouraged? What do you foresee as your greatest obstacle in recovery? What is your greatest asset for overcoming that obstacle?

8. Be patient with your progress toward being yourself. Do you see your present struggles as an invaluable way to learn about and become yourself? Can you see self-knowledge and personal growth as a journey? Do you believe in progress, or do you feel caught in self-defeating behaviors?

THREE

THOSE MOST VULNERABLE TO TRAUMA
A Heart Close to Breaking

No problem can be solved with the same
level of consciousness that created it.
—ALBERT EINSTEIN

"Is everyone traumatized when they discover their partner's affair?" people ask me. In working with patients who have been wounded by an infidelity, I have observed that all are hurt, but some appear more vulnerable to being deeply traumatized than others. Several factors influence their ability to cope with the devastating discovery of their partner's affair. The intensity of the trauma and the ability to rebuild their lives appear to be a function of their personalities, temperaments, and personal histories in relationships. I would like to describe some of the characteristics of these less resilient individuals who appear more prone to suffer post-infidelity stress disorder. Those most vulnerable are:

1. The overdependent

2. Those with a fragile sense of self

3. Those locked in a pattern of abusive relationships

As you read my descriptions of these various personalities and hear their stories, listen for a ring of truth, however faint, and see what you might learn about yourself.

1. The overdependent

Many idealize love, believing they will find all their happiness through their partner. As the following two stories illustrate, those who find their identities and life meaning in their partner's love are vulnerable to a personal collapse when the relationship ends.

JENNIFER'S STORY CONTINUED

Jennifer felt a burst of self-confidence when she told Bruce to leave the house after discovering the affair. Her confidence was fueled by her rage. She kept asking herself, "How could he do that to me and my daughter?" In the first few weeks when Bruce begged to return home, Jennifer maintained her resolve and refused to talk with him until he was ready to be honest with her. In a strange way she sensed strength she had never felt before. It was the first time she had ever really asserted herself with Bruce. She had trusted in his strength and self-confidence, which made up for the lack of these qualities in herself.

After a few weeks, Jennifer's resolve began to fade. Anxious thoughts filled her mind. "I have never lived alone in my life. How can I survive without Bruce? How will I ever support myself?" Self-doubt had always ruled Jennifer's life, and she often struggled making decisions for herself. She had surprised herself at her decisive action in demanding that Bruce leave.

Jennifer also thought about her childhood. She had two younger sisters she often babysat for. Jennifer was a compliant child who always wanted to be helpful to her mother. She was her mother's shadow. Her father was a domineering man who ruled the household with an iron fist, drank every weekend, and became mean. Jennifer remembered trying to be quiet and hiding in her room when her father was in his mood. When her father drank, she wanted to become invisible. Her mother was a quiet, mousy woman. She waited on her husband and never spoke up to him, even when he became angry and disciplined the children harshly.

During therapy, Jennifer recalled an incident that made her see her father and herself in a different perspective. When Jennifer was ten years old, her father's younger sister died of cancer. Her father was devastated, and she saw the depth of his grief and fear. For more than a month after his sister's death, her father gathered the family every night to sleep together in the living room. He said he was afraid of something terrible happening to his wife or children, and he could not tolerate losing them. Years later, Jennifer realized that behind her father's tyrannical exterior was an anxious and frightened man.

She also realized the impact of living in a household pervaded with fear. She grew up a fearful person who never had confidence in herself. She always looked to others for reassurance. She was afraid of asserting herself and thought of others as superior to her. It was no surprise to her that she idealized Bruce and put so much trust in him, even though she later discovered he did not deserve it.

ROGER'S STORY

Roger was married fifteen years when he learned his wife was having an emotional affair with her boss. His wife had been friends with her boss for many years. Roger always felt threatened by their relationship, but his wife ridiculed him for his suspiciousness. One night he intercepted a romantic email to his wife from her boss and knew that their friendship had crossed the line. When he confronted his wife, she confessed with much anguish and tears. She acknowledged that she had been unhappy for many years in their marriage. She felt ignored, and her boss gave her the attention she craved. Roger admitted that he was a quiet, laid-back person who had few interests. He just liked to watch TV, whereas his wife was an outgoing, social person. Roger felt guilty for neglecting her. He acquiesced when she begged him to remain in the house while she decided whether to continue the marriage or move in with her boss who was in the process of divorce.

Roger admitted that he was terrified of losing his wife and living alone. He was enraged at her betrayal and had nightmares about it, but his fear of being alone was stronger. He also blamed himself for her infidelity because he felt guilty for neglecting her. He said, "I know what she did was not right, but I share some of the blame." He also asked her to stay because of his firm belief in the commitment of marriage for life.

While sorting out his conflicting feelings about the marriage, Roger reflected on his childhood. His father was a strict Lutheran pastor. The family gathered every evening for Bible reading and study. His father often lectured the family on Christian teachings and the right way of living. The rules of the house were clear and strict. Roger often bemoaned that he did not have the freedom to stay out and go places, like his friends. Yet Roger never questioned his father's authority. He knew that if he ever spoke up to him, he would be disciplined severely. His older brother challenged his father on one occasion, and memories of the ensuing beating were etched in his memory. Roger lived in fear of his father's righteous wrath and submitted to his authority. He later learned through therapy that he also lacked confidence in himself and never learned to think for himself.

Like Jennifer and Roger, those who find their identities and self-worth in their partner's love live in a house built by their partner, not themselves. They have receded into the background and let their partner make the critical decisions that shape their relationship. They are so dependent on their partner that they lose themselves. They believe, "My partner is everything; I am nothing." When they discover their partner's infidelity, they suddenly realize they have been living with a stranger and feel frightened and lost.

When you are captivated by the romantic view of love that promises salvation through the love, attention, and affection of another, you are at risk of being disillusioned. You may come to believe that your partner provides you with strength against the harsh realities of life. He becomes your safe haven. Your partner's love relieves you from the burden of loneliness and gives your life a sense of meaning. It follows that when your partner's love is questioned, your sense of meaning and value are lost. In Shakespeare's romantic tragedy, Romeo and Juliet were completely absorbed in their love for each other. When Romeo thought Juliet was dead, he took his own life because he could not imagine life without her.

When the awakened Juliet discovered her dead Romeo, her only recourse was likewise to end her own life. Similarly, when your love has failed you, you may believe your life is over.

Seduced by the romantic view of love, you not only see your partner as all powerful and indispensable for your happiness but tend to see yourself as helpless and dependent. Seeing your complete fulfillment in a loving relationship, you tend to seek the approval, attention, and affection of another to feel good about yourself. You also tend to surrender to your partner to feel loved. Love comes to mean sacrificing yourself for a higher ideal. But underlying this self-sacrifice is the belief, often unacknowledged, that you are worthless, incomplete in yourself. Feeling weak, you find your strength through another's love. You might believe you are lost and found by the other's attention and recognition.

Those who idealize love and sacrifice themselves to maintain a relationship are really dependent personalities. They exhibit an excessive need to be taken care of and do not believe they can survive on their own. The following are some of the characteristics of dependent personalities, which make them vulnerable to being traumatized by a failed relationship. Those who are dependent:

- feel inferior and see others as superior.
- have difficulty trusting themselves to make decisions.
- constantly seek reassurance from others.
- fear confrontation and have difficulty asserting themselves.
- would rather be a follower than a leader.
- avoid taking initiatives for fear of making a mistake.
- cannot stand being alone.
- are afraid of rejection.
- tend to cling to those who are close to them.
- have a desperate need for approval.
- feel helpless and believe they need others to care for them.
- lack self-confidence and avoid taking responsibility for activities.

2. Those with a fragile sense of self

While the overdependent seek to find their identity through the love of their partner, those with a fragile sense of who they are seek to build their self-esteem in a variety of ways, which inevitably fails. They may compulsively seek recognition through appearances, accomplishments, power, or relationships. In relationships, they seek a refuge from their lifelong sense of personal insecurity. They demand too much from their partners and become disappointed, resentful, and disillusioned. Some hide their insecurity behind a facade of achievement, like Rick in the following story, or display it openly, like Renee.

RICK'S STORY

Rick flew into a rage and began throwing things when he discovered his wife was having an affair with her coworker. He screamed at his wife, clenched his fists, and wanted to hit her. As happened so often in the past, his wife screamed back at him, insulted him, and shouted, "I had the affair because you're such a lousy husband." Feeling enraged and helpless, Rick stormed out of the house.

In therapy, Rick tried to sort out the pieces of his life and marriage. He realized that his marriage had always been volatile. Even while dating he and his future wife argued constantly. Because both of them were so sensitive and easily offended, they reacted with hostility to any disagreement, even over minor matters. Rick saw his wife as cruel in knowing exactly how to push his buttons, and he reacted with predictable hurt and outrage. After each outburst, both felt remorse and made up but eventually repeated the all-too-familiar pattern. Rick came to believe that their mutual arguing and anger became the glue for their relationship, a way of keeping connected.

Rick also realized that he related with his wife in a way he observed in his parents. His parents argued all the time, about everything. Rick remembered always being scared as a child. He was especially afraid of his mother's anger; she frequently and unexpectedly raged out of control. She was especially harsh in disciplining him and his two younger brothers. Rick's father was often out of town for business for extended periods of time. When his father left, he would tell Rick

45

that he was "the man of the house" in his absence because he was the oldest child. Rick took pride in having such responsibility placed on his shoulders but also felt overwhelmed by it.

When Rick grew up he was very successful in business. He began his own company and was admired by all his employees for his wisdom and sense of fairness. As much as he was admired by others, Rick felt a sense of emptiness inside. He thought of himself as a fraud who fooled everyone with his business and social successes. No one, except his wife, suspected his deep insecurity about himself. His ongoing marital conflicts reinforced his sense of personal worthlessness.

RENEE'S STORY

When Renee learned that her husband of twenty-five years was leaving her, she took an overdose of pills. She survived because her oldest son happened to come home and find her unconscious. She was rushed to the hospital and later transferred to a psychiatric unit for severe depression. Renee admitted that she had never been happy in her marriage. She saw her husband as having a double personality. At times he appeared to be outgoing and self-confident, and at other times he was depressed, impulsive, and insecure. He had engaged in a few sexual liaisons during their marriage, but Renee tolerated the "bad husband" because she also saw his good side. She thought of herself as his indispensable safety net during his rough periods. But when he announced that he was leaving Renee for another woman, Renee felt overwhelmed and had no reason to live.

Renee had always been an extremely insecure, moody person, and she could trace the roots of her insecurity to her childhood. Her father was a mean alcoholic. The whole household lived in fear of his outbursts of temper. At night, when he came home drunk, he used to sneak into Renee's bedroom and fondle her. Renee pretended she was asleep but used to imagine herself in another place when the abuse occurred. Renee was so terrified of her father that she never told anyone about the abuse, although she suspected her mother knew. Her mother was a depressed, submissive woman. Renee always harbored an intense anger against her mother for not protecting her.

At a young age, Renee found consolation in art. Her uncle, a sensitive and melancholic man, taught her how to paint. While drawing she could retreat into her own safe world of the imagination and shut out painful thoughts and feelings. She could also express her pain and anger and feel soothed through the creative process. Renee thought of herself as damaged by her father's abuse and mother's neglect. She was easily overwhelmed by even the smallest disappointments. Her moods and temper were out of control. Often the pain she felt in the pit of her stomach led her to frequent thoughts of suicide and several attempts. She always returned to her art to keep from falling apart.

Rick and Renee live life on the edge. Like Humpty Dumpty sitting on the wall, they do everything in their power to keep from falling and shattering into a million pieces. For those with such a fragile sense of themselves, their relationship is like a house of cards, an unsteady structure always on the verge of collapsing. It is never really a secure place because they feel so insecure inside. They see themselves as incapable of creating a stable partnership yet hope that the relationship will be a sanctuary. When they discover their partner's affair, the truth of how estranged they are from themselves is revealed and they fall apart.

When you have such a fragile sense of self, the world is a dangerous place. You feel vulnerable to stress and disappointment. Sensitive to being hurt, you are always on guard. Even though in lucid moments you can appreciate that people may not intend to hurt you, you tend to personalize their behaviors. You may entertain high expectations about how you want to be treated and react with intense pain to even the slightest disappointments. Your emotional well-being increasingly depends on how others respond to you. If you pay close attention, you notice that your self-esteem rises with praise and falls with criticism.

Even though your life may appear okay on the surface, in your quiet moments you admit that you feel empty inside and surrounded by a void. To maintain yourself, you create the scaffolding of a normal life. For example, you may invest yourself in work, in projects, in looking good, in being popular, in having money, in being admired, or in being loved. The list of external props for your life can be limitless. Even though you would like to believe you can fool others, you know in your heart of hearts you cannot fool yourself. You may secretly consider yourself a fraud. You are aware that all the outward appearances of success and confidence disguise a weak and helpless person who despises his vulnerability. When you invest your personal security and self-esteem in another person, the end of that relationship destroys your fragile self-image. You may be traumatized and feel as though you are falling apart.

In the psychological literature, those with such a fragile sense of self have significant personality disturbances. In the *Diagnostic and Statistical Manual of Mental Disorders,* they are identified as borderline personalities, who have extremely unstable moods and relationships, or narcissistic personalities, who are preoccupied with their sense of self-importance.[1] The following are some characteristics of these insecure personalities. Those with a fragile sense of self:

- feel empty or bored almost all the time.
- have out of control moods.
- are oversensitive to criticism and are easily offended.
- cannot control their temper, which is frighteningly intense.
- are terrified of being abandoned.
- feel extremely high or low in their relationships.
- hate themselves and often think of harming themselves.
- are impulsive and engage in self-destructive behavior.
- cannot tolerate being alone.
- need constant attention and admiration.
- believe they are special and have perfectionist expectations of themselves.
- have difficulty understanding others' feelings.
- are hypersensitive to others' reactions and to criticism.
- compare themselves with others and often feel envious.

3. Those locked in a pattern of abusive relationships

History tends to repeat itself, and those who are ignorant of it are condemned to repeat it. Those who have grown up in abusive households relive that experience in their relationships, unaware of the cost to themselves, until a crisis occurs. The discovery of an affair can trigger that crisis, releasing a flood of accumulated pain, as the following stories illustrate.

STACEY'S STORY

Stacey felt stuck in her seven-year marriage that she knew was a mistake a month after the wedding day. Her husband was a charming man, and he convinced her to move with him to a new city after they had been dating for only a few months. Stacey was infatuated with his charm and confidence. After the wedding, her husband became moody and withdrawn and drank more heavily. Stacey quickly found a sales job and made new friends. Her husband became jealous and berated her for her time away from him. He demeaned her and called her names. As time went on, his possessiveness became intolerable. When she defended herself, he became physically abusive. Stacey wanted to leave him, but she was frightened of what he might do. It was only after she discovered his affair with her best friend that she had the courage to leave him.

Even after separating from her unfaithful husband, Stacey was preoccupied with the pain of being betrayed. She thought of herself as damaged goods and blamed herself for being an inadequate wife. She was confused about herself. She could not understand how she could be so successful and confident in her work and so blind and weak in her relationships.

During therapy, she bemoaned all her terrible choices in men and asked, "How could I be so stupid and not see these men for who they were?" Right out of high school she lived with a man who was an alcoholic, was extremely jealous, and had a temper. She felt imprisoned in that relationship. They broke up because he finally left her for another woman. Shortly after that relationship ended, Stacey dated another man who was so insecure and possessive that he tapped her phone. He stalked her for months after she broke up with him. For a while she dated a man who treated her like a queen and wanted to marry her. But she was bored with him and ended the relationship.

After a few months of therapy, Stacey realized that she was attracted to men who reminded her of her father. Her father was injured at his factory job and received disability. He spent most of his day drinking and became a tyrant at home, while Stacey's mother worked. He used to beat Stacey and her brother and sister over trivial things. Her mother was a weak, depressed woman who also endured her husband's rages and assaults. Stacey realized she re-created what was familiar to her in her relationships with men.

RON'S STORY

Ron was devastated when his younger wife left him for the party life. When Ron married Janine he saw her as a spoiled child but expected her to grow up. He was attracted to her youthful exuberance and carefree attitude. Ron was a serious person, and he appreciated Janine's fun-loving nature. At first, they enjoyed going out to dinner and the movies together. She seemed to cling to Ron and look up to him, since he was ten years older. However, as time passed, she became bored and restless. Ron worked long hours. Janine complained that he was always tired and did not want to socialize as much as she did. She began going out to the bar with some younger friends she met at work. Her drinking increased, and she stayed out later and later. Ron complained, and heated arguments ensued. Finally, she announced that she did not want to be married anymore and had found someone else.

Ron had flashbacks of his previous marriage to a woman he described as "exotic and electric." Their sex was wild, and they enjoyed experimenting with drugs together. They had a son, and Ron became resentful when his wife spent more and more time away from home. She loved to shop, spending more than he believed they could afford. Ron felt exploited financially. They had many heated arguments about her spending and neglect of their son. She left Ron one day without a word because she claimed she had fallen in love with another man. It took several years for him to recover from the hurt of their divorce. He sensed he was reliving the trauma with Janine's departure.

In therapy, Ron described himself as a "Gemini personality" because there were two sides to him. He had a strong sense of responsibility and duty yet loved excitement and adventure. He realized that he was attracted to women who brought excitement into his life. He also realized in treatment how his love choices were opposite to his parents in some ways, but alike in others. His parents were quiet, conservative, and old-fashioned. They were always busy and never paid much attention to him or his brother. Ron never felt close to them. When he was sexually abused by his babysitter, he never considered telling his parents about it. He suffered in silence. Ron felt emotionally neglected by his parents as he had by his spouses.

After the honeymoon phase of their relationships, both Stacey and Ron in the above stories realized that their marriages were a house of horror, not the enchanting place they expected. Those with a history of being maltreated or abused in relationships hope that their marriages will be different from all their previous relationships and sacrifice themselves to make it work. They believe, "As an individual, I will become nothing, in order to keep the relationship; I will not count the cost to myself." When they discover their partner's infidelity, their hopes for someone different from the past are dashed. They may continue to sacrifice themselves to maintain the relationship until the unfaithful partner leaves. In the process, they experience the accumulated impact of all the previous interpersonal traumas.

Like Stacey and Ron, you may have felt stuck in relationships that over time came to resemble prisons. Initially, you were swept away by infatuation and dreams of passionate romance. You found your partner exciting, or maybe challenging. Perhaps you could not spend enough time together because you had so much fun doing almost anything. But soon the thrill disappeared. It may have been as quickly as after the wedding day when another side of your partner's personality emerged. You began to see your partner as more demanding, unreasonable, and even possessive, sensing that only his needs were important, while you were being used. Your needs and desires were increasingly pushed into the background, and you found yourself sacrificing more and more for his happiness. It may have dawned on you that you did not seem to have any rights in the relationship. As your partner's demands, demeaning behavior, name calling, or even physical abuse escalated, you felt helpless to escape. Because you felt so bad about yourself and so frightened to be assertive, you resigned yourself to the prison of the relationship.

Patrick Carnes, an international expert on addictions, describes what happens in relationships where one person exploits the other for his own purposes: an addictive relationship develops. The violated partner forms a "betrayal bond" with the hurtful partner and feels powerless to escape, much like the experience of addiction. They suspect the relationship is harmful to them but still cling to it, as if in a drugged state. They derive an unhealthy pleasure in surrendering themselves to the will of another, viewed as all-powerful.[2] Those who have a history of being betrayed by significant people in their life, often beginning with their parents, tend to repeat that pattern in their relationships. They might choose partners who replicate the mistreatment, abuse, neglect, and betrayal they grew up with. They become addicted to what is familiar, terrified to change it. The experience of being exploited and betrayed is then reinforced by deep shame, the belief they do not deserve better, and a fear of being abandoned. When they discover the infidelity of their partner, the reservoir of buried feelings from so many previous betrayals bursts the dam.

Those caught in a betrayal bond:

- are accustomed to accepting broken promises by others.
- feel stuck and helpless to do anything about their partner's destructive behavior.
- have an exaggerated sense of loyalty to their partner.
- hide their partner's faults when others point them out.
- become defensive when anyone questions their partner or their relationship.
- believe they can change their partner through love.

- excuse their partner's destructive, exploitive, or degrading acts.

- seem addicted to excitement in relationships and are bored with those who treat them well.

- keep their partner's destructive behavior secret from others.

- submit to even the most unreasonable demands by their partner.

- are terrified of being alone.

- feel a sense of shame at being exploited but cannot admit it to anyone.

- enjoy, yet hate, their partner's possessiveness.

For those who have sought their identity and sense of security in the relationship, the consequences of betrayal can be especially devastating. Those who dependently cling to love, have a fragile sense of self, or have had lifelong experiences of being exploited in relationships are at risk of suffering post-infidelity stress disorder. They may feel helpless and hopeless and believe their lives are over. Nevertheless, from the depths of despair, the ground is fertile for a new life to blossom. That is the miracle of recovery.

SOME DOS AND DON'TS FOR RECOVERY

1. Attend to your tender spots revealed by the betrayal. What is most hurtful about your partner's infidelity: the deceit, the loss of support, the hurt pride? What is your predominant feeling: loneliness, fear, anger?

2. Do not ignore your pain. How do you cope with pain: by withdrawing, becoming angry, clinging to others for reassurance? Do you see the present pain as temporary or lasting? Do you tend to suppress the pain or indulge in self-pity? Can you honestly and courageously face this painful moment, realizing that it will pass?

3. Have confidence in your inner strength. What personal strengths have you discovered through this painful experience? Are you more

resilient than you expected? Do you see yourself as a survivor or a helpless victim?

4. Acknowledge your weaknesses. What weaknesses have become evident through this experience? Are you a dependent person, expecting happiness from others? Are you a person with a fragile sense of who you are, constantly looking for reassurance from others? Are you a person accustomed to being victimized by others?

5. Trust your ability to learn new ways of coping. How have you coped with problems in the past? Do you believe you have the ability to cope with your partner's betrayal? Can this painful experience be the occasion for you to learn new, more effective ways of coping?

6. Maintain hope in recovery. Have you succumbed to despair, resigned to being a victim in life? Do you recognize a hidden potential for growth that may be activated by this crisis? Do you have hope of building a life beyond the pain of the present moment?

FOUR

ADULT CHILDREN OF UNFAITHFUL PARENTS
The Pain Goes On

*Insanity: doing the same thing over
and over again and expecting different results.*

—ALBERT EINSTEIN

Infidelity spans across the generations. If you have had an unfaithful partner or been unfaithful yourself, there is a possibility you have
experienced infidelity within your own family of origin. You may be an
adult child of an unfaithful parent. You may have been traumatized as
a child by your parents' behavior and not been aware of its impact on
your life and how you relate to others. Even if you do not recall parental infidelity, it may be beneficial to explore your childhood memories
and their impact on your current relationships. Furthermore, if you are
in a current infidelity situation, you might want to explore its possible
influence on your children, so you can help heal their wounds. Many
of the couples who come to me with marital problems also have memories of their parents experiencing similar conflicts or infidelities. Many
complain they were traumatized as children and have difficulty trusting
others and forming stable, intimate relationships as adults. Later in life,
these individuals manifest some of the symptoms of post-infidelity stress
disorder described in the first chapter. The following is a list of those

55

symptoms with one addition, which merits discussion here because of the strong correlation between trauma and addictive behaviors.

1. Exposure to a life-threatening event

2. Intense fear and helplessness

3. Re-experiencing the event

4. Avoidance of reminders of the event

5. Emotional numbing

6. Heightened anxiety

7. Irritability and rage

8. Addictive behaviors

In the following elaboration of these symptoms, you may recall some memories from childhood or become more sensitive to what is happening with your children as you struggle with your partner's infidelity.

1. Exposure to a life-threatening event

Imagine the impact on a child who discovers a parent's infidelity. Depending on the age, the child may not have much understanding of what is happening in the family. Nevertheless, a child is like a sponge soaking up all the anxious and hostile feelings between his parents. He is exposed to their fighting and feels their rage. In light of the secrecy and deception that accompany every affair, he may not know directly about the affair or recognize the source of his parents' anger, anxiety, or depressed mood. The impressionable youngster may feel neglected because of his unfaithful parent's absence from the home and from his wounded parent's preoccupation with the betrayal. Undoubtedly, he feels intense anxiety about the potential breakup of the family and loss of a parent. As an innocent child, he grows up in an atmosphere of betrayal, deception, hostility, and insecurity, without the ability to comprehend what is going on. He may feel shame because of his unfaithful parent's behavior and think he needs to hide it. He may want to protect his hurt parent and seek revenge on the unfaithful one. Imagine its impact on his conscious and unconscious perceptions about committed relationships as he grows into adulthood. Growing up in a family with an unfaithful parent may not be a threat to his physical life, but certainly to his psychological well-being. If you grew up in a house affected by infidelity, you may recognize this child in you. If you are trying to cope with your partner's affair, you may be able to better understand how it may be affecting your children.

2. Intense fear and helplessness

If your parent had an affair, there was likely considerable disruption in your home, over which you had no control. An emotional storm was unleashed, and you were left adrift in the wreckage of your parents' marriage. Perhaps you felt the tension and hostility in the home but could not understand it. Your parents undoubtedly argued about the affair and perhaps threatened divorce. They may have tried to keep their fighting and the affair secret, but you may have picked up the signs of trouble. In the midst of all the turmoil, you probably felt helpless and frightened about your future. (Perhaps you can see a glimpse of that fear in your children's eyes.) To cope, as children naturally do, you may have blamed yourself. You imagined that if you had been a better behaved child your parents would not have had this problem. Without knowing it, your experience of helplessness, fear, and insecurity was shaping you to assume a victim role in life, as these stories illustrate.

Diane, a forty-year-old woman, complained, "I don't have a voice. I'm always second-guessing myself about any decision I make and let others lead me around. I don't even have confidence in my own opinions. I feel like such a wimp." Diane related how insecure she felt growing up. Her mother had several affairs and divorced her father, who was alcoholic. Her mother always lied about her relationships with men and blamed her father for her unhappiness. Diane grew up in an atmosphere of deception that interfered with her ability to trust her perception of the truth.

Jimmy, a thirty-year-old man, came to therapy because he felt so self-conscious around women. He commented, "I was always shy as a child and had crushes on girls, but I was always terrified to approach them. I've had a couple of long-term relationships with women that have not worked out. It seems I'm attracted to troubled women who eventually leave me." Jimmy recalled accompanying his father to the home of another woman and her family when he was a child. He imagined they were just friends until his mother divorced his father and he married his lady friend. His mother remained bitter for years about the infidelity. And Jimmy came to share his mother's bitterness and mistrust.

3. Re-experiencing the event

Those who have been traumatized often relive the horror of the event in nightmares and flashbacks. However, there is another way to relive a horrifying experience in order to gain a sense of mastery over it: relive it in daily life. The psychological term to describe this reliving of the trauma is called "repetition compulsion." In an unconscious effort to heal the wound, traumatized people relive the experience over and over with the hope of a different result. They re-create similar situations in their own relationships, choosing to repeat the familiar rather than try to experience something different. They prefer the known to the unknown, which provokes anxiety.

How does this repetition compulsion affect people touched by infidelity? If you grew up in a home in which a parent was unfaithful, there is a good chance that either you will marry someone who becomes unfaithful or you will have an affair. That may seem strange because you assume that you would want to avoid at all costs what was so painful in your childhood. Actually, the opposite occurs. There is a strong tendency to re-create in your adult relationships the pattern of relating that you observed as a child. Your parents provided a powerful model of how men and women interact. You choose the known, rather than the unknown, with the secret fantasy that you can make it different. If you identify with the parent who was victimized, you may marry an unfaithful person. If you identify with the unfaithful parent, fascinated with his power and freedom, you may choose to have an affair. Aware of the profound influence you are having on your children, you likely want to help them avoid making the mistakes you did. The following stories illustrate how history repeats itself.

Richard, a man now in his fifties, had divorced his unfaithful wife after a brief marriage when he was in his twenties. For many years he was single and dated many women but claimed he could never find the right person to settle down with. In therapy, because of his lack of connection with women, he observed, "I don't think it's a coincidence that among the four boys in our family three married women who cheated on them and the other never married." He recalled that a family friend, a policeman, came often to have coffee with his mother while his father was working. One night, he saw his mother and the man kissing passionately, while both were intoxicated. He never talked with his mother or father about the event but never forgot it. The seeds of mistrust in women were sown.

Peter, a hard-driving businessman who traveled frequently, came to see me because of marital problems. He and his wife argued constantly about even the most trivial matters. He commented, "My wife and I are both jealous people. Throughout our relationship we fought about each other's friendships with members of the opposite sex. I believe my wife has been unfaithful, and so have I. When I travel I meet women in the bar and we spend the night together." Peter related that his father was often away on business and told him to be "the man of the house" while he was away. He recalled that his mother was always moody, irritable, and angry when his father was gone. He later learned that his father had an ongoing affair with a woman in one of the cities he visited on business.

4. Avoidance of reminders of the event

It makes sense that if something is uncomfortable and painful you avoid it. You have to touch a hot stove only once to learn to keep away from it. If you experienced the turmoil created by infidelity in your parents' marriage, you may cope with the pain of betrayal by avoiding intimate relationships. Similarly, your children, witnessing the turmoil caused by your partner's affair, may become extremely cautious about getting close to people. The trauma of betrayal makes an indelible mark on the psyche. The specter of infidelity may haunt you in all your relationships, although you may not be fully aware of its ghostly presence. One way to find safety is to avoid getting too close to the flames of intimacy that could burn you. But the consequence is a life of loneliness.

Celeste, an attractive middle-aged woman, came to therapy because she could not connect with men in her life. Because she was such a beautiful and engaging person, men were drawn to her. Celeste reflected on herself: "It seems I'm attracted to men who refuse to make a commitment. We only get so close. Then he backs off and says he is not ready." Celeste came to realize that she was attracted to emotionally unavailable men with whom she could feel safe because there was no real possibility of intimacy, which she believed was dangerous. She acknowledged that she was the one afraid of commitment. She admitted that she was ashamed of her mother, an emotionally unstable woman, who sought the attention of men and was eventually abandoned by her husband. Celeste realized that she sabotaged her relationships much like her mother.

5. Emotional numbing

In a household where a betrayal has occurred, an emotional storm rages, sometimes below the surface, which can engulf all the family members, including the children. If you grew up in such a household, perhaps you could not escape the angry outbursts, tearful pleading, anxious fretting, or even physical fighting of your parents over the affair. Even if your parents kept their disagreements private, you could not completely escape the atmosphere of tension and hostility. As a frightened child, one way of coping may have been to withdraw into yourself to find safety. If you observe closely, perhaps you can see signs of your children running for cover to escape the tension in the home. One patient told me how she had a hiding place under the stairs where she daydreamed while her parents fought. Another patient told me how he learned about his mother's affair when he was twelve years old. He listened attentively at the top of the stairs one night while his parents screamed at each other about the affair, but he afterward chose not to think or talk about it and claimed he had no feelings about the infidelity. Shutting down your feelings as a child may have been an effective way of keeping yourself from being overwhelmed. The danger, of course, is that the emotional detaching becomes a way of life, as the following stories illustrate.

An elderly gentleman, Lee, came to see me because he was not sure he wanted to remain married. He had become actively involved in his church and was facing himself honestly for the first time in his life. He confessed, "I have never loved anyone in my life and don't think I know what love means. I've been married twice but never felt close to either woman. I haven't seen my children in years." Lee recognized his emotional withdrawal and was disturbed by it. He acknowledged that he drank for years to numb himself and decided to stop. Together, we explored his childhood. Lee felt that he raised himself because his parents were so neglectful. His alcoholic father accused his mother of being unfaithful and frequently flew into rages and beat her. He realized that he grew up terrified of getting close to people because he never wanted to experience the emotional chaos of his parents' marriage. For the first time in his life, Lee admitted his fear of intimacy and wanted to overcome his sense of detachment.

Melissa, a middle-aged woman, came to therapy because her son complained about how she treated him while growing up, but she had no recollection of the events he reported. Melissa was married to a man for fifteen years and discovered he was unfaithful, but only after he divorced her and married the other woman. She dated several men who mistreated her and decided, "I can't trust myself to choose the right kind of guy, so I just keep to myself now." Melissa complained that she could hardly remember anything about her father who died when she was ten years old. The only memory she had was of him being drunk and arguing with her mother. Her older sister told her many years later that their parents argued about their father's affair.

6. Heightened anxiety

Children expect their homes to be places of safety from a world that can be challenging and threatening. However, if an infidelity occurs, that sense of security vanishes. If you grew up in a household touched by infidelity, instead of feeling peace and comfort at home with attentive parents, perhaps you experienced agitated, angry, worried parents who were preoccupied with their own problems. You may have lived with the constant threat at home of the family falling apart and breaking up. You may even have been frightened by escalating violence between your parents that may also have been directed at you or your siblings. In short, the home was transformed into an unsafe place. Perhaps you can sense your children's insecurity, their fear of the family falling apart. If you grew up with a sense of insecurity, you may spend your whole life looking for a relationship that can provide safety, yet never trust it because you are so acutely sensitive to the dangers of intimacy.

Carol and Paul came to see me for marital counseling. Carol insisted that Paul had an affair in the past and was meeting with other women secretly. Paul protested his innocence and felt helpless to reassure his suspicious wife. Carol admitted she could not prove his infidelity but was certain she was picking up signs of it in his behavior. She said, "I know I am a needy person and need reassurance of my husband's love. People have betrayed me in my life, and I always expect the worst to happen. I couldn't trust my mother, so how could I trust anyone?" Carol related that both her parents were unfaithful and lied about all their extramarital activities. She never knew what was true growing up and came to mistrust her own perceptions of reality. She lived in constant fear; the anxiety about being betrayed, humiliated, and abandoned never left her. Her husband, who was really an honest and trustworthy man, could never convince her of his faithfulness.

7. Irritability and rage

Those who have been traumatized often react with intense anger because their well-being has been threatened. They are fighting for their survival. The anger energizes them and makes them feel powerful in the face of their sense of being victimized. If you were raised in a home in which there was an infidelity, you likely are well acquainted with rage. You probably saw anger expressed in a variety of ways, in cold withdrawal, in angry verbal outbursts, and even in violence. You may have experienced anger as a fascinating, powerful, and frightening emotion. As a child, the displays of anger were also confusing and dangerous, as you witnessed its destructive consequences. (Perhaps you are noticing an increase in your children's aggressive behavior, suspecting they are reacting to their insecure home life.) As you grew into adulthood, you may have developed an ambivalent relationship with anger yourself. You learned either to suppress it because it was so frightening or to indulge it because it made you feel so powerful.

Those who grew up in hostile home environments precipitated by infidelity often learn that relationships involve a fight for power and control, as this case illustrates.

Alice, an accomplished businesswoman, came to therapy because she was unhappy in her marriage. Her husband had a brief affair, and they reconciled after it ended. However, the bitter fighting continued. Their relationship had become a battleground. She lamented, "I don't know how to stop the fighting. My temper is so out of control, and I hate it. I can see I am pushing my family away, but I don't know how to let go of my anger." She related that she had a distant relationship with her parents. They fought all the time over her father's affair when she was a child, and her mother never hid her bitterness. Alice said, "I wish they had divorced and ended all the fighting." Alice realized that she was re-creating her parents' antagonistic relationship with her husband. She began to recognize the hurt, sadness, and fear behind all her anger.

8. Addictive behaviors

There is a strong link between trauma and addiction. Nearly 90 percent of those who engage in addictive behaviors have experienced some trauma in their lives, particularly in childhood.[1] An addiction is a compulsive behavior that fills a void in the person's life. It is a way of gaining pleasure quickly and avoiding pain. The addictive behavior, such as drinking, using drugs, gambling, shopping, eating, and sexual acting out, is a way of numbing the painful feelings resulting from the trauma. It is no wonder that so many war veterans also abuse substances.

If your parent suffered the trauma of infidelity, there is a good chance that he compensated for the pain with some addictive behavior, such as drinking or drug use. You may then have suffered a double absence of your parents, through the trauma of betrayal and through the addiction. That loss may have influenced you to numb your feelings with addictive behavior. Perhaps, if you are now a parent agonizing over your partner's infidelity, you may be noticing your teenage children beginning to experiment with smoking, drinking, and drug use and suspect they are trying to escape. Furthermore, with the infidelity of a parent, you likely experienced much confusion around sexuality. Because of their hostility toward one another, your parents probably did not express a healthy and playful affection toward each other. Sex may have become associated with betrayal, secrecy, and forbidden behavior. Perhaps you are disturbed that your teens are becoming more sexually active, in imitation of your unfaithful partner. This confusion about sex may lead to a sexual addiction later in life, as these stories illustrate.

Ray, a young professional, came to see me with the complaint of excessive drinking and promiscuous behavior. He was engaged to a woman and acknowledged that these behaviors sabotaged his relationship with her. Ray confessed, "I know that I am out of control with my drinking. I am usually a shy person. But when I drink, I am the life of the party and love the attention of women. We almost always end up in bed together. The next day I feel miserable and hate myself for what I did the night before." Ray was aware that his parents had a poor sex life and showed little affection toward each other. He had vague recollections of his parents arguing about his mother's affair, and his older sister later told him how she enjoyed their mother's pornographic material at a young age.

Larry, a staunch Catholic, came to therapy because his wife caught him using Internet pornography. He stated, "I feel ashamed about the pornography and having to keep it hidden from everybody. I stay up late and feel tired the next day. I want to stop but don't know how." During the therapy sessions, Larry became aware of how much he disengaged from his feelings and lacked intimacy with his wife. They were committed to each other, but closeness was lacking. Larry did not see his use of pornography as being unfaithful but acknowledged how it strained his relationship with his wife. He recalled that his mother drank heavily, went to bars alone, and flirted with men. He suspected she may have been unfaithful. His parents showed little affection to each other, and Larry discovered his father's cache of pornography when he was a young teen.

The trauma of betrayal has a long reach. It is not limited to the couple whose relationship is disrupted by the infidelity. The children of unfaithful parents also experience its devastating grip, which may be a cause of great guilt for you as a parent. These children relive in their own relationships as adults the interpersonal distress they experienced growing up, and as they become intimately involved with others, the seeds of betrayal blossom. In my clinical experience, children raised by unfaithful parents either marry unfaithful partners or engage in affairs themselves. Furthermore, they experience the range of traumatic symptoms as they become emotionally involved with others, feeling intense mistrust, anxiety, anger, and emotional numbing, and engaging in addictive behaviors. If you have experienced parental infidelity, you may feel caught in the web of your parent's sins, but there is hope for escape, healing, and genuine growth. Acknowledging the traumatizing effect of your parent's infidelity and its impact on your current relationships can be a significant first step in your own recovery. Recognizing the damaging effect of your partner's infidelity on your children can also be the beginning of a healing to prevent them from re-creating your nightmare in their future relationships.

SOME DOS AND DON'TS FOR RECOVERY

1. Be curious about the influences on your life. Do you think about your childhood and its influence on who you are today? What experiences from the past most shaped you? How were you nurtured as a child? Do you have difficulty remembering much of your childhood?

2. Have the courage to explore the painful times as a child. What has been most hurtful about your upbringing? What was your relationship like with your parents, your siblings? What was disappointing about how you were raised?

3. Do not blame your parents for who you are today. Are you angry with your parents for their neglect or mistreatment? Do you hold a grudge against them? Do you feel trapped by the messages they gave you growing up? Do you feel helpless to disengage from their influence?

4. Allow yourself to grieve the losses from your childhood. What did you miss most growing up? How did your parents fail to give you

what you needed? How have these losses affected you as an adult? Were your parents faithful to each other?

5. Appreciate what you learned from your parents. What did you like most about your parents? What do you consider their greatest gift to you? Do you allow yourself feelings of gratitude?

6. Have confidence in the healing power within you. Do you see yourself as a damaged person because of what you experienced growing up? From where does your desire for healing come, if not from within you?

7. Do not wallow in guilt for the impact of the infidelity on your children. Can you appreciate how they are reacting? Can you try to find a way to help them, instead of being stuck in self-blame? How can you be a sensitive, nurturing parent to them in this difficult time?

PART TWO

STEPS TO RECOVERY
FROM THE TRAUMA

FIVE

STAGE 1: CALMING THE EMOTIONAL STORM
Finding a Safe Haven within Yourself

Resolve to find thyself . . . he who finds himself loses his misery.
MATTHEW ARNOLD

The first step in the recovery process is to acknowledge the full impact of the betrayal so that you can learn to calm the emotional storm that has been unleashed. Those who have been traumatized typically alternate between periods of emotional numbness and periods of feeling overwhelmed. As the initial shock recedes, the uncontrollability of their moods dominates them. When you first discover your partner's infidelity, you may be outraged, then withdraw into a stunned silence. However, as the impact of your partner's infidelity sinks in, you may become flooded with feelings that threaten to engulf you.

The shocking discovery also reveals your typical ways of coping with trauma, which must be examined and worked through for healing to occur. All of us have developed over time ways of protecting ourselves when threatened. These coping styles have their roots in childhood. In the midst of a crisis, we revert to these automatic defensive responses. For example, we may tend to bury painful feelings, to withdraw into activity, or to indulge in emotional outbursts. We may either fight against or surrender to the storm. Our defensive maneuvers, however, are only relatively effective in protecting us. In the midst of an overwhelming crisis, such as the discovery of a betrayal, the cracks in our defensive armor become visible. This crisis may be a challenge and an opportunity to learn new, more effective coping skills. We develop inner strength by facing adversity, not avoiding it. Ultimately, it is only embracing the full range of our feelings with honesty, courage, and gentleness that will lead to our inner healing and wholeness.

JENNIFER'S STORY CONTINUED

When Jennifer allowed Bruce to return home, she insisted he sleep in the guest room. She told him she needed time to decide whether she wanted to be married to him. When she was in the grip of rage over what he had done, she was convinced she wanted a divorce. She was so angry she could kill him. When she thought about their fun times in the past and imagined life without him, she was overcome with anxiety. How could she survive as a single parent? But could she ever trust him again? She knew she could not think clearly with all the emotions and terrible thoughts swirling around in her head.

Jennifer hoped that Bruce's return would allow them to talk calmly about the affair. She needed to understand why he did what he did. It never occurred to her that he could be so insensitive, spiteful, and deceitful. In her worst nightmare, she never imagined he would be unfaithful. Who was the man she married?

Jennifer became obsessed to learn all the details about the affair and what her husband was thinking. Did he love the woman? Did he share with her intimate details of their life? How did he act with her? What did they do together? Jennifer was always the one to bring up the affair for discussion, and Bruce was reluctant to talk about it. Jennifer bombarded him with questions about exactly what happened. When Bruce remained vague about the details, she became enraged and screamed at him. The angrier she became, the more he withdrew into silence and eventually erupted into anger. He admitted that he felt guilty and did not want to dredge up the sordid details, which he insisted would only make her feel worse. Jennifer wanted him to know how hurt, angry, and bitter she felt. She wanted him to understand the full impact of his actions on her and their daughter. However, with each fruitless encounter, Jennifer became more frustrated and enraged. She felt less secure about herself and their future together.

Jennifer realized she was in an emotional storm. She thought of herself adrift on a tiny boat in the ocean during a storm, with waves crashing about her. She feared being swamped by the raging waters and losing herself in the deep. Her feelings vacillated wildly. At times she felt numb, dead inside, and thought about nothing. She walked through the day in a fog. In the evenings she drank to keep calm and forget. At other times, her feelings of anger and fear erupted, and she was frighteningly out of control. She directed her fury at Bruce, screamed at him, and berated him for the pain he caused. "How could you have done that to us?" Often she focused her anger on herself for being so blind and stupid. She thought about what a terrible wife she had been that her husband would seek the comfort of another woman. There were also moments when she was in the grip of fear and had panic attacks, especially thinking about her uncertain future. And always, there was the sadness about the loss of their "perfect life." She was afraid she would dissolve in a pool of self-pity.

Jennifer was fortunate that she had Jane as a good friend. As she became more depressed, Jennifer withdrew from everyone. But Jane always kept calling and encouraged Jennifer to talk about what was going on with her. Jane kept telling her that she needed to seek counseling. Finally, Jennifer agreed and said, "I'm at my wit's end. I'll go crazy if I don't get help."

When I meet in therapy with patients who have been traumatized by the discovery of their partner's affair, I encourage them to talk about its impact on their lives. Some are emotionally shut down, afraid of being flooded by their painful feelings. Eventually, most pour out feelings of rage, fear, sadness, guilt, shame, and profound disappointment, like Jennifer. I explain to my patients that they have been traumatized and that what they are experiencing is not unusual for someone who has experienced the shock they received. I assure them that they are not going crazy and that recovery is possible, although it will take time.

My first piece of advice, if you feel caught up in the initial emotional storm, is not to make any major life decisions, especially about the marriage. You should also avoid making any other significant decisions, for example, regarding finances or living arrangements, because the noise of the emotional turmoil is too loud to hear your own thoughts clearly. Until your feelings quiet down, you are likely not able to think clearly about what you really want or what is in your best interest. Remember that recovery is a process that takes time. The first step in that process is to acknowledge the reality of the affair and its emotional impact on your life, and begin to calm the storm.

THE BRAIN ON HIGH ALERT

You may be frightened by the intensity of your emotional reactions and how out of control you might feel. You may believe you are drowning in your emotions. You may also question your sanity because of the persistence of unwanted thoughts and an inability to think clearly. My patients often find it helpful when I give them a brief sketch of how the brain reacts to cope with trauma.[1] The human psyche is astounding in its ability to protect itself and to adapt in order to survive.

With the introduction of a new technique called neuroimaging, researchers discovered a way of monitoring the activity of the brain and studying it. They are able to capture movements in the brain in colored pictures. When we use our brain, there is a rapid movement of electrical impulses and chemicals through an intricate web of neural connections within our head. The brain comprises many structures that function in specific ways to register sensations and produce thoughts, feelings, and behaviors. Many parts of the brain work together in a coordinated fashion to produce complex behavior. With the current technology, neuroscientists are able to study how the brain operates when an individual thinks, feels, and acts in a variety of conditions. They have noted that significant changes occur in the brain, particularly when intense emotions are experienced.

When these scientists studied the brain and emotions, they learned that three structures were predominantly involved in the processing of emotions: the amygdala, the hippocampus, and the neocortex. The amygdala is a small walnut-sized structure in the midbrain that responds rapidly to any perceptions of danger. It has an important role in detecting signals of fear, generating fear, and activating a defensive response, such as fight-or-flight reactions. The hippocampus, another area in the midbrain, is involved in storing memories of facts or events. The neocortex, the newest and most developed part of the brain, is in the frontal area, behind the forehead. The neocortex processes information that it receives from the senses and other parts of the brain. It is the control center that evaluates information, plans for the future, makes decisions for action, and regulates the emotions.

When we experience a stressful, threatening event, our brain responds almost instantaneously to activate defensive measures. The amygdala becomes hyperactive at any signal of danger. It immediately sends input to the neocortex for further processing. The neocortex never operates in isolation but rapidly connects with the hippocampus, which stores memories of previous experiences. Input from the hippocampus helps assess the danger and measure the response, based on the stored memory of previous experiences. Meanwhile, signals are sent through the amygdala to the sympathetic nervous system and the hypothalamic-pituitary-adrenal axes (HPA), causing an increase in heart rate, respiration, muscle tension, body temperature, and blood pressure. The hormones adrenaline, noradrenaline, and cortisol are released throughout the body to increase alertness and prepare for emergency action. This is the startle response that prepares to counter danger.

The increased arousal serves a survival purpose. It enables us to defend ourselves through fight, flight, or freezing. If the perceived danger is great enough or persistent enough, the brain adapts itself to the situation and operates under permanent high alert. There are actual measurable changes in brain functioning that inhibit the shutdown of the stress reaction system. That is why those who have been traumatized find it nearly impossible to relax or feel safe. Their brains will not allow it. Furthermore, with the persistent state of emergency readiness, the body can become exhausted and develop stress-related symptoms, such as back pain, hypertension, ulcers, and even cancer.

You may want to give up, thinking, "If the brain is so locked into this stress response, what hope is there of change?" Recently, brain researchers have discovered that the brain has a remarkable ability to adapt and recover. They call it "plasticity." They observed that the brain is able to regenerate itself and develop new internal connections. Through the use of the mind, the cycle of fearful reaction locked in the brain can be broken.

RECOVERY: A WAY THROUGH, NOT A WAY OUT

When you are flooded with feelings of fear, rage, and sadness, you may believe you are having a breakdown. You might think you will fall apart and never pull yourself together again. But the reality is that you will survive the pain. I tell my patients that what they are experiencing is not a breakdown, but a breakthrough of intense feelings that can no longer be suppressed. What has broken down is their old ways of coping, learned from childhood. I assure them that these feelings indicate that they are alive, not dead inside, like they think. The good news is that you can learn to manage your feelings and even learn from them. Your admission of powerlessness over your emotions is the first, and often necessary, step on the journey of recovery.

There are many strategies you can use to release yourself from the grip of overwhelming feelings. I assure you that you are not as helpless as you think in the midst of the emotional storm you are experiencing. For one thing, you are free to assume whatever attitude you want toward both your feelings and thoughts. As much as you might identify with your feelings in the midst of a life crisis, you are not your feelings. You can stand back and observe yourself feeling what you feel and thinking what you think. If you pay close attention, you notice that your feelings and thoughts pass, like clouds in the sky swept along by the wind. However, in the midst of your deepest distress, they may seem like a permanently stalled storm front.

One problem that many of you may face is that you never learned how to manage your feelings effectively. From childhood you developed strategies for coping with distressful events and your reactions to them. These defensive maneuvers were partially a result of your own temperament and partially from the role models you observed growing up. The ways you manage painful feelings, of course, are relatively effective in the midst of life's difficulties and help you survive the normal ups and downs of life. However, when you are faced with a traumatic event, such as the discovery of your partner's infidelity, you may feel overwhelmed because your usual ways of coping are proving inadequate. The trauma reveals chinks in your armor and challenges you to develop more effective coping skills.

From my clinical experience, there are three typical attitudes toward negative feelings that ultimately increase their grip on us. First, we may judge and condemn them as negative and struggle to overcome them. For example, we may hate our anger, be afraid of being overwhelmed by it, and become depressed over the ongoing struggle. In the struggle we learn that other negative feelings emerge, and the battle becomes an unwinnable war with new enemies. Second, we may try to ignore or repress painful feelings. We deny reality and pretend that the feelings do not exist. However, the more we suppress the feelings, the more pressure builds for them to emerge in indirect ways. Like a pressure cooker, the suppressed feelings sooner or later seep out or blow off the lid. For example, repressed anger emerges as an irritable mood and is often directed against innocent parties, like other family members, friends, or even the dog. Finally, we may choose to indulge the emotions. We believe that by ventilating them we release the steam and they dissipate. However, the opposite occurs. Expressing unwanted feelings reinforces their strength. For example, when anger is expressed in an outburst, other outbursts are provoked, and our tendency for tantrums is reinforced.

Explaining attitudes toward emotions to my therapy patients, I use the image of a waterfall. I tell them: "Your feelings and accompanying thoughts flow like a river over a waterfall. You can ignore or try to stop the flow, but, obviously, that will not work. The current keeps flowing. Or you can jump into the waterfall, be swept away, and risk drowning. An alternative is to stand behind the waterfall and observe the flow, seeking to understand what it means for your life."

Instead of being threatened by your feelings, it may be helpful to view them as natural reactions to life situations and simply relax with them. As difficult as they may be to live with, they are your friends, not your enemies. Your emotions contain energy that gives you a sense of vitality and can motivate you to action. However, they must be directed into constructive, rather than destructive, channels. In order to release the energy of your emotions, it is necessary to acknowledge the feeling and accept it. Next, you need to explore its meaning and understand why you feel the way you do. And finally, you can decide how to express what you learn in the most effective way that is also in your best interest. It is my firm conviction that, with practice, you can learn to channel the energy of the feeling for your own and others' well-being. To release the positive energy of your emotions, especially those experienced as negative, you will need to move from avoiding, to tolerating, to embracing them.

Steps to a healthy relationship with your feelings:

1. Pay close attention to your emotional reactions without judging them.

2. Acknowledge your feelings, without suppressing them.

3. Try to understand your reactions in the context of your life history.

4. Decide how to express your feelings appropriately.

Frequently, those who have been traumatized develop an aversion toward their feelings because they are so painful. They have difficulty processing their feelings because they avoid exactly what they need to do. They believe they cannot just stop and listen to themselves. For example, Dale, whose wife left him for another woman, commented, "I keep busy and running around so I don't have to stop and think. When I stop, I get overwhelmed by terrible thoughts and feelings." The following are typical emotional responses to the discovery of infidelity:

1. Numbness/denial: shutting down

2. Anger: closing off

3. Fear: backing away

4. Sadness: coping with loss

The following are brief explanations of the survival purpose and consequences of expressing these emotions.

1. Numbness/denial: shutting down

When you first learn of your partner's affair, you may well experience shock, feeling driven into a stunned silence. You may shut down to protect yourself from being flooded with emotion. One patient described it as "hibernating, sleep walking." Nothing seems real, and you may even take some comfort in the sense of disbelief.

Because your feelings are so painful, your first reaction is, naturally, to seek relief. An age-old remedy for pain relief is using alcohol or drugs. Alcohol and many drugs are anesthetics and tranquilizers. They are mood-altering substances that reliably provide temporary relief. However, the painful reality, although escaped momentarily, remains; problems still need to be faced. Using alcohol or drugs to cope can lead you to believe the illusion that recovery is the absence of pain and prevent you from the hard work of problem solving. Furthermore, the prolonged use of alcohol or drugs to cope may also develop into an addiction, which will make you more out of control in your life. The literature documents the high incidence of addictions among those who have been traumatized.

2. Anger: closing off

There may be moments that you think you cannot contain the rage you feel inside at being betrayed. At times, you might want to seek revenge on your partner for the harm she has caused. You want to inflict pain on the person who has caused you so much suffering. At other times, you may hold your feelings in, become irritable, and even blame yourself for being so blind and easily fooled.

You may be reluctant to give up your anger because it feels empowering. Anger gives you the sensation of strength so you can protest, "Never again," much like the Jewish people who never want to forget their rage about the Holocaust. You close yourself off to the pain with a wall of anger. Yet, if you stop to consider, you are also aware of the cost to your personal happiness in being angry. It robs you of your sense of inner peace. When you strike out in anger, even if you believe the other person deserves it, pangs of guilt usually follow eventually. Punishing others inevitably results in self-punishment. There are also physical consequences of anger, as documented by the medical profession. For example, internalized anger has been associated with back pain, cancer, heart disease, high blood pressure, gastric ailments, and a compromised immune system. The vengeful act also creates hostile relationships. Outbursts of anger provoke retaliation and begin an endless cycle of retribution. In the end, we all become victims of our anger. One patient came to the conclusion that her hatred for her unfaithful partner was like taking poison and expecting her partner to suffer.

3. Fear: backing away

After discovering the affair, you may feel thrown into chaos and uncertainty about your life. Your plans for life together with your partner have been shattered. Perhaps your assumptions about who your partner is and what you thought your relationship was have been destroyed. You may feel you have to start over with your life and be uncertain about what you will do. Self-doubts may also arise about your ability to cope with the new situation, with life on your own, with the burdens of unknown responsibilities.

Uncertainty about the future and self-doubt about your own competency can become the breeding ground for crippling anxiety. Fear and anxiety are normal reactions that protect you from danger. You naturally back away from what threatens you. Realistically, there are threats in life, and these emotions are early warning signals of danger. As explained earlier, these reactions are built into the nervous system for survival. However, when the imagination takes over and begins to exaggerate the dangers, you may begin to panic. You may question yourself and become paralyzed with fear. You may well ask: "How will I survive on my own? How can I ever trust anyone again? How can I keep from falling apart with all the stress I feel?"

It is important to remember that fear is about what might happen in the future. Of course, the future does not yet exist and is unknown. However, we imagine that terrible things will happen and that we will be helpless to cope. Fear and anxiety are in the imagination. They are about things that are not facts of life, but about what we imagine. In fear we cling to our assumptions about the future as if they were facts. Consequently, fear thrives in darkness and ignorance, in the unquestioning acceptance of these often pessimistic projections of our own minds. If we try to pretend we are not afraid, paradoxically, the fear grows. Anxiety seeps into the feigned ignorance.

4. Sadness: coping with loss

When you allow yourself to stop and think about the betrayal, you may experience a deep sadness that can become a debilitating depression. You have experienced a death, not a physical death, but the end of a relationship that provided you, to some extent, with a sense of security, meaning, and joy in your life. Sadness is a natural reaction to loss. You have lost a familiar life with your partner, trust in that person, and even confidence in yourself. When you think about the past and all the happy times together, your sadness may deepen because you know that those joys can never be recovered with your partner. You have been robbed of the consolations of a loving memory of your partner due to the betrayal. Finally, you may believe that a sense of security in any future relationship has been taken from you.

Sadness underlies many of the emotions we discussed earlier. Anger, fear, guilt, and denial may be ways of defending yourself against the full weight of sorrow about the tragedy of life. In acknowledging sadness you admit the impermanence and insecurity of life that ultimately ends in death. All relationships are terminal because they end with your partner's death or your own. The separation forced upon you by the betrayal anticipates the unavoidable dying that is part of living.

As mentioned previously, you may well experience a grieving process in recovery from the trauma of betrayal. While Dr. Kübler-Ross spoke about stages of grief in dying, I do not think of discrete stages in emotional recovery, but an overlapping and repetition of the various emotions of denial, anger, depression, and fear over time. Deep personal wounds heal gradually as we adjust to loss and feel sadness. Embracing, not avoiding or fighting, this painful grief process is an essential step in recovery and personal healing.

The ultimate goal of recovery is well illustrated in the traditional story of the poisoned tree. On first discovering a poisoned tree, some people see only its danger and try to avoid it. Their immediate reaction is, "Let's cut it down before we are hurt." Other people, upon encountering the tree, do not hate or fear it. Instead, they see it as a part of nature that must be respected. They build a fence around the tree so that others may not be poisoned. They think, "Let us not cut down the tree, but have compassion for it because we share the same nature." A third group approaches the tree and proclaims, "This is perfect. I was looking for a poisoned tree." Instead of destroying or avoiding the tree, they pick the poisoned fruit, investigate it, and look for ways to use the poison as a medicine to heal themselves and others. A mature emotional recovery involves acknowledging, embracing, exploring, and appreciating your painful negative emotions in order to transform and release their energy for a fuller life.

SOME AIDS FOR RECOVERY

The following are some tools to assist you in your emotional healing:

1. Undertake therapy: a companion for the journey

If you feel traumatized by your partner's infidelity, you will benefit from individual therapy to help untangle the knot of distressful feelings and thoughts. When you consider seeing a therapist, you may experience some reluctance. First, you may think your partner has the problem because she did not live up to her commitment. That is true, but it does not detract from the fact that you are in pain and need help for yourself. Second, you may also think that you have enough close friends or family who can support you. Of course, their support is essential. However, family and friends are not objective, and while they may encourage you to ventilate your feelings, they are not qualified to help you understand and work through them. If you are in physical pain, you do not hesitate to see a doctor. By the same token, if you are in emotional pain, which can be worse, why hesitate to see someone who can help you find relief?

You may no longer feel safe and secure because your comfortable world has fallen apart. The therapeutic relationship can provide a safe haven for you to re-establish trust in yourself and others. It is important that you find a therapist who is competent treating relationship issues and with whom you feel comfortable. It is also important that you have confidence in the person's ability to help you explore and understand yourself. Admittedly, therapy with a competent professional requires a significant investment in time, energy, and finances. If at all possible, I encourage you to make that investment and assure you of a rich return in contentment and self-knowledge.

Psychologists today recognize that there is a vital link between feelings, thoughts, and behavior. Our emotional reactions are influenced by the way we think about events in our lives. We interpret interactions with others and events almost instantaneously, based on prior experience. These thoughts arise automatically, and we may have little awareness of them. We develop a belief system about who we are, and our place in the world relating to others, based on a lifetime of experience interacting with the significant people in our lives. Our spontaneous thoughts and feelings lead to behaviors. As the word "e-motion" suggests, our feelings are impulses to action. If we feel anxious, it is because we anticipate a dangerous situation without the necessary resources to cope with it. Consequently, we take evasive action to protect ourselves. If we feel angry, it is because we perceive a present threat to our well-being and are energized to defend ourselves. If we feel sad, it is because we acknowledge a significant loss and seek comfort. The way we interpret a situation and our ability to respond determines our emotional reaction. A competent therapist can help you understand how your thoughts and feelings affect your behavior and well-being.

When Jennifer first came to therapy, she was nervous and embarrassed. She felt ashamed to talk about such personal matters as the betrayal by her husband. She was a private person and didn't want others to know about what she perceived as a personal and humiliating failure. After settling down a bit, she began to talk about her overwhelming fear. She was so frightened about what the future would be without her husband, raising their daughter alone. Jennifer said she had not had a good night's sleep since discovering the affair. She had anxiety attacks throughout the day whenever she thought about the affair and her future. Her heart raced and she could hardly breathe. She thought she was having a heart attack and admitted that her heart was broken. Her mind also was out of control, filled with worries and preoccupied with what her husband had done to her and their daughter.

I invited Jennifer to be aware of the automatic thoughts that accompanied her anxiety attacks. At first she could only identify her mind as "blank and racing." As she stopped to consider, she became aware of thinking: "My life is over. I'm such a failure. How can I survive alone? What did I do wrong to deserve this?" We examined together the various thoughts that emerged and questioned their validity. Did these thoughts really make sense to her when she examined them closely? We uncovered a personal belief about herself that she hardly recognized, the belief that she was a weak, powerless, and worthless person. We also explored the roots of this belief in her childhood. Her father was moody and demanding, controlling the household with his explosive temper. Her mother cowered in fear, believing that her main job in life was to serve her husband. Jennifer realized how much she had become like her mother and needed to assert herself more with her husband.

2. Join a support group

You may feel isolated in your pain, believing that no one will understand. Your family takes sides, and because of your depression, you may withdraw more and more from your friends and normal activities. The sense of being alone and isolated will only increase your emotional pain. However, there are many support groups in the community, which are free or have a minimal cost and can bring you together with others who may be suffering similar emotional distress. It is a great consolation to know that you are not alone in your pain.

One of the most popular and available support groups is through the Twelve Step Program, a guide to personal conversion. The program is spiritual and God-focused, but not attached to any specific religious group. You may identify such groups only with alcoholics or drug addicts, but the program has expanded to assist people with a wide range of problems. Through decades of personal experience, the use of the twelve steps has shown to be a powerful tool in recovery from intransigently painful behaviors. Originally started in the

1930s as Alcoholics Anonymous, a self-help group without professional involvement, the program now reaches out to those addicted to gambling, eating, sex, and spending, and to their families. Groups have also arisen in many communities to support those who are addicted to emotional states they cannot seem to escape. They are called Emotions Anonymous. These groups can be helpful for some, especially those who feel trapped in their emotional storm. They can benefit those who sense their anger outbursts, unremitting depression, and anxious obsessing about the affair are out of control, like an addiction. The steps of recovery begin with an admission of powerlessness over any emotional state, progress through a request for God's help and an honest self-examination, and end with a reaching out to others. Working the steps with the support of others in similar emotional pain can be extremely liberating. Participating in these groups, you may be surprised to learn how many others are struggling with the deep wound of betrayal.

3. Keep a journal

An effective way to calm the emotional storm through self-awareness is to keep a journal of your thoughts and feelings. The process is simple. Get a notebook, sit in a quiet place, and pay attention to what you are experiencing in the moment. Begin writing whatever comes to your mind, any thoughts, feelings, memories. Let the words flow without censoring or judging them. If the feelings that emerge through the writing become too overwhelming, just stop the exercise. Be gentle with yourself. Those who have been traumatized frequently become flooded by painful feelings and become frightened of drowning in them. Keeping a journal, which is a personal diary of your experience, helps to unfreeze the feelings that keep you stuck. In writing, you let your feelings flow. The process of writing also enables you to bring the power of your mind into the healing process so that you do not drown in your feelings. You begin to gain some perspective on your passing thoughts and feelings that gives you a sense that you are in control of your life. My patients have related that this stream-of-consciousness writing has been immensely valuable for knowing and calming themselves.

4. Take medication: a tool for recovery

There are occasions when I recommend that my traumatized patients seek a psychiatric evaluation to assess their need for medication. When you are feeling so overwhelmed, anxious, or worried that you can hardly function; when you are so depressed that you cannot sleep or eat and lack energy; when you are so distraught that you think suicide is the only escape; when you are so irritable and angry that you are afraid you cannot control your rage—then I would recommend that you consult with a psychiatrist. Your primary care physician may prescribe an anti-depressant, tranquilizer, or sleep aid, but I suggest you see a psychiatrist who is a specialist with psychotropic medication. The psychiatrist is better informed about the variety of medications available and can monitor more closely and accurately your response to the medications and make appropriate adjustments. He will also hospitalize you if you are suicidal and need a temporary safe environment for your recovery.

I remind my patients that medication can be an important tool for recovery but caution them that it is not a magic pill that will solve their problems. If you are feeling so flooded by your emotions that you are not able to think clearly enough to work through personal and marital issues, you need some emotional calm that medication can provide. Recovery requires work, taking an honest, and often painful, look at yourself and your relationship.

5. A personal exercise: follow your breath

A powerful way to reconnect with yourself and calm the emotional storm is with a meditation following your breath, which comes from the Buddhist tradition. This exercise encourages you to become an observer of your feelings to avoid the pitfalls of either ignoring or identifying with them. It helps you to focus on the present moment to bring yourself to peace, and eventually insight. Much of our emotional turmoil results from our inability to live the present moment fully. Often, we mentally live in the past and ruminate about regrets, lost opportunities, old wounds. Preoccupied with the past, we live an "if only" life. Or we live in the imagined future, caught up in our plans, hopes, and worries. Then we choose a "what if" life. Living in either the past or the future, we miss the magic and wonder of the present moment. If we have been traumatized by an infidelity, our roller-coaster thoughts and feelings cast us into different time zones. We become obsessed with the betrayal that happened and worry endlessly about what we will do.

This exercise can also help you to relax in your body. When you experience emotional distress, you may be surprised at the amount of tension you hold in your body. This muscular tension keeps you from relaxing with your mind and feelings. Often our lives are so frenetic, so driven to produce and accomplish tasks, we never learn to relax. We never take the time to stop and learn to release the buildup of stress. We pay a severe price for this neglect of ourselves. The constant tension produces a wide variety of medical illnesses, such as heart disease, high blood pressure, gastric problems, ulcers, back and joint pain, and so forth, and interferes with our happiness.

To help keep you in the present moment, to help let go of the anger about the past and worry about the future, I recommend that you make a commitment to a daily exercise of following your breath. Think for a moment what your breath means. Breathing is something you do every moment of your life. Without breath, there is no life. Your breathing reminds you that you have a body that needs to be cared for. You breathe in air, which comes from outside you, to keep you alive. That which keeps you a living person connects you with all of nature. Plants produce oxygen, which enables animals, other humans, and you to survive. There is a dynamic, free, and fresh quality about air, which is stirred up to become wind, penetrating closed-in places, or even a powerful hurricane. Breath is also sacred, putting you into contact with the Divine. The Hebrew word for "spirit" is the same word for "breath." God's breath hovered over the waters at creation, and God breathed His life into the human form.

The procedure for this traditional practice of following your breath is simple:

1. Find a quiet place. Sit in a relaxed position with your back and head straight. The erect posture is important to allow the free flow of your breath. You may sit in an upright chair with your feet firmly planted on the floor or in the traditional lotus position with your legs crossed. Place your hands on your knees with the palms

upward in a receptive position. Either close your eyes or focus on a point immediately in front of you.

2. Next, breathe deeply from your abdomen. Do not take shallow breathes from your chest. Breathe regularly and focus your attention on your body. Slowly scan your body with your mind, beginning at the top of your head and proceeding to the bottom of your feet. Notice the areas where you feel tension in your muscles. Pause when you discover an area of tension and tell yourself to relax. Breathe slowly, sense a feeling of warmth, and feel the tension easing, like a rubber band unwinding. When you feel relaxed in that area, move on with your mental body scan.

3. Now focus all your attention on the rising and falling of your breath. Follow closely the sensation of your breathing. You will immediately notice how distracted you are by intrusive thoughts, how difficult it is to focus your attention only on your breath. Some practitioners label this the "wild monkey mind." Just observe your mind tending to get lost in the avalanche of thoughts.

4. When you are distracted by the thoughts, gently refocus your attention on your breathing. Avoid struggling with the unwanted thoughts. Just acknowledge their presence, perhaps saying to yourself, "a thought," and let it pass without dwelling on it. Maintain a relaxed posture in both your mind and body.

Practice this simple procedure every day, if possible, to make it a habit. You may begin with a five-minute practice and gradually increase the time you spend in this meditation. The first thing you will notice is how difficult it is to sustain your attention and discipline your mind. But the calmness you experience and the connection with yourself will astound you if you persevere. The meditation helps focus the mind on the present moment, rather than dwelling on an uncertain future with anxiety or a painful past with regret and sorrow.

Some who have been traumatized may find this practice too overwhelming at first because intrusive thoughts are so powerful in filling the silence. Be gentle with yourself and do not force yourself to be still if it is too stressful. You may instead choose to walk in a peaceful place and try to follow your breath as you saunter.

6. Pray from the heart for the gifts and fruits of the Spirit

Jesus taught the power of prayer, promising, "Ask and you shall receive; seek and you shall find; knock and it shall be opened to you" (Luke 11:9). In ordinary times, we ask for fulfillment of our needs of the moment, for example, that we get the job we want, pass an exam, or enjoy good health. But in the extraordinary time of crisis, our attention is initially focused on getting immediate relief. However, as we pray more deeply, we may be drawn to consider a larger perspective, thinking about what is most important in our lives, not just for the moment. The crisis of infidelity encourages us to consider that larger perspective, and Jesus invites us to do the same when he adds, "How much more will the heavenly Father give the Holy Spirit to those who ask Him" (Luke 11:13).

Prayer of petition is common to all the spiritual traditions. Buddhists pray for release from the craving, hatred, and delusion that causes suffering and ask for the *paramitas*, or perfections, that bring liberation. Similar to the gifts and fruits of the Holy Spirit in the Christian tradition, they pray for generosity, proper conduct, renunciation, wisdom, energy, patience, truthfulness, determination, loving-kindness, and equanimity. In the Native American tradition, shamans are sought out to pray for healing and for wisdom in times of decision.

While in the midst of your emotional and mental turmoil following the discovery of your partner's infidelity, have you considered praying for the gifts and fruits of the Spirit? These gifts, if fully embraced, produce not only relief from suffering but also wholeness, happiness, and peace.

Take a moment now to relax in a quiet place. It is important that you assume a comfortable posture. Whether you sit, kneel, stand, lie down, or walk does not matter, as long as you are relaxed and attentive. Consciously place yourself in God's presence, however you conceive Him, fully aware of His love and promises of assistance. Be aware of the presence of His Spirit in your heart. Now ask God directly for the gift of fortitude, which is the courage to face the threats to your security and not give up. Allow yourself to feel, without being too overwhelmed, the reactions of hurt, anger, fear, and sadness. However, offer these feelings up in a spirit of confidence that you are bearing them with God's, or the Great Spirit's, strength and courage. Let yourself feel fortified for a few moments, sensing an inner energy and determination to persevere. Knowing that God is generous in giving His blessings, ask also for the gift of temperance, which is the ability to keep your balance in the midst of the emotional storm. This gift is similar to the *paramita* of equanimity, which is the acceptance of unceasing change with steadiness and renunciation, restraining our passionate craving and aversion. Be assured that with God's strength you are able to withstand the storm, as Jesus' disciples did in that storm-battered boat while Jesus slept. Be confident you will reach the far shore of recovery and peace, if you are willing to persevere and make the effort.

Recovery is a journey that begins by embracing our feelings with honesty, courage, and gentleness. Such a journey can be perilous, with many unexpected turns. There are many ways to respond to the pain of betrayal that can divert us from the path of recovery. We may suppress the painful feelings, allow ourselves to be overwhelmed by them, or act them out in making rash decisions. We may be tempted to act precipitously, by leaving our unfaithful partner in anger or clinging to her in fear. As distressful as these overwhelming emotions are, embracing them in an effort to understand them becomes an opportunity to practice and grow in the virtues of fortitude, temperance, energy, and determination. Furthermore, a wise companion, social support, and a reliance on our spiritual resources can offer strength and guidance for integrating our feelings, thoughts, and decisions toward building a new life.

SOME DOS AND DON'TS FOR RECOVERY

1. Don't make any rash decisions. Do you tend to act impulsively, without considering the consequences? Do you make decisions when upset? When you are upset, do you have difficulty stopping to think things through?

2. Accept your struggles for recovery as normal. Are you impatient with yourself because you feel the betrayal so intensely? Are you impatient to get over the pain? Do you think you are abnormal because you hurt so badly and for so long? Do you believe you can learn new, more effective ways of coping?

3. Don't indulge your anger and retaliate. Do you have a temper? Does your anger feel out of control? Do you want to seek revenge on your unfaithful partner?

4. Don't bury or fight against your feelings. Are you down on yourself for what you feel? Do you tend to ignore your feelings? Do you feel in a constant battle with yourself over your uncomfortable thoughts and feelings?

5. Don't minimize or exaggerate the personal impact of the infidelity. Would you rather just forget about what happened and move on with your life? Do you complain excessively about what you suffered? Does self-pity dominate your life?

6. Treat your feelings as friends, not enemies. Do you hate what you feel? Do you think you can learn from your feelings and gain important information about yourself? Do you listen carefully to your feelings, as you would a close friend? Do you take all your feelings seriously, especially the uncomfortable ones?

7. Focus on self-care and take time for yourself. Do you believe you deserve the time you take for yourself? Do you focus more on caring for others than yourself? Are you your own best friend?

8. Seek support and guidance through therapy and self-help groups. Do you believe you deserve the care of others? Can you trust others enough to let them help you? Are you willing to let others know you, or is that too frightening? Do you expect others will reject you if they really get to know you?

9. Pray as if everything depends on God, however you conceive Him; work on recovery as if everything depends on you. Do you believe in the power of prayer? Are you willing to put energy into developing the virtues needed for recovery?

10. Cultivate the virtue of fortitude—courage. Do you see the decision to invest in your own recovery as a courageous act? Do you see it as an invaluable opportunity to become a courageous person?

SIX

STAGE 2:
UNDERSTANDING YOUR
UNFAITHFUL PARTNER
Why? . . . Why Me?

Those things that hurt, instruct.
—BENJAMIN FRANKLIN

After initial shock and disbelief, when the mind clears, your question most likely is "why?" Why did the affair occur? What happened and what led up to it? Why now? Why did this happen to me? Those who have been traumatized experience cognitive shock. Their assumptions about life that provided a sense of consistency, predictability, and security have been shattered. They can no longer trust their perceptions and judgments about the world and themselves. Similarly, after discovering the affair, your mind may swirl with unanswered questions and you might become obsessed with finding answers. You may feel so driven to find answers because your familiar world has been shattered and you are filled with anxiety and dread. What you assumed to be true about your partner, yourself, and your relationship has been revealed to be a lie. And what can be most unsettling about the affair are the lies and deception by your partner to engage in and maintain the infidelity. A massive betrayal of trust has occurred.

SOME SHATTERED ASSUMPTIONS

1. About your partner's character

2. About the security of your relationship

3. About your own self-confidence

4. About your perception of reality

What are some of the assumptions that may have been shattered? First, what you believed about your partner is tragically called into question. You were undoubtedly drawn to your partner because of qualities that you admired in her, such as her honesty, charm, intelligence, humor, sensitivity, and so forth. As you got to know your partner, you probably became aware of idiosyncrasies, annoying habits, and character flaws, but, up to this point, nothing so serious that you wanted to end the relationship. In all likelihood, you never imagined she could be so deceitful, insensitive, and cruel as to betray you. Otherwise, you never would have made a commitment to her.

Second, your beliefs about your relationship may have been destroyed. Whether you are married or in a stable relationship, heterosexual or homosexual, you undoubtedly assumed a degree of commitment from your partner. You probably talked explicitly about the nature of your relationship, about being exclusive, not having sex with others, not revealing personal secrets, your future together. Many mutual expectations became clear as the relationship unfolded and crises arose. Crises likely led you to talk about your differing views, desires, and expectations and to seek a common ground. But underlying all the discussion was a mutual trust in each other's honesty, which has been strained to the breaking point.

Third, uncertainties about what you believe about yourself may have been exposed. For example, before the discovered affair, you may have seen yourself as a confident, secure, insightful, trusting person. You felt capable to manage your life, with all its ordinary surprises. But with the shocking revelation of the affair, your world has been turned upside down and you may feel in an emotional free fall. You may question your ability to cope, wondering, "What's wrong with me? Will I survive this? How could I have been so blind?"

Finally, you may now question your sense of reality. You probably felt a sense of security in your relationship, acknowledged some problems as everybody has, and were generally at peace with yourself in your personal universe. You saw the world as a friendly place in which your needs were met, for the most part. However, after the betrayal with your partner's lies and deceptions, you may no longer trust your perceptions and judgments. You may wonder—if you were so wrong in trusting your partner, how could you possibly be right in trusting your ability to see reality clearly? You may believe that your world has now been transformed into a hostile, unsafe place in which you feel helpless to recognize dangers and protect yourself.

As much as you want to understand what your partner did and why, you may surprisingly discover in yourself a reluctance to know the truth. You might prefer the comfort of denial. One patient told me, "I prefer not to look at things too closely. I'm more comfortable with the unknown than the known. The known may be worse than I imagine, and I may have to do something about it." He pretended that if he did not know it, it did not exist. To talk about the infidelity is too painful because it makes it more real. It inflames the wound.

Because you have been betrayed, you may no longer trust your partner or believe he will be honest. If he covered up the affair, you assume he will lie about what happened. He may even offer some excuses to justify his behavior, or even blame you. Such dishonesty will only deepen the hurt and distrust. Furthermore, if you inquire about the affair, you may be confronted with your partner's defensiveness, and you do not want to engage in more arguments with him.

Furthermore, if you are honest with yourself, you may recognize that you want to stay angry to feel powerful and in control, or even self-righteous. Your anger may have become a safe haven, to protect you from further harm. You may not want to make the effort to understand your partner or give him a chance to make excuses.

BENEFITS OF UNDERSTANDING YOUR PARTNER

1. To relieve self-blame

2. To make sense of your world again

3. To give up the grudge against your partner

4. To begin an honest self-examination

5. To grow in wisdom

Are there any real benefits to understanding your partner's harmful behavior? I believe there are. First, at some level you may blame yourself for your partner's infidelity, believing that you somehow drove her into the arms of another. You might ask yourself, "Why me? What did I do to deserve this? Was I that terrible a partner?" You might possibly consider her unfaithfulness as a reflection on you and your adequacy as a partner. You might imagine that somehow you are responsible and think, "If only I had been more attentive, affectionate, worked less, had better sex, then she would not have strayed." You may well wonder, "What was so wrong with me that she chose another?" The benefit of understanding what led your partner to the affair can help to relieve that self-blame, by giving you a more realistic appreciation of the distribution of responsibility.

A second benefit is appreciating that the affair did not occur out of the blue. Something in your relationship and in your partner prepared for that catastrophic event, although it may not be so clear at first. One of the most unsettling aspects of discovering your partner's infidelity is its unpredictability. The dream of what your life together could be has been shattered. All of us have an imaginary film in our mind's eye of how we want our lives to proceed. No one expects a partner to betray them. Such an unpredictable catastrophe creates anxiety about what other terrible things could happen. Our assumptions about a stable, familiar, and happy life together, forever, have been undermined. What else can happen? Our assumption about our relationship as a safe haven has been belied. How can we ever trust anyone again? Understanding what led up to the affair can help make sense of it and give some measure of comfort in the rationality of the universe.

Third, understanding can help you give up your anger. Because of the seriousness of the betrayal and threat to your well-being, you may feel consumed by rage. Your anger is a wall that protects you from further harm. However, as time passes, you may begin to realize that the rage also imprisons you. It deprives you of contentment and peace and isolates you from others who may not understand your irritability. As many under stress do, you may even suffer physical symptoms, such as back and stomach pains, sleeplessness, and muscle tension. In short, you may not like the person you have become, an angry person. Further angry expressions toward your unfaithful partner will only inflame the anger and its poisonous effects on your life. This may be difficult to hear in the midst of your rage, but the only escape from your wrath will be through acceptance and forgiveness. Understanding your partner's involvement in the affair can help you begin to appreciate her humanness, without excusing the action, and develop some empathy. That empathy, the ability to put yourself in another's shoes, is an essential step in the process of acceptance and forgiveness.

A fourth benefit, also difficult to acknowledge and accept, is that through understanding your partner's behavior you are better able to give up blame and engage in an honest self-examination. Blame does not change what has happened. It only imprisons you in anger and keeps you from looking honestly at yourself and your life. I want to emphasize that no one is responsible for his partner's infidelity. Your partner is responsible for his behavior, and nothing you ever did could justify the betrayal. However, the infidelity may expose an underlying and unacknowledged weakness in your relationship. The infidelity may be a symptom of some deeper problems that are crying out for attention. Perhaps both of you were dissatisfied but did not address it honestly with each other. Understanding your partner and giving up blame will free you to look at yourself honestly, without self-blame, as to how your actions in the relationship may have contributed to the dissatisfaction you both experienced.

A final, surprising benefit of grappling with the truth of your partner's infidelity may be that you grow in wisdom and understanding. Without even knowing it, you may have become complacent in your relationship and clung to the comfortable security of your routine lives. You may have grown to accept many beliefs about yourself, your partner, and your relationship that were distorted and gave you a false sense of security. Your perceptions may have been clouded by your need to romanticize and idealize your life. You may have come to take for granted the good things you were enjoying in the relationship. As painful as the discovery of the affair was, it can be an opportunity to grow in wisdom and understanding. What knowledge you gain will be precious, because it will be purchased at a high price, with much effort and soul-searching. For many, it may be the first time they make a long, hard, honest scrutiny of their lives.

Like Jennifer, you may have struggled in vain to have an honest conversation with your partner about the affair. Fueled by your anxiety, you might obsess about the affair and ruminate about possible reasons. Your anger will probably make you persistent in trying to find out from your partner the details of what happened and why. However, you may discover that the more you push your partner to know the truth, the more he may resist, pushing back. Naturally, you are frustrated by your partner's defensiveness, which is likely motivated by his guilt and shame. He may say he is withholding the details to spare you the pain, but the truth is he is attempting to spare himself the humiliation of his betrayal. The reality is that he will speak honestly only when he is ready to accept responsibility for his behavior.

TYPICAL PATTERNS OF INFIDELITY

Infidelity exposes massive cracks in the foundation of a relationship, which may not have been recognized but are revealed through the affair. That is one reason why the discovery of an affair is so shocking. In most cases, it shouts out, "Something was wrong in our relationship, and I didn't even know it!" An affair is never a healthy choice and is almost always a symptom of a deep underlying problem in the relationship. It arises from dissatisfaction in the relationship and usually reveals the personality conflicts of the offending partner.

Why would anyone choose to break such an important promise to someone he loves? Based on my clinical experience, I will say that in most cases the choice for an affair is a flight from the struggles of intimacy. To sustain a committed relationship requires much maturity and hard work. It is a demanding, complicated process to love and be loved, to be able to stand on one's own and yet be emotionally connected. A mature relationship demands endless give-and-take, the courage to express honest feelings, and the fortitude to negotiate differences of opinion and desires. It requires fully accepting oneself and the loved one, including differences in feelings, desires, and opinions. Because two unique individuals choose to be together, inevitable misunderstandings and conflicts arise that need to be resolved. Furthermore, to risk loving another exposes one to the possibility of being hurt; it is safer not to care. The decision to engage in an affair is really an avoidance of a commitment to any one person, because it involves choosing to be with two part-time partners.

INSECURE ATTACHMENT STYLES

As the popular song lyrics express it, there are "fifty ways to leave your lover." Certainly, there are countless ways of disconnecting in a relationship. Attachment theory, a theory about bonding in relationships, suggests a helpful way to understand and group together some of the major ways that people connect and disconnect in relationships. John Bowlby, an ethnologist, observed how animals care for their young, and, in the process, an attachment bond develops between them. He further noted that whenever there was a danger, a survival response was activated that maintained the protective closeness between the mother and her offspring. He called it an "attachment system." Bowlby saw a similarity between the interaction of animals with their young and how human beings form strong affectional bonds to specific people. Through emotional bonding with the mother, a child feels a sense of security that allows him to venture out and explore his environment. In stressful times of separation, he relies on his trust in his mother's protective presence.[1]

Based on Bowlby's theory, researchers devised experiments to validate his insights. Mary Ainsworth and her colleagues observed mother-child interactions under controlled conditions and developed a technique called "the strange situation." She observed brief separations and reunions between mothers and their one-year-old children and noted their differing behaviors. Some ways of interacting during the separation-reunion appeared to be more effective in relieving anxiety in the child than others. She observed that most children responded with a "secure style." The child showed signs of distress when the mother withdrew but quickly approached her and settled down when she returned. Other reactions appeared to reveal a continuing sense of insecurity in the child, even after reunion. Some children displayed an "avoidant style." These children experienced some distress at their mother's leaving but seemed to reject the mother upon her return. Other children showed an "anxious-ambivalent style." They demonstrated a high level of distress during the separation and a mixture of approach and rejection upon reunion.[2]

Further research suggested that the attachment styles, learned through the repetitive interactions between the primary caregiver and the child, persist into adulthood in their most significant relationships. Some adults feel secure within themselves. They can easily stand on their own and yet are able to maintain an emotional connection with their partners. They can negotiate the emotional space in their relationships, respecting each other's differing needs for closeness and distance. Others feel varying degrees of insecurity in their relationships, reacting to stressful interactions by an avoidant or anxious style. These insecure individuals tend to act in extremes, either detaching emotionally or clinging to their partners. Bartholomew and Horowitz undertook an experiment examining the attachment styles of young adults and noted a third way that insecure individuals react in stressful interactions with their partners. They develop a "dismissing style" in which they fight against close relationships.[3]

In working with couples struggling through an infidelity, I have observed three typical ways that unfaithful partners disconnect in their relationships. They flee the demands of an intimate relationship, the stressful give-and-take of negotiating emotional space. Their disconnection reveals the underlying sense of insecurity they feel within themselves and their relationships. Through their infidelity, these individuals engage in the following behaviors.

1. Flight, which is similar to the avoidant style and reveals a fear of closeness.

2. Fight, a version of the dismissing style, which suggests a relentless turf battle.

3. Cling, which is like the anxious-ambivalent style, manifesting a fear of autonomy.

Interestingly, these three patterns of disconnection have been observed by others in the past. Karen Horney, a renowned German-American psychologist, explained that neurotic people resolve and express their inner conflicts in their relationships by (1) moving away from others (flight), (2) moving against others (fight), or (3) moving toward others (cling).[4] There is a parallel between these three styles of disconnecting with Buddha's insights twenty-five hundred years ago. He said there are three root causes of suffering that condition interactions with others: (1) greed or excessive attachment (cling), (2) hatred or aversion (fight), and (3) delusion, living the illusion that we are separate from others (flight).

THREE PATTERNS OF DISCONNECTING THROUGH AN INFIDELITY

It is important that you understand not only the immediate circumstances that may have influenced your partner's decision to be unfaithful but also her personality weaknesses that are revealed through her choice. It would be beneficial for you to know what drama was playing out in her mind through the affair so you can know your part in the play. You were obviously an unwilling participant but need to know how you were unwittingly drawn in. Understanding your partner's behavior will also be important for your decision about whether you want to continue the relationship. Can the damage be repaired? Is she a trustworthy person? Can you ever trust her again? If you choose to reconcile, you will need to know what issues within your partner, yourself, and your relationship demand attention. The following three stories illustrate typical scenarios of infidelity.

1. Flight from closeness: Bruce and Jennifer's story

Bruce was a football star in high school and enjoyed the attention he received. He was handsome, charming, and extremely popular, especially with all the girls. He loved to flirt, and many girls swarmed around him, seeking his attention. Bruce dated many girls but was never serious about settling down and going steady. He just wanted to have fun. When he noticed Jennifer at a party, he was attracted to her quiet beauty and wanted to get to know her. He had recognized her from a few classes and saw her as a reserved, conscientious student, sort of his opposite. Bruce surprised himself when they began dating and he fell in love with her. She was a steady person who balanced his wild and adventurous style. After dating a couple of years, at times from a distance while in college, they were married.

Bruce and Jennifer quickly settled into the routine of marriage and career. He became a stockbroker and enjoyed success because of his natural sales ability. They had a daughter, who was the love of his life, although he was so busy with work that he regretfully did not spend much time with her. Bruce put his energy into pursuing his career, which led to swift advancement at his office and a position as a vice president.

Bruce was a person who was easily bored and always liked to be on the go. In contrast, Jennifer was a stay-at-home kind of person. He relied on her stability to maintain the home front. However, as time passed, his boredom with the routine of married life increased. Jennifer complained about how much time he spent away from home, and their arguments increased. Bruce was experiencing enormous pressure at work to produce in his new position. He complained that Jennifer did not understand what it took to succeed in his business. As the tension increased in their marriage, the frequency of sex declined.

In order to escape the pressure from home, Bruce spent more time at work and went to a bar after work to unwind. He worked more closely with his secretary, who gradually became his confidante. He complained to her about his work pressures and wife's lack of understanding, and she offered a consoling ear. Sometimes they went out together for a quick drink, and Bruce decided not to tell Jennifer about their socializing outside work. Bruce was aware that he was developing feelings for his secretary and kept them secret. Then one evening, when Bruce was feeling stressed out, they went to a motel and slept together. He was aware that they had crossed a line in their relationship and felt a terrible guilt. But their friendship and occasional sex continued.

After Jennifer discovered his affair and threw him out of the house, Bruce eventually sought therapy for himself. He came to realize how emotionally aloof he had always been in his life. He loved the limelight and attention but never allowed himself to be really close to people. Without knowing it, he had become like his parents who both worked and had little time for him. He was an only child and spent a good part of his childhood in day care. His parents spoiled him with material things and took him on fancy vacations but never spent much time really talking with him.

Those like Bruce fear being emotionally close in a relationship and seek a comfortable distance from others in activities or isolation. Because of their fear of intimacy and desire for freedom, they withdraw more when they feel pressured from their partner to relate. They may maintain a facade of confidence and be charming and outgoing, but deep down they feel insecure about themselves. They feel unworthy of love and look to others to provide them with approval. They fear being criticized and not living up to others' expectations of them. They deny their own dependency needs because they are afraid if others really know them they will be rejected. So their relationships remain superficial. Their avoidance of closeness is a way of protecting themselves from the pain of emotional neglect as children. An affair becomes attractive to them because it provides an escape from the demands for intimacy from their partner. Furthermore, they may enjoy the affection, admiration, and approval of their mistress without having to make a commitment.

2. Fight for control: Sam and Laura's story

Sam and Laura met in high school and were immediately drawn to each other. They seemed to have a love-hate relationship from the outset. The good times together were fantastic, and the bad times, horrendous. Both were outgoing and popular, associating with a wide network of friends. Unfortunately, however, both were insanely jealous.

The slightest attention either paid to anyone else led to verbal, and sometimes physical, brawls. They separated numerous times while dating but soon discovered that they could not live without each other. Shortly after graduating from high school, they were married in an elaborate Italian wedding.

Not surprisingly, their bickering continued into the marriage. Sam was a successful businessman and prided himself on his accomplishments. Laura stayed home to care for their two children and worked part-time. Since both were proud and stubborn people, they often argued, both insisting they were right. Their disagreements became shouting matches and endless cycles of blame. They enjoyed an active social life, with many friends. Sam spent time with his business associates, golfing and hunting, while Laura enjoyed luncheons with her friends. Their socializing became grist for the mill of their regular arguments. Laura accused Sam of flirting, while Sam became convinced that Laura was cultivating male friendships at work.

When Sam was on one of his many business trips, he met a young woman who captivated him. Their friendship developed through numerous phone conversations, which Sam kept secret from his wife. Sam arranged for meetings out of town with his new girlfriend, and soon their relationship became sexual. Sam justified it in his own mind with the idea that he was giving Laura some of her own medicine for having so many male friends.

Sam was very familiar with power struggles. His parents were both accomplished professionals who competed with each other in daily life. Their marriage seemed to be one unending disagreement, and anger the glue to their relationship. Both had to be right, and there was no compromising, because it meant defeat. His father, an attorney, admitted that debating made him feel alive. Sam often felt like a spectator to their numerous fights and just tried to stay out of harm's way. Meanwhile, he was engaged in his own battles with his three brothers, with whom he competed in sports and other arenas.

Sam's marriage to Laura can be likened to two scorpions trapped in a bottle. Those like Sam and Laura fear being dependent on others and create distance in their relationships through competition and hostility.

They mistrust others and seek control and power to maintain a sense of safety in relationships. These are success-driven people. From all outward appearances, they are self-confident and exude personal strength. However, beneath this facade is an insecure person who feels extremely vulnerable in relationships. They fear being exposed as a fraud and then exploited. Their sense of security depends on their maintaining an air of independence, strength, and invulnerability. These individuals never felt close to their parents and believed they had to fight to preserve their sense of integrity. Their childhoods were often power struggles, and they came to see others as untrustworthy and rejecting. They may initiate an affair, as did Sam, to retaliate against perceived injuries from their partner. The affair further creates the image of independent action and maintains emotional distance in the marriage. Keeping it secret is also a triumph over the partner.

3. Clinging to love: Sarah and Bill's story

Sarah and Bill were married for nearly twenty-five years. For most of the time, it was an emotional wasteland for Sarah. Her husband never talked and was a control freak. He was a policeman who claimed he knew how tough and dangerous life was and said he wanted to protect Sarah. He ended up protecting her by keeping her in a prison of his control. Bill made all the decisions around the house without consulting Sarah. He kept a tight rein on their finances. Sarah had to beg him for money to pay for even the smallest expenses. For the most part, Sarah became compliant but nursed a secret resentment at being so dominated and voiceless.

Her only consolation was their son, to whom Sarah devoted her life. Bill worked long hours, and she cared for their son and the home. When their son left for college, Sarah felt desperately alone and isolated. At about the same time, one of her husband's colleagues, a fellow police officer, began stopping by for coffee. Sarah looked forward to his visits because he was a sensitive man who listened to her. He began to come by more frequently, and their friendship grew. Sarah was desperate for some attention and recognized that she was developing feelings for him, which she kept from Bill. Over time, as their emotional connection deepened, they had occasional sex. Sarah felt guilty but enjoyed the affection. She was terrified of leaving Bill and breaking up the family.

Sarah recognized that she was a person who had an insatiable need for affection and was confused that she married such an aloof and controlling man. As a child, she was "Daddy's little girl" and enjoyed spending time with her father. He was a quiet, passive, and accommodating man. Her mother ran the household. She was a domineering, controlling, and aggressive woman whom Sarah felt she could never please. She longed to be close to her mother but always felt rejected because her mother was such a harsh taskmaster. Sarah realized she had married someone like her mother but hoped her love could transform her husband into someone more like her father.

Those like Sarah long to be loved and fear standing on their own. They are dependent personalities who are preoccupied with maintaining close relationships, even at the cost of themselves. They exhibit strong needs for attention, affection, and support. They see themselves as helpless and unlovable and others as providers of care, comfort, and protection. Fears of being abandoned dominate them because they do not really believe they can survive emotionally on their own. In relationships, they tend to be passive and submissive because they do not want to jeopardize the protective presence of the other. During their childhood, their parents were often overprotective of them and never encouraged them to assert themselves. In many ways, they look for a nurturing parent in their marriages. They may become involved in an affair, as did Sarah, to assert themselves with a controlling spouse and express their resentment indirectly. They may also find another to whom they can cling, to provide security when they feel unappreciated in their marriage.

OTHER TYPES OF AFFAIRS

The typical ways of disconnecting described above are certainly not an exhaustive depiction of the variety of infidelities. However, they illustrate how problems in intimate relating may come to light through the action of the unfaithful partner. The following are some other typical patterns that arise more directly from the personal dispositions, that is, from the impulsiveness, compulsiveness, or decision of the one engaged in the affair. In contrast to the previous patterns, the infidelity reflects more clearly what is missing in the offending person than in the relationship and may suggest a different response on your part.

1. The impulsive infidelity: the one-night stand

Some infidelities are isolated events in which the involvement is limited to sex, without any emotional intimacy. Usually, a set of external circumstances creates the environment for an impulsive act that both partners agree was out of character. For example, Ted had been married for ten years. He admitted that he and his wife had their ups and downs in their marriage but claimed he was generally happy. He had never even considered being unfaithful to his wife. Ted often traveled for business and dreaded the time away from his family. He had always been a social drinker but noticed that his drinking had increased over the past couple of years. He drank heavily on weekends and occasionally when he was away on business trips. Before one trip, he had a major argument with his wife and left, stewing about how he had been wronged. After dinner with clients at the hotel, he decided to relax at the bar. To unwind, he began ordering cocktails, one after another, and conversed with an attractive woman who was also away on business. As they drank together, becoming more intoxicated, she invited him to her room for a nightcap. The next day Ted could hardly remember the details of how they ended up in bed together.

The discovery of a one-night-stand affair is so devastating because often the betrayal is unexpected and out of character for your partner. Perhaps you would never have believed your partner capable of such behavior, but after the discovery you are not so sure it could not happen again. It is important to understand the circumstances surrounding the sexual behavior, which may be an impulsive act. Often, the person's ability to make good decisions is compromised by alcohol or drugs. The impulsive sexual encounter may reveal another problem that has been ignored, an alcohol or drug addiction. Unless the addiction is addressed, your partner will continue to be at risk of further impulsive sexual acting out.

2. Compulsive infidelity: a sexual addiction

The sexual acting out may be part of a pattern of behavior that existed long before you met your partner. Often, because of shame, that behavior was a carefully guarded secret. For example, Allen came to therapy because he complained, "I'm oversexed." He related that he and his wife of five years had periodically engaged in group sex with their neighbors. Both loved the sexual excitement and adventure, which they believed improved their sex life together. However, he and his wife reacted differently to the occasional encounters. He wanted them to last longer and occur more frequently. The more they argued about it, the more she was determined that the group sex would stop. Allen came to me because he wanted to preserve the marriage. He related that he was exposed to his father's pornography at eight years old. His father was a quiet, withdrawn man whose only apparent interests were using pornography and going to nude bars. Allen became preoccupied with sex at an early age, indulged in Internet pornography, and went to nude bars, like his father. Allen was a handsome man who enjoyed flirting with women. Before being married, he had a knack for enticing girls into having sex but observed in himself that he was emotionally detached from them. After marriage, his preoccupation with women and desire for sexual adventure only increased. His fantasy dream of group sex was fulfilled when his wife agreed to participate, but her desire to stop the group encounters caused a crisis for them in their marriage.

The most lucrative business on the Internet is pornography. My patients have told me they can find whatever they desire to indulge their fantasies. The number of people and the extent of their use of Internet sex, in a variety of forms, are revealing a sexual problem of epidemic proportions. For some, sex can be like a drug to which they are addicted. The excitement of sex serves a purpose in filling a deep void in their lives. The sex-addicted person struggles with emotional intimacy and finds a substitute in sexual stimulation. These individuals feel powerless to control their addictive behavior, which is really a compulsion.

If you discover that your partner engages in extramarital sexual activity and does not seem able to stop, despite the negative consequences, he may have a sexual addiction. Because it is an addiction, it is helpful to be aware that you are powerless to stop the behavior.

All your confrontations, pleadings, and efforts to monitor, control, or punish his sexual acting out will not work. It will only lead to resentment on his part, and an angry sense of helplessness on yours. His sexual acting out will end only when he admits a problem, is motivated to change, and seeks help for himself. Unless he is committed to a personal recovery program, he will likely continue to relapse, despite his best intentions to stop.

3. Terminal infidelity: the exit affair

There are times when someone becomes involved in an affair because he has decided to leave the marriage. He may not be fully aware of his decision at the time or may just be reluctant to file for divorce. In any event, the affair signifies the end of the relationship. For example, Larry had been married for nearly thirty years but never felt happy. His wife was an emotionally unstable woman who had been hospitalized many times for depression and suicidal attempts. Larry took care of her but felt drained as the years passed. He thought of himself as her designated caretaker but resented the role and complained of feeling neglected. Over the years, he consoled himself with several affairs, which he scrupulously kept hidden from his family. He justified the affairs in his own mind as necessary emotional respites from the wasteland of his marriage to a sick woman. Finally, he met a woman who he believed understood him and genuinely cared for him. When he moved in with her, his infidelity became public and he announced the end of his marriage.

When your partner refuses to give up his relationship with the third party, despite your protests, it is a clear sign that he has decided to leave the marriage. In that case, no reconciliation is possible, even if you want it. Obviously, a stable, committed relationship requires the free consent and commitment of both parties. If one person does not accept the condition of exclusivity, it is obvious that the relationship cannot survive.

It is also essential that the offending partner learn from the affair, why he became involved with another outside his committed relationship, what dissatisfactions led him to stray, and how he contributed to the breakdown of the relationship. Unless he discovers the answers to these important questions, he will be handicapped in either reconciling with his partner or pursuing another relationship. Without accurate self-understanding, he will repeat the same unhappy dance with another partner, with likely the same result. The qualities of alertness, curiosity, openness, honesty, and gentleness in self-exploration are as important for the unfaithful partner as for the wounded one. The following suggested aids for the offended partner's recovery can also be useful for the offending partner's self-examination.

SOME AIDS FOR RECOVERY

The following are some aids to gain a new understanding, a different perspective.

1. Undergo therapy to know yourself

In the initial stage of recovery, you attempted to calm the emotional storm. In this second stage of recovery, which is seeking understanding, I recommend that you continue in individual therapy. Even though the emotional storm has been stilled somewhat, though not entirely, you need to engage your intellect to understand and learn from what happened. You need to understand more deeply your partner, yourself, and your relationship before you can make a wise and informed decision about what you want to do about the relationship. There are two choices: separation or reconciliation. Until you are comfortable in your knowledge of what led to the breakdown in the relationship, you cannot be secure in making a decision, the next step in recovery. A competent therapist is an invaluable aid in this work of exploration.

I further recommend, if he is willing, that you invite your partner to join you for some sessions together to explore what happened. For an accurate understanding, it is important for you to appreciate the total context of his decision to be unfaithful. For example, you will want to know what stresses he felt in his life, what dissatisfactions in the relationship he experienced, what he was thinking, what was attractive about the other person, and what personality weaknesses he displayed in the choice. These are difficult issues that are helpful to explore with a trained professional who can maintain a safe environment, to avoid the hostile reactions you may experience in your personal conversations with your partner. You may also have to face the possibility that your partner has no clear idea of why he did what he did.

2. Expand your journal

Continue paying close attention to your experiences and get into the habit of writing daily what you discover about yourself. During this stage of self-exploration, I recommend that you begin to reflect deeply on your relationship with your partner to gain a new perspective on yourself, your partner, and your relationship. Imagine you are writing an autobiographical relationship history, and try to write as honestly as you can. Look back on your relationship and ponder these questions. How did you meet? What was your first impression of your partner? What attracted you to him? What did you like about him? What did you dislike about him? What was your experience dating him? How did your relationship progress? When did you decide to make a lifelong commitment to each other? Did you have any reservations or concerns about living together? Were you always happy and satisfied in your relationship? When did your feelings change? What was going on in your life together at the time? What are you dissatisfied with now? What do you value in your partner? This honest exploration of your relationship may be difficult because you may tend to obsess about the affair. However, if the obsessing continues, you will likely remain stuck in blaming your partner and feeling like a helpless victim. Turning your attention to understanding your relationship is an essential step toward self-healing and gaining a sense of control over your life.

Essential Qualities for Gaining Self-Knowledge:

1. Alertness to your experience
2. Curiosity about yourself and your reaction
3. Openness to all you discover
4. Honesty about what you see in yourself
5. Gentleness with yourself

3. Continue with your group support

Because of the betrayal, you may feel a profound sense of helplessness and isolation, which is common to those who have been traumatized. Your once friendly, comfortable, secure world has now become a hostile, insecure place. Your natural tendency to protect yourself may lead you to withdraw from social interaction. Trusting yourself and others may feel threatening. Participating in a caring group, such as group therapy, a twelve-step group, a prayer group, or a support group for the divorced, can help you reconnect with others and yourself. The care and understanding of others in the group can empower you to trust yourself and others again. The group can become your safety zone where you can gain self-confidence to venture out into the world again.

Remember that the betrayal thrived in secrecy and drew its power in deception and manipulation of the truth. By openly talking about what happened, bringing it into the light of day, you begin to destroy its hold on you.

4. Pray from the heart for the Spirit's gift of understanding and knowledge

When you are caught up with analyzing what went wrong with your relationship, it is easy for your prayer to become overintellectual. You spontaneously pray from your head and not your heart. Obsessing about the affair, as mentioned above, can be a way of protecting yourself from your painful feelings. In the same way, this intellectual avoidance can creep into your prayer. Instead, in praying for the gifts of the Spirit, allow yourself to feel deeply from your heart.

An old Sufi tale, recorded by Shah, expresses this truth about authentic prayer. Someone approached a madman who was weeping bitterly and asked, "Why do you cry?" The madman responded, "I'm crying to attract the pity of His heart." The other commented, "Your words are nonsense because He has no physical heart." The madman answered, "It is you who are wrong, because He is the owner of all the hearts in the world. Through your heart you can make your connection with God."[5]

Now, find a quiet place where you can relax and not be distracted. It is helpful to establish a regular location where you are drawn more readily into a calm and prayerful attitude. Think of this place as your personal sanctuary, the place of refuge where you meet God, however you conceive of Him. Be aware of God's loving presence and promise to give whatever you ask of Him. Begin by allowing yourself to experience the doubt and uncertainty that is currently dominating your life. Acknowledge the destruction of your former beliefs about yourself, your partner, and your relationship. Recognize the struggle in your mind to know the truth, just as Jacob wrestled with the angel to receive his blessings. Feel the sense of despair and resignation welling up within you. It is important that you feel deeply your emptiness before you can experience God's fullness. After spending time with your doubt and despair, begin your prayer of petition. Your prayer will have a greater sense of urgency if you first allow yourself to feel your pain. From your heart, pray for understanding and knowledge both of your partner and yourself, which is similar to the *paramita* of truthfulness. Do not ask simply to know what your partner did and why he did it, but beg God to help you know the deeper truth about both of you. Pray that you may know yourself and your partner as God knows you. Ask for divine insight. Both you and your partner participate in the Mystery of God's life. You may ask God for qualities of alertness, curiosity, openness, honesty, and gentleness that you can open your heart to His truth. Pray also with the Psalmist that you may know yourself and your partner as God knows you. In that prayerful self-knowledge you will realize at a heartfelt level that you are children of God, fundamentally good in your nature.

In the Hebrew Scriptures, the Psalmist chants:

> *O Lord, you have probed me and you know me;*
> *You know when I sit and when I stand;*
> *You understand my thoughts from afar.*
> *My journeys and my rest you scrutinize,*
> *With all my ways you are familiar.*
> *Even before a word is on my tongue,*
> *Behold, O Lord, you know the whole of it.*
> *Behind me and before, you hem me in*

And rest your hand upon me.
Such knowledge is too wonderful for me;
Too lofty for me to attain (Psalms 139:1–6).

Someone's choice to have an affair reveals her insecure attachment in the relationship. It is her way of disconnecting from the give-and-take of intimacy, which requires the ability to be emotionally connected, maintain a sense of autonomy, and negotiate differences in the relationship. An unfaithful partner attempts to regulate the emotional closeness/distance in the relationship by becoming involved with a third party. There are many reasons for and ways of disconnecting. Those who are overdependent and cling to others may choose an affair partner who will support them when disappointed in their primary relationship. Those who fear being close and losing themselves enter affairs to create distance and retaliate in the power struggle with their partners. Finally, those who are emotionally detached maintain and increase the emotional distance in their relationship by pursuing another. Facing your doubt and despair courageously can become an opportunity to deepen the virtues of understanding, knowledge, and truthfulness that will guide you through recovery. Understanding your partner can be a gateway to understanding yourself, which is the next essential step in your own recovery.

SOME DOS AND DON'TS FOR RECOVERY

1. Don't try to seek safety in ignorance. Do you tend to sweep problems under the rug? Do you avoid what is uncomfortable in your life? Do you believe that ignorance is bliss?

2. Face your questions squarely. Looking back, did you have questions about your partner that you ignored? If so, why did you put on blinders? Do you believe that ultimately the truth will set you free?

3. Don't stay imprisoned in blaming yourself or your partner. Are you holding a grudge against yourself or your partner? Who is your anger hurting? What purpose does the blaming serve?

4. Maintain a sense of curiosity about your partner and yourself. Do you tend to be inquisitive or judgmental in the face of uncertainty? Do you believe that your curiosity will eventually be rewarded with knowledge of the truth? Or do you believe that you are condemned to uncertainty and ignorance?

5. Trust your own perceptions and insights. Do you believe enough in yourself that you can see what is true and what is not? Do you think you are able to untangle the lies in your relationship? Do you see yourself as a perceptive, intelligent person?

6. Listen and learn from your partner. Can you set aside your anger enough to listen to your partner? Even though he has deceived you, can you glean some truth in what he says? Do you want to understand your partner? Can you learn something about yourself from your partner?

7. Keep an open mind for new perspectives. Do you believe you can learn something new from the experience of betrayal? Do you feel free to explore the meaning of what happened? Is it too painful?

8. Allow yourself to feel empathy for yourself and your partner. Are you closed off behind a wall of anger? Can you see yourself and your partner as two suffering people? Can you be gentle with yourself and your partner? Despite the anger, do you have any tender feelings toward your partner?

9. Seek to know ever-deeper truth about yourself and your partner. Are you only preoccupied with what happened and why? Do you desire to know yourself and your partner as God, the Omniscient, or the universal life force, knows you? Do you accept your fundamental goodness and ultimate unknowability?

SEVEN

STAGE 3: SEEKING
SELF-UNDERSTANDING
The Truth Will Set You Free

*Your task is not to seek love, but merely to seek and find all the
barriers with yourself that you have built against it.*

—RUMI

Your natural curiosity to understand why your partner was unfaithful can easily become an obsessive pursuit. You may feel a sense of
urgency to know all the details about the affair, the other woman,
and your partner's thinking and behavior. However, it is likely that
you will soon discover this search for the truth is not satisfying. Your
partner may become defensive because he feels attacked. The knowledge you acquired about what happened might not ease the pain. In
fact, it may even increase your anxiety and anger at being betrayed.
The search may become endless because you can never learn enough
details to be at peace.

While normal for a period of time, obsessing about the affair can
never result in the truth that will set you free. Even though your
obsessing may seem like a genuine expression of emotion, it is really
an avoidance of the deeper anguish you feel about the betrayal. Most
likely, fear and anger about the collapse of your world underlie your
preoccupation with your hurt feelings and your partner's behavior.

The obsessing keeps you frozen in blaming your partner, and even yourself in a subconscious way. You might continue to see your partner as the guilty and powerful persecutor, and yourself the innocent and helpless victim. However, such a view of the situation keeps you feeling weak, helpless, and out of control.

Truth-seeking pundits observe that the truth will set you free, but first, it will make you miserable. The freedom you seek is purchased at a price: an honest self-examination. That is the third step on your healing journey. As much as you may find yourself resisting this suggestion, I believe it is important to seek the truth about the infidelity in the broader context of your relationship with your partner, instead of narrowly focusing on the act of infidelity. In the process, you begin to look honestly at how you and your partner were interacting in your relationship, acknowledging the strengths and weaknesses of both. Let me emphasize that no matter what your weaknesses are, you are not responsible for your partner's unfaithful behavior. There is nothing you did or could do that would justify infidelity. Only your partner is responsible for his actions, as you are for your own. Nevertheless, a full appreciation of the truth of what happened will entail your taking an honest, and perhaps painful, look at how you interacted in the partnership.

I have observed over and over how the distortion and denial of reality go hand in hand when an affair is involved. The unfaithful partner distorts the truth, while the wounded one denies it. For example, a young woman came to see me because she had learned that her husband had a six-month affair shortly after they were married. After a brief separation, she decided to remain with him. A year after the affair, she was distressed because her husband was insanely jealous, monitored her activities, and accused her of being unfaithful. The woman insisted that she was faithful, although her husband didn't believe her, and she told him that she resented his suspiciousness and possessiveness. I inquired about the woman's reactions during the turmoil of their marriage. She claimed she was not angry about her husband's betrayal and had forgiven him. She also claimed she had had no suspicions that he was seeing another woman for weekly sexual encounters when they were first married. I observed the irony of their mutual blindness. Her husband saw something that was not there, while she did not see something that was. He projected his own unfaithful behavior onto her, while she projected her innocence onto him. Both denied reality to serve a purpose, to protect themselves from painful truths about themselves. He did not want to admit his own insecurities and bad behavior, while she did not want to see how insecure, dependent, and helpless she felt with him.

How will the truth set you free? The truth about your partner and yourself provides a firm foundation to decide about the future of your relationship. You can readily see the importance of understanding your unfaithful partner but may understandably object at the suggestion that you need to focus attention on your own behavior in the relationship. After all, you may think, he was the one who engaged in bad behavior. He is the guilty party. Nevertheless, to fully understand the truth and the complete context of what happened, you will need to see clearly your role in a relationship with an unfaithful partner, without blaming yourself for his infidelity.

BENEFITS OF SELF-EXAMINATION

1. To give up self-blame

2. To learn about yourself

3. To take responsibility for your own life

4. To make an informed decision about your future

Perhaps taking a long look at yourself may lead to a painful self-examination. You may enter dark places in your heart you have avoided, especially if your life has been satisfying and comfortable. But I am convinced the work is worth the effort and necessary for personal growth. It will set you free from any illusions you may have had about yourself and your relationship. Naturally, you will embark on this journey of self-appraisal only if you believe the benefits outweigh the pain and effort. What are the benefits of this painful, yet liberating, self-exploration?

First, while you may be consciously consumed by the blame toward your unfaithful partner, you may also blame yourself at some level. Your rage at your partner may hide your self-blame. You may secretly wonder why she found another more attractive than you. You may ask yourself, "What's wrong with me? What did I do to drive her away? How could I have been so blind about her behavior? How could I have been deceived so easily?" Such gross self-accusations, if honestly admitted, are obviously unfair. However, that does not mean that you were the perfect partner at all moments in the relationship. No one is. Acknowledging your weaknesses and accepting them with humility can relieve the pressure of an exaggerated, yet disguised self-blame. As Alexander Chase observed, "To understand is to forgive, even oneself."[1]

Second, when your partner explains what led to the affair, she will undoubtedly focus on what has been dissatisfying to her in the relationship. You may take that as her way of excusing herself and blaming you. However, you can also take what she says and evaluate its truthfulness, accepting what applies and rejecting what does not. It can be an opportunity to learn about yourself. What you hear from your partner may be painful in its accuracy about your faults. But living with illusions about yourself destroys your happiness to a greater degree. Recognizing and admitting your faults marks the beginning of your own liberation. While you cannot change your partner, you can change yourself. Furthermore, in the process, you will undoubtedly come to recognize that you were not entirely satisfied in the relationship and played a role in your mutual unhappiness. Perhaps something was missing for you, even before you discovered the infidelity. Acknowledging honestly your own suffering and unhappiness in the relationship before the discovered affair can help you replace your harsh self-judgment with empathy.

Third, continuing to focus on what your unfaithful partner did and the pain it caused will only increase your sense of helplessness. There is a danger that you will become stuck in seeing yourself as a victim and her as a powerful persecutor. If you assume a victim identity you may reinforce the belief that other people and what they do to you can make you who you are. You also affirm that the painful past in which you were victimized is more powerful than the present healing moment. You may continue living in the past, letting the pain control your life. However, by taking an honest look at yourself and accepting responsibility for your part in problems in your relationship, you actually empower yourself. In shifting your attention from your partner's behavior, over which you have no control, to your own, over which you do have control, you gain a sense of inner strength. By actively taking responsibility for your behavior and for yourself, you can release energy to transform your life. One woman told me she was awakened to taking responsibility for herself and stopped blaming her unfaithful husband when she read a statement in a Dr. Phil book. In his blunt manner, he explained: no one held a gun to your head and told you to marry him.

Finally, self-understanding will provide you with the essential information to make a wise choice about your relationship, whether to continue or end it. If you choose to continue the relationship, you want to know what part you played in the conflicts and unhappiness you both experienced so you can rebuild the relationship on a firmer foundation. If you choose not to stay together, you want to learn about your ways of interacting with others so that you do not repeat the same mistakes in future relationships. I often counsel my patients, "Unless you understand your part in the failure of the relationship, you will repeat the same dance with a different partner." Through awareness and a commitment to change, you can overcome the tendency to re-create the pattern of your past relationships.

TYPICAL PATTERNS OF RELATING WITH UNFAITHFUL PARTNERS

An affair reveals an insecure attachment in your relationship. As explained in the last chapter, there are typical ways that unfaithful partners disconnect. They may flee from intimacy out of a fear of closeness; fight against intimacy by engaging in power struggles; or cling to others because they fear standing on their own. Emily Brown, writing about the treatment of infidelity, described similar patterns. She observed that some couples avoid conflict because of fears of asserting themselves, some avoid intimacy through constant battling, and others detach emotionally from their partners and engage intimately with a third party.[2]

PATTERNS OF DISCONNECTING

1. Clinging to love

2. Fighting for control

3. Fleeing from closeness

Having been so deeply wounded by infidelity, you may also have disconnected from your partner, perhaps without knowing it. If you look honestly at yourself and your relationship, you may discover that you felt insecure at some level, even before the discovery of the affair. You may realize that you avoided the struggle for a healthy intimacy, in a way similar to what you observed in your unfaithful partner. You might discover tendencies in yourself to cling, fight against, or flee from your partner, which contributed to your mutual dissatisfaction in the relationship. It is my firm conviction that unless you work out your personal struggles with intimacy, odds are you will repeat your disconnection in other relationships. The following three stories illustrate typical scenarios.

1. Clinging to love: Jennifer and Bruce's story

After discovering Bruce's affair with his secretary, Jennifer was in shock. She had imagined they had a perfect marriage. Of course, they had their ups and downs, like everyone else. But Jennifer thought they were both happy together and deeply in love. She could not understand how something so good went wrong. She became obsessed with understanding why Bruce was unfaithful and what happened with his secretary.

When her depression deepened and she became frustrated with Bruce's defensiveness in talking about the affair, she sought help for herself, at the urging of her friend. Initially, in therapy she could only talk about the affair and the pain and outrage she felt. After some encouragement, she began to explore her relationship with Bruce.

Jennifer confessed that she never had any reservations about marrying Bruce because she was so infatuated with him. With some gentle prodding to look back in hindsight with the knowledge of his infidelity, Jennifer admitted that she was jealous of the attention he received from other women. Bruce liked to flirt and sought the limelight in whatever he did. She saw herself as an admiring bystander. After they were married for a year, Bruce threw himself into his profession as a stockbroker. He began spending more and more time at work. Jennifer complained about feeling neglected but distracted herself with caring for their daughter, doing housework, and working part-time at a bookstore. Sometimes Bruce would stay out late without calling. Jennifer became upset but never challenged him with any determination. Their sex life declined after the birth of their daughter because they were both too tired. Jennifer never imagined that Bruce was spending time with another woman.

After several months of examining her life in therapy, Jennifer came to the realization that her naïveté served a purpose. She had not wanted to pick up on the signs of Bruce's emotional withdrawal and infidelity. It was too scary for her to admit that he could leave her for another woman. She did not think she could survive on her own. She also began to realize how dependent she had become on him, afraid to confront him and tell him how neglected she felt. She faced her own discontent in the marriage and admitted her loneliness and anger at being neglected. Bruce had been absent a long time before the affair. Jennifer lamented, "I could only give him love, but the other woman obviously gave him the admiration he needed."

Reflecting back on her childhood, Jennifer realized that she had become a compliant child to cope with her father's demandingness and unpredictable temper. She always wanted to please him but never felt like she succeeded. She began at an early age to feel inadequate and worthless. Her mother was extremely submissive to her father, and Jennifer discovered that she had identified with her in her own marriage. She became the devoted and unquestioning wife and submissive to Bruce. She also realized that she intuited Bruce's unacknowledged neediness and became his caretaker. She was always there to support him, be available to him, and admire his achievements. Suddenly, it dawned on her that her father was an insecure man who hid behind a facade of strength, and her mother was a silent pillar of support. She had unknowingly re-created her parents' marriage in her relationship with Bruce.

Those who cling to love, like Jennifer, find their meaning in life through their love relationships. They value harmony and may hide any dissatisfaction and conflict behind a facade of niceness. They do not want to rock the boat, because of their fear of being cast overboard. In reality, they feel weak and inadequate inside and hope to draw strength from their partner. They do not believe they can survive on their own. Consequently, they often choose as a partner someone who embodies qualities they admire and lack in themselves. They are often drawn to aloof, assertive, and apparently independent partners. In some ways, they marry a parent for whom they sacrifice themselves to gain approval and a sense of security. They need to be needed and find their value in serving their partner and the children. Their partner may seek an affair because he feels the need to create some distance. Those who cling to love often ignore signs of the infidelity, unconsciously telling themselves, "I don't want to know." Ignorance is safer than knowledge for them because of their desperate fear of being abandoned or of having to take decisive action. When the affair is finally realized, they fall into despair, wondering, "How will I ever survive?"

Robin Norwood, in her book *Women Who Love Too Much*, insightfully describes women who desperately cling to love. These women believe that loving somebody is the most important thing in life. However, they are living an unrecognized "rescue fantasy" in their romantic pursuits. These women grew up in dysfunctional families where their emotional needs were not met. They grew up feeling empty and worthless inside but discovered a way of feeling good about themselves by taking care of others. In their relationships, they become caregivers, sacrificing their own needs for others. Consequently, they are drawn to emotionally unavailable men whom they try to change through their love. They marry men who are troubled, distant, moody, unpredictable, and needy. They are bored by honest and dependable "nice guys." Unconsciously, these women want to re-create and relive their lost childhoods to regain a sense of self-worth. They desperately seek to control their men and their relationships under the guise of "being helpful." Their fear of abandonment makes them long-suffering in trying to maintain an unhappy and doomed relationship.[3]

Contrary to the stereotype of the independent male, it should be noted that many men also cling desperately to love and seek to rescue their needy partners.

Another name that describes the type of relationship in which one person devotes herself to serving another while neglecting herself is "codependency." Those who cling to love are prone to codependent, addictive relationships. All of their attention is focused on their partner, whom they hope will bring them joy in life. When they are in love, they feel intensely alive, special, a whole person. Their partner becomes the center of their world, and they willingly sacrifice themselves to keep him happy. However, there is a neediness, a desperate clinging quality to their involvement in the relationship because it is motivated by a deep-seated fear of being abandoned. These people feel empty and incomplete inside and believe that the relationship will make them whole and happy. The relationship is like a drug that anesthetizes them to their inner pain. When they feel loved and appreciated, they are "high." But when there is conflict in the relationship and their partner steps back, they feel lost. They experience withdrawal symptoms and desperately seek to bring their partner back, to get their "fix," while denying the emotional pain they are experiencing.

There are, of course, degrees of clinging to relationships, and, if you see a glimmer of yourself in the above portrayals, you may not readily identify with all the characteristics. However, the above accounts describe the dynamics of dependent relationships where you may seek to fill an inner emptiness through your partner. Confronting honestly your overdependent tendencies may be an opportunity to discover your unrecognized strength and goodness. If you want to work on this, try thinking through the following:

1. You need to pay close attention to yourself, to your thoughts, feelings, and desires. When you were a child, your parents probably dismissed your needs in many ways. If that was the case, you grew up imitating them in ignoring yourself. It will certainly be an unfamiliar experience to stop and think about your own desires, but take the risk.

2. While you have learned to dismiss yourself, you may have allowed others not to take you seriously. Learn to be honest about what you want and to express it openly. Learn to assert yourself and take yourself seriously, so that others will also.

3. Because you have ignored yourself for so long, you may have become deaf to the voice within you. Learn to listen and trust your perceptions, intuitions, thoughts, and judgments about yourself and others. You have a truth within you that you have hidden. Learn to trust yourself and give voice to what you discover.

4. You have viewed others as superior to you and allowed them to control your life. Now learn to take responsibility for your own life. Listen to your own desires, consider what is in your own best interest, and take action.

5. The guiding fantasy of your life has been that being loved will make you happy. Develop more realistic expectations about your relationships. Your relationships do not define you. You are who you are, not a reflection of another's approval. Freely engage in the give-and-take of relationships you choose as healthy and fulfilling.

6. Develop self-confidence. One recently divorced woman told me her theme song was "I Will Survive."

7. Learn to enjoy your own company. You may have associated being alone with loneliness and isolation. That is because you felt so empty inside. Instead, learn to value your time alone and the richness of your own experience.

8. Take the word "can't" out of your vocabulary. The more you think you cannot do something, the more you imagine yourself as disabled and the more you limit yourself. Instead, use the vocabulary of willing: "I choose or don't choose" to do something. These words reflect an inner sense of personal empowerment and responsibility.

9. Cultivate the virtue of courage. Recognize how fear has dominated your life and decisions and make a resolution to go beyond the fear.

You may come to the realization that you have been living in fear your whole life, without even knowing it. The affair and your traumatic response may have revealed the underlying fear that has ruled your life. That painful experience may be a blessing in that your ignorance about what has been motivating you is exposed and you can begin the process of recovery with eyes wide open. The antidote to fear, of course, is courage. Courage is not being fearless but refusing to allow your fear to enslave you and moving beyond it. Courage involves acknowledging and facing your fears, which reside in the imagination about possible outcomes in a future that does not exist. In the grip of fear, you imagine terrible things will happen. However, if you act and those terrible things do not occur, your fear will diminish. As a result, you will gain a realistic sense of mastery over your life.

2. Fighting for control: Laura and Sam's story

When Laura met Sam, she knew she had met her match. She had many boyfriends in high school, but she quickly became bored with them. They were "nice" boys who doted on her. But she liked the challenge that Sam presented. He would not accept her moodiness and attempts to bully him. She admired his willingness to fight back. Laura admitted that their relationship was tumultuous from the beginning, but it was also exciting, and never boring. She and Sam were both outgoing and popular. They had many friends and were always on the go socially. Laura was petite and attractive, a fiery redhead. Guys were attracted to her, and she enjoyed their attention. Because she flirted and had so many male friends, Sam became insanely jealous. She was also jealous of his many female friends. Their relationships with others were a constant source of tension and arguments that led to numerous separations.

They always came back to each other. They learned that they could not live with or without each other. When they were married, Laura was not surprised that the drama of frequent bickering continued. As vehemently as they argued, they always made up eventually; the "makeup sex" was incredible. They continued to argue about their associations and declared friendships with members of the opposite sex. But Laura admitted that she was stunned when she learned about Sam's affair with a woman he met on a business trip. He had gone too far.

Laura could not tolerate the infidelity and sought help for herself. She could not decide whether she wanted a divorce. Sam agreed to give up the other woman but admitted he was uncertain about the marriage. Laura was an emotionally volatile woman who reacted quickly and intensely to any situation. Therapy became for her a challenge to stop and think about her life for the first time. After many months of treatment, she became aware of how much she distracted herself from her real feelings by the constant activity and emotional drama of her relationships. She had imagined that her emotions ran deep because she was so emotionally reactive. However, she discovered that beneath the stormy surface was a huge reservoir of unacknowledged pain. She realized that she had never been emotionally honest with Sam. The anger hid what she was really feeling but did not recognize.

Laura began to examine the roots of her anger and resentment. She was the youngest of three children. Her brother had a chronic serious illness, and her sister was rebellious, in and out of trouble with the law. Laura complained, "I always felt alone as a child because my parents were so preoccupied with my sick brother or troubled sister." Her father was an imposing, domineering man who put all his energy into running his business. When he was home, he tried to run the household as an efficient business organization but encountered the resistance of his children and argumentative wife. Laura never felt close to her mother, who withdrew into her own world but occasionally emerged to battle with her husband. Because Laura was so outgoing and attractive, she learned to gain attention through her beauty and personality. She also flew into rages, like her parents, which made her feel powerful, because she got what she wanted. She admitted that secretly she imagined others would hug and console her when she was so upset. Exploring her childhood, it was not difficult for Laura to understand how she was drawn to someone like Sam who was as volatile as she and her parents. The anger, arguing, and flirting were a means of keeping an emotional distance from each other and avoiding the deep pain of neglect while growing up.

Those who fight for control in relationships, like Laura, fear getting too close and depending on others. Their anger is a way of protecting themselves from being exploited. They view relationships as power struggles in which they must fight to maintain themselves and avoid being taken advantage of. If they surrender themselves in love, they fear losing control and losing themselves. They need to appear tough and hide their softer side. However, their dependency becomes evident when they continue in relationships that become destructive to their well-being. They alternate between attacking and submitting to the attacks of their partner and claim they feel alive when there is drama in the relationship. They experience much ambivalence in their marriage and secretly tell themselves, without admitting it to their partner, "I hate you, but I can't live without you." Their slogan is: "I fight, therefore I am." All the aggression hides the sense of powerlessness they feel inside. It covers up all the pain they feel about being neglected or even abused as a child. Naturally, they choose a partner in marriage who will battle them, against whom they can both win and lose. Either or both may engage in affairs as acts of spite and retaliation in the ongoing battle. Unlike the clinging spouse, they are hypervigilant to signs of infidelity and offer the challenge "I dare you to leave." However, when the affair is discovered, the facade of toughness may collapse, revealing the hurt and powerlessness they feel inside.

For those of you who realize your tendency to engage in power struggles in relationships, the crisis of a discovered affair may be an opportunity for you to become acquainted with the neglected side of your personality, your disowned softer side. The following are some suggestions for the recovery of your true self:

1. Learn to manage your anger. Expressing anger has probably always been easy for you, but controlling it has not. Become aware of the impact of your anger on others, how it alienates them, pushes them away, and invites retaliation.

2. Pay close attention to your feelings. You are probably so accustomed to reacting with anger that you never stop to look closely at the feelings that underlie the anger. Anger is a secondary emotion. The root of the anger needs to be acknowledged before it can be healed.

3. Learn to develop a sense of empathy for yourself. You are angry about something, perhaps a huge reservoir of unacknowledged pain from your childhood that is warded off by your anger. Be gentle with yourself in letting yourself be aware of your pain.

4. Work on expressing intimacy in all your relationships. Because of your need to defend yourself, you have not let people know how you really feel. Learn to take the risk of making yourself vulnerable in your close relationships.

5. Learn to talk about your pain and trust that others will care. That is a huge step for you. It will feel unsafe for a long time to talk about painful things because you have been so guarded your whole life. You view admitting hurt feelings as a weakness, but actually, it takes courage to be so honest.

6. Undertake experiments in relationships of letting the other person take control and set the agenda periodically. You may surprise yourself that it is a relief not to be so burdened with responsibility.

7. Learn to compromise in decision making. You may have thought you always needed to be right. It was a sign of weakness to be wrong. Take the risk of acknowledging and negotiating differences in your relationships.

8. Focus on how you can love your partner, rather than on how he has failed in loving you.

9. Cultivate the virtue of patience. With diligent effort, learn to tolerate what does not happen according to your plans. Acknowledge and put aside your angry reaction.

3. Fleeing from closeness: Bill and Sarah's story

When Sarah announced to him that she wanted a divorce because she was in love with another man, Bill was in shock. He could not believe it. They had been married for twenty-five years, and Bill imagined that their marriage was like everyone else's who had been together for so many years. He had worked long hours, while Sarah was staying home and cared for their son. Within a couple of weeks, the shock wore off, and his emotions exploded like a time bomb. Bill was enraged, especially when he learned that his wife's lover was a fellow police officer. It was a double betrayal, by his wife and his coworker. He was also surprised at how frightened and lonely he felt at the prospect of losing his wife of so many years. He had become accustomed to having her around and later admitted that he had taken her for granted.

Bill did not want the marriage to end and pleaded with Sarah to reconsider. They both began therapy, and Bill came to realize how lonely, neglected, and unhappy Sarah had felt for many years. She often complained about his drinking and about feeling alone. Bill also began therapy for himself because he felt so desperate about his marriage ending. When Sarah and Bill were first married, he thrived on the attention she paid him. But soon thereafter, he started to feel smothered by her constant demands that he spend more time with her. He withdrew more and more into his work and spent his free time with his fellow officers, who were much less demanding. Furthermore, Sarah did not like his drinking and often nagged him about it. In contrast, his friends were fun and enjoyed partying.

In therapy, Bill also began to explore his childhood. He was the middle of five children and considered himself "lost in the middle somewhere." Both his parents drank heavily. His mother was a mean drunk, while his father was mostly a happy drinker. Nevertheless, there were times when his parents fought viciously, and Bill remembers trying to hide and become invisible. Bill felt closer to his father, who was easygoing and fun loving. His mother, on the other hand, was domineering and cruel. She punished the children harshly and mercilessly. Bill came to realize why he was so attracted to law enforcement. During the sessions, Bill explored how his profession as a police officer had interfered with his marriage. He worked odd-hour shifts, volunteered for overtime, and socialized after work with his colleagues. Bill realized that the Fraternal Order of Police had become his substitute family. As a policeman he felt a sense of belonging with his fellow officers that he never felt at home. He also gained a missing sense of power with the authority of his position. And he liked the clear rules and guidelines. Bill also appreciated how he chose as a wife a meek, submissive woman, who was the opposite of his mother. His wife was a woman with whom he could feel superior. Furthermore, he realized that he had detached from his wife and children, just as his alcoholic parents had.

Those like Bill who detach in relationships value their freedom and fear losing themselves if they get too close with loved ones. To protect themselves and safeguard their freedom, they keep their emotional distance. They take pride in their self-sufficiency and independence and often feel superior and unique. They put their energies into their own pursuits, such as work, hobbies, or even caring for others. They are often workaholics and perfectionists who overdevelop the intellectual side of their personalities. However, beneath this facade of self-sufficiency is an insecure person who fears depending on others. They deny any feelings that will connect them with others, because they see relationships as chains. Growing up, because their parents may not have been emotionally available to them, they learned that they could count only on themselves. Other factors can certainly contribute to learning to detach to survive, such as the childhood experience of serious illness, family disruption, or extended separation from the parents. When their partners complain of feeling neglected, they ignore it as a sign of their partner's weakness and neediness. They respond to threats of infidelity with a feigned nonchalance, "I don't care." They often choose partners who cling to them and represent their disowned dependency needs. Their partner may pursue an affair as a cry for attention. When the affair is discovered, their facade of cool detachment may collapse, and they are flooded by fears of being abandoned, as they were in childhood.

If you tend to flee intimacy, you may live an illusion that you do not need others. You may have become disconnected from your feelings and desires, which engage you with others. Your partner's affair can become a wake-up call, an invitation to awaken yourself to your deep longings for closeness. Here are some suggestions to begin recovery:

1. Pay close attention to your feelings. This may be a new experience because you are so accustomed to living in your head and losing yourself in activities.

2. Pay attention to your body. Because you are so accustomed to ignoring your feelings, you may not even be able to identify a feeling. You can begin by noticing your physical reactions to situations, the tension in your neck and stomach discomfort, for example. Feelings are expressed through your spontaneous bodily reactions.

3. Once you identify your emotional reactions, make the effort to share your feelings with others. It may be awkward because you have never learned the language of emotions. Those who care about you will welcome your effort.

4. Allow yourself to grieve your childhood losses. One way you have learned to cope is to detach from memories, painful feelings, and uncomfortable thoughts. Undoubtedly, there is much sadness in your life that has been bottled up.

5. Give up your fantasies of perfection. You live in the world of "shoulds," with overdeveloped ideas of how you, your life, and others should live. Remove the word "should" from your vocabulary. Your ideas about reality interfere with your experiencing life as you live it.

6. Learn to have empathy for yourself and others. You can be very demanding of yourself and others because of the high standards you maintain. Try not to take those standards so seriously, develop a sense of humility, and give yourself and others a break.

7. Learn to relax and enjoy yourself, especially with others. If you take so seriously yourself and your ideas of how life should be, you lose the capacity to have fun.

8. Live the present moment fully. If you live in your head, you are preoccupied with future plans or past events and not fully engaged in life. Only the present moment exists. Life and a sense of vitality unfold from the present.

9. Take the risk to connect with others. You tend to isolate yourself to feel safe but in the end suffer loneliness. See a therapist or join a support group, or both, to find a safe place to explore your fears of intimacy and experiment with new behaviors.

10. Cultivate the virtue of wisdom, which acknowledges your connection with others and mutual dependency.

If those who have been unfaithful have any hope of reconciling with their partner, they need to understand clearly the pain they caused by their infidelity and communicate to their partner their heartfelt understanding. Often, the offending person is so caught up in blaming his partner for his unhappiness in the relationship or so captivated by the romance of his affair that he does not recognize the consequences of his behavior. He may even become impatient when his partner expresses the pain and harm caused by his actions. He may adamantly refuse to accept responsibility for his behavior and flee a sense of guilt. However, unless he reaches out to his offended partner with empathy, he will remain a prisoner of his guilt and blame. Recovery for the unfaithful person requires, as for his wounded partner, an accurate understanding of himself and his partner and a full acceptance of personal responsibility for his actions.

SOME AIDS FOR RECOVERY

In this wintertime of your recovery, you continue to withdraw in order to contemplate and learn from your painful experience. You seek the wisdom of an honest and accurate self-knowledge.

1. Continuing therapy: focusing on yourself

As explained previously, an affair is a symptom of an insecure bonding in the relationship. In therapy it is important to explore what the discovered affair reveals about your partner, yourself, and the way you have related with each other. In working with patients who have been traumatized by a discovered infidelity, I invite them to explore three questions about themselves: (1) Why did you choose this partner who turned out to be unfaithful? (2) What was the quality of your interactions with this person? (3) Was your way of interacting familiar from your childhood experience? I urge my patients to be aware of the way they interact with others and of how their personal histories shape and guide them.

I invite my patients to take a close look at the history of their relationship. Frequently, the offended partner exclaims, "I had no idea that the affair was going on." She also adds, "I never imagined he was the kind of person who would betray me." Together we examine her proclaimed ignorance to see what we can learn about her, about what she knows but thinks she does not know. For example, regarding one's choice of a partner, Freud observed that unconscious childhood fantasies influence the choice of a mate. He contended that there were two types of marital choice. Either we fall in love with someone like ourselves or we choose someone who acts like a parent toward us, providing support and nurturing.[4] The person chosen like ourselves may exhibit qualities that we have, once had, wish we had, or existed in family members. He affirmed that we always choose the kind of mate we need to complement our personality features. Often our reasons for choosing our mate remain hidden to us. However, what we are really looking for must come to light in order to avoid repeating a similar choice in the future.

I also invite my patients to explore the ways they connect, disconnect, and reconnect with their partners. An intimate relationship is like a dance where both partners move together in rhythm, but their movements may be more or less in sync. What do they talk about and what do they avoid discussing? How do they talk, listen, and respond to each other? In attending closely to their interactions, patterns of relating become apparent. Do they tend to avoid conflict or relish it? Do they tend to cling to each other, push each other away, or go back and forth? What automatic thoughts about themselves and their partners emerge in the communication? What is the primary tone of feeling in their relationship? What are the sensitive issues? I ask my patients to be attentive to the patterns of their communicating and further explore how they learned to communicate the way they do. Inevitably, this leads to a consideration of how their parents related in their marriage. I tell my patients, "For better or worse, your parent's marriage is the model for your own marriage. You may choose to be different, but the shadow of their marriage is always in the background." We further explore how the patient interacted with his parents and siblings. How we related to significant people in the past sets the pattern for future relationships.

Individual therapy can be extremely helpful to explore these complicated relational issues. Occasional couple's therapy sessions with your partner can also be helpful. As the saying goes, you can learn more from your enemies than from your friends. Your friends may tell you what you want to hear, while your enemies will tell you about your dark side. At this point, you're likely see your unfaithful partner as an enemy, rather than the trusted friend you thought. Listen carefully to his feedback about what he did not like about you in the relationship and try to glean some truth about yourself that was hidden. Furthermore, pay close attention to what bothers you about your partner. It is another avenue to self-knowledge. Often what we despise in others we hate in ourselves, but disown. Unconsciously, we project our faults on them and criticize them for what we dislike in ourselves. I remind my patients, in a humorous way, "If you spot it, you got it."

2. Autobiographical journaling

Continue to write down your spontaneous thoughts and feelings. I recommend that you focus your attention also on your personal history, particularly the significant relationships in your life. What is your earliest memory as a child? How did your parents treat you? Did you feel mistreated, neglected, or abused? Or did you feel secure and cared for? How did they pay attention to you, encourage you, and show affection? How did you respond? What feelings and needs were ignored, and how were they dismissed? How did you cope with it? What were your parents like? What did you like about each parent? What did you dislike about them? How did you get along with your siblings? What was your parents' marriage like? How did they display affection? How did they make decisions and plan for the future? How did they resolve disagreements? Who had the power in decision making, or was it equally shared? Were they faithful to each other? You might review other significant relationships in your life, such as your close friendships and previous romantic involvements. Did you feel emotionally close to these people and believe you could trust them? What kind of people have you been attracted to? How did the relationships begin, progress, and end? These are just a few suggestive questions to stimulate your reflections about your life and relationships. The goal of this exercise is to learn more about yourself by becoming aware of the repeating patterns in your relationships. What you learned in childhood you will re-create in your future relationships and marriage.

3. Self-help groups

Your honest and fearless self-examination may lead you to the conclusion that you, your partner, or a family member is addicted to alcohol or other drugs. In fact, there is a good possibility that someone within your family is addicted. Research has consistently shown that those who have suffered traumas are prone to addictive behaviors to ease the pain and fill the void.

In my practice, I have observed a recurring pattern in couples who have experienced infidelity. On the one hand, the unfaithful partner frequently abuses alcohol or drugs. The use of substances facilitates his sexual acting out by impairing his judgment and decreasing his inhibitions. Many affairs begin at the bar or while drinking. On the other hand, the offended partner often exhibits codependent traits. She tends to live in denial and focus more attention on caring for others than herself. She makes excuses for her partner's behavior and is afraid to assert herself.

If you discover an addiction, or even a tendency to abuse substances within yourself, your partner, or a family member, I recommend that you participate in a twelve-step group. These groups have proven to be more effective than individual therapy in addressing addictive behaviors. The twelve steps address the underlying attitudes and behaviors that keep the addictions going. Furthermore, the honest exchange of ideas and support from those who share the same struggles with addiction contributes immeasurably to recovery. If you are abusing substances or think you might have a problem but are unsure, you can join Alcoholics Anonymous or Narcotics Anonymous. If your partner or family member abuses alcohol or drugs, I recommend that you join Al Anon or Codependents Anonymous (CODA), which will help you to recover from your tendency to become overinvolved in their behavior and neglect yourself. If you grew up in an alcoholic household, you can attend Adult Children of Alcoholics meetings to learn its impact on your current functioning. Those who grow up in alcoholic families often have difficulty acknowledging their feelings, trusting others, and knowing what is normal.

4. A personal exercise: Tonglen

There is a traditional Eastern practice that can help you courageously face and give up your pain. It is called *tonglen*, which literally means "sending and taking." The exercise fosters unconditional acceptance, which confronts our natural tendency to flee from what is uncomfortable and seek pleasure, at all cost. Such a flight from unpleasantness can interfere with our personal pursuit of the truth about ourselves, because we do not always like what we see, preferring to ignore or resist it. The *tonglen* exercise also reinforces our connectedness with others, because what we all have in common is suffering and the desire to transcend it. *Tonglen* is a breathing exercise that involves taking in what is bad, painful, or undesirable and sending out what is good, peaceful, and life giving.

To perform this exercise, sit in a quiet place, relax your whole body, and close your eyes. Breathe slowly and deeply, concentrating on each breath. Allow yourself to feel completely relaxed with a sense of openness to all that is. As you inhale, think about taking in your own suffering and pain. Feel deeply the misery of the moment, perhaps all the anger and hurt you feel at being betrayed. With each exhalation, focus on sending out peace, relaxation, and joy. Allow yourself to feel empathy toward your own suffering, both past and present, and think of extending relief to everyone who shares the same pain. Open your heart to both the pain and joy, completely and unconditionally accepting yourself. Also realize that accepting yourself, if it is genuine and complete, inevitably overflows into acceptance of others. As you progress in this exercise and as you feel ready, allow yourself to feel the pain of your unfaithful partner, realizing that his behavior was a self-defeating way of coping with his own suffering. You are both connected in suffering. Breathe in his pain, and exhale peace toward him and to all who share the unhappiness of betrayal.

5. Prayer from the heart for the Spirit's gift of self-knowledge

Go to your place of prayer and put yourself in God's loving presence. It is helpful to establish a regular time for prayer, perhaps in the early morning or before bedtime, so that the activities of the day do not distract you from this essential, life-giving practice. Think of your prayer time as retreating to an oasis where you are nourished by the water of eternal life, much like the Samaritan woman who met Jesus and came to faith at the well. Allow yourself to acknowledge your self-doubt and self-blame about the affair. If you have become aware of faults that may have contributed to the strain in your relationship, do not hide from them. Acknowledge the continuous threat of self-deception. As the prophet Jeremiah has observed, "More tortuous than all else is the human heart, beyond remedy. Who can understand it? I, the Lord, alone know the mind and test the heart" (Jeremiah 17:9-10). With a spirit of humility, ask God for the gift of self-knowledge, which is similar to the *paramita* of truthfulness. Beg God to free you from any illusions you may have about yourself and help you to know yourself as He knows you. Despite your preoccupation with what is wrong with your life and yourself, you may be surprised to discover the depth of God's love for you as you are, with all your faults. That awareness will give you the courage to face and correct those self-defeating attitudes and behaviors. Before concluding your prayer time, relax for a few moments in the awareness of God's abiding wisdom and love and thank Him for His help.

Recovery entails giving up your preoccupation with the harm done by your unfaithful partner and the view of yourself as a helpless victim. It requires a shift of focus toward self-understanding and responsibility for your own behavior, without blaming yourself for the infidelity. Such a shift empowers you to rebuild your life on a firmer foundation, with or without your present partner. An honest and humble self-examination, often painful, is an opportunity for personal enlightenment, for cultivating the virtues of knowledge and truthfulness. You may be surprised to realize that you were holding yourself back in the relationship, rather than being fully and maturely invested—much like your partner. Three common patterns of disconnecting are by clinging to love out of fear of being independent, fighting against intimacy by engaging in power struggles, and fleeing from intimacy because of fear of closeness. Seeking the truth reveals how you have been shaped by all the significant relationships in your life. It is the best preparation for making a wise, well-informed decision about whether to continue or end the relationship with your unfaithful partner.

SOME DOS AND DON'TS FOR RECOVERY

1. Pay close attention to your reactions, especially the distressful ones. Do you tend to ignore your feelings by keeping busy? Do you avoid discomfort at all costs? Do you seek to feel good all the time?

2. Don't reject any thoughts or feelings as negative. Are you judgmental about your thoughts and feelings? Is your life governed by many "shoulds"? How do you distinguish positive and negative thoughts and feelings?

3. Maintain an attitude of curiosity about your reactions. Is self-knowledge an important value for you? Are you preoccupied with changing what you do not like in yourself without making the effort to understand yourself? Are you quick to judge yourself? Do you see

your painful reaction to this life crisis as an opportunity to deepen your self-knowledge and grow as a person?

4. Be honest with yourself. Can you be both honest and gentle with yourself? Can you acknowledge what you do not like about yourself, and equally, what you appreciate about yourself? Do you tend to exaggerate or minimize your strengths and weaknesses?

5. Explore the chain of thoughts and feelings that arise. Can you be an impartial observer of yourself and your reactions? Does it take too much effort to understand yourself? Do you believe you can learn something new about yourself that will give you a fresh sense of freedom?

6. Be attentive to patterns in your reactions. Do you tend to be a dependent person, looking to others for approval? Are you an angry person who has to be right and fights for control? Do you tend to withdraw from others and live in your own world? Do you believe you can modify your self-defeating patterns of behavior?

7. Be inquisitive about your childhood. Are you curious about how your upbringing influenced your present attitudes and behavior? Can you remember much about your childhood, or is it a blank? Are your memories predominantly happy or sad? What is your earliest memory, and how would you characterize it?

8. Accept responsibility for your own behavior. Do you tend to blame others for your behavior? Do you view yourself as a powerless victim who cannot change his life? Do you look for guidance more from others than yourself?

9. Cultivate the virtues of self-knowledge, honesty, and truthfulness. Do you believe that authentic happiness comes from being true to yourself, even if it is painful? Do you prefer to seek a life of comfort, avoiding pain at all costs? Can you identify ways you tend to avoid painful truths about yourself?

EIGHT

STAGE 4: MAKING A WISE DECISION
To Be or Not to Be . . . with Your Partner

As soon as you trust yourself, you will know how to live.
—JOHANN VON GOETHE

When you discover your partner's infidelity, you hit a crossroad in your relationship. The discovery creates a crisis that can be resolved only by making a decision because your relationship with that person can never be the same. Those who have been traumatized often think of their lives in terms of before and after the traumatizing event. Before, life was simpler and more predictable. But after the event, all has changed. Assumptions about yourself, your partner, and your relationship together may have been shattered. Pandora's box has been opened. As much as you may wish it, you can never pretend that the affair did not occur. Its specter, unfortunately, will always haunt you.

You are left with a decision with only two options: Do you want to stay with your partner or leave him? Because of the serious consequences of the decision for yourself, your family, and your children, you want to make a careful, well-considered, and wise decision. Such a decision can be made only after you have calmed the emotional storm and achieved some understanding of your partner, yourself, and your relationship.

While the decision about remaining in or leaving your relationship can be reduced to an either-or decision, you will make the decision in the context of a renewed self-understanding. The decision to be or not to be with your partner requires a change of heart, a personal conversion that is the essence of recovery. In the self-confrontation provoked by the trauma of the discovered infidelity, you may become aware of self-defeating patterns of behavior in your relationships and make a commitment to change. You may come to realize that unless you change the way you relate to yourself and others, you will repeat the same painful, unsatisfying dance with any partner you choose.

As Dr. Kübler-Ross observed, in the dying process there is a stage of bargaining in which those facing death bargain with God to spare them. In your recovery from the trauma of infidelity, you may engage in a similar grieving process and find yourself bargaining with yourself. You may ask yourself, "Do I really have to make this difficult decision? Is there anything I can do to avoid it?" After taking an honest and courageous look at yourself, you may also ask, "Do I really have to change myself?" Often the honest self-examination reveals what you do not like to see in yourself, that you have faults that contributed to the unhappiness of your relationship. Perhaps you would like to blame only your unfaithful partner, but honesty may impel you to admit that you have failed in some way. You might be faced with your self-defeating ways of relating with others and with your resistance to change. You may find yourself hanging on to old attitudes and patterns of behaving. As I tell my patients in the midst of treatment, "You can expect that you will feel caught between two stools and don't know where to stand. You've learned what behaviors don't work, but don't know how to replace them." You are squarely confronted with your fear of change, of creating a new future for yourself, and may bargain with yourself to find a shortcut, a way of avoiding the insecurity of change.

IS DIVORCE INEVITABLE?

If your partner has been unfaithful, is divorce eventually inevitable? Some justify divorce only for the three big A's: adultery, alcoholism, and abuse. They say it is intolerable to stay with someone who has been unfaithful and advocate immediate separation. Others insist on the sanctity of marriage and believe that any problem can be worked through with enough love and commitment. Research indicates that some choose to continue the relationship with their unfaithful partners, while others do not. One older study of affairs reported that one-third of those interviewed were eventually divorced as a direct result of an infidelity.[1] A more recent study by Lawson indicates that the marriage ends for almost half of those having affairs.[2] It is difficult to obtain accurate and consistent data regarding infidelity because of the large variety of types of affairs, whether long- or short-term, single or multiple, sexual or emotional. Typically, your reaction is related to the type of affair. For example, you may tend to view a one-night sexual encounter more readily as a forgivable mistake than a long-term emotional/sexual affair. Nevertheless, when you have discovered your partner's infidelity, you must make a difficult decision about the relationship based on your own values, appraisal of yourself and your partner, and determination of what is in your own best interest.

DO I NEED TO SEPARATE FROM MY PARTNER TO MAKE A GOOD DECISION?

Making a conscientious decision will take time. How long depends on your ability to sort through your issues honestly. Patients sometimes ask me about the advisability of separating from their partner for a period of time. For some individuals, a separation can be helpful, or even advisable. They may be so distraught, so caught up in the emotional storm, that they need time apart from their unfaithful partner to find a measure of calm. The sight of their partner provokes flashbacks, with overwhelming feelings and rage. They may also need time to sort out their thoughts and feelings, preferably with the help of a therapist, without feeling the pressure of their partner's presence and questions. Hopefully, the time apart will allow both parties to slow down sufficiently to undertake an honest self-examination. They will both experience what it will be like living apart, if they choose to divorce. The separation may also impress upon the unfaithful partner the seriousness of the betrayal and its impact on you.

If you choose to separate in order to care for yourself through the immediate crisis, I recommend that you decide how long the trial separation will last, from a few weeks to several months. It is important that you minimize contact with your partner or mutually decide to have no contact so that you can experience the full reality of being separated. In my experience, a no-contact separation of several months' duration is useful in several circumstances: when you are so enmeshed with your partner that any contact will activate old self-defeating patterns of interacting, when you are so under the influence of your partner that you cannot make an independent decision, when you are so consumed by anger in your partner's presence that you cannot think clearly, when you are so terrified of being alone that you are incapable of making a wise decision. Of course, if you feel physically threatened, I recommend an immediate separation to protect yourself.

BARRIERS TO WISE DECISION MAKING

In order to make a wise, rather than an impulsive or ill-considered decision, you will need to calm yourself enough to consider some serious personal questions. For example, you can benefit from asking yourself the following: What do I really want? What are the pros and cons of staying in and leaving the relationship? What is the impact of staying or leaving on me and my children? What is in my/our best interests? Can I ever feel secure with this person again? Do I really love him? What do I need to change in myself to make this relationship work? Am I willing to work at making the changes? Is my partner a trustworthy person? Can I be assured this betrayal will never happen again? What does she need to change to make this relationship work? Is she willing to make the effort? What do I need to do to prepare myself for living on my own if I decide to leave?

These are difficult questions to answer honestly. In my clinical experience, those who have been traumatized have a particular difficulty answering them, mostly because they do not trust themselves. There are several reasons for this. First, you may have grown up in a household where your parents either ignored your needs, mistreated you in some way, or modeled unhealthy ways of interacting. Perhaps you were never encouraged to pay attention to your feelings, desires, or opinions and were even discouraged from expressing them. Consequently, you may have grown up ignoring yourself, just as your caregivers did. You have not learned to trust your perceptions of yourself or have the language to express yourself. Furthermore, you may have grown up unaccustomed to pursuing what you really want in a direct way. Second, more immediately and as a direct result of the deceptions you experienced with your unfaithful partner, you may question your own perceptions of reality. Perhaps your partner lied to you or even ridiculed you for your suspicions. As a consequence, you grew to doubt yourself and even feel guilty for questioning. You learned to submerge what you experienced and perceived in order to maintain the relationship, unaware of how your partner was manipulating the truth for her own advantage. Third, because of the betrayal, your assumptions about relationships have likely been shattered, resulting in a profound self-doubt. Finally, you may have become stuck in your recovery and believe yourself incapable of making a wise decision about your future. The following are several ways you may be stuck in a stage of recovery:

1. Caught in the emotional storm

2. Trapped in obsessive thinking

3. Frozen in a self-defeating pattern of relating

1. Caught in the emotional storm

You may become sidetracked in your recovery because you are still caught in the emotional storm of the traumatic discovery of your partner's affair. Like many who have been traumatized, you may still feel so overwhelmed with pain and confusion that you cannot think clearly. You may feel in the grip of powerful, uncontrollable feelings that rule your life. You might feel helpless and not know where to turn. Naturally, when your pain becomes so overwhelming, you may seek a way of escape, perhaps turning to alcohol or drugs, as many do. Or you may try to distract yourself with activities, such as shopping, gambling, or work. In such a fragile emotional state, even the smallest disappointment can cause a tidal wave of emotion and tears. You may still feel like you are drowning in a sea of emotion, being swept along by currents that are deep, hidden, and threatening. In the grip of these powerful emotions, you are unable to step back and reflect on what is happening to you and what you want in your life. You can see the forest, but not the trees.

You may see yourself as too emotionally disabled to make a wise decision about your relationship, or about any significant matter. There is a double danger at this point. The first danger is that you will act impulsively and short-circuit a healthy decision-making process. You may leave your partner in anger or cling to him out of a sense of fearful desperation. In my clinical experience, such a pattern of being ruled by emotions, unable to make a deliberate decision, is more common with women, because they tend to be more in touch with their feelings. A second danger is that you will become numb and withdraw from the rigors of the decision-making process, as the following case illustrates.

Allysa is an example of an emotionally stuck person. She brought her husband, Jim, to therapy because she could not get over his affair the year before. They had been married for four years, and their relationship had been marked by frequent arguing. When they were separated after an argument, Jim was intoxicated one night, met an old girlfriend at a bar, and engaged in sex with her. After they got back together, Allysa learned about Jim's sexual encounter and was furious. For a year they argued vehemently about the incident, and Jim could not reassure her of his remorse and commitment to her. Allysa began drinking heavily, and her hurt and rage often exploded when she was intoxicated. I tried to explain how the drinking prolonged the emotional turmoil and reduced her ability to think clearly about their marital problems. But Allysa persisted in her drinking and painful confusion. She was unable to quiet her emotions enough to look honestly at herself, her partner, and their relationship in order to make a wise decision about their future together.

2. Trapped in obsessive thinking

A second way you may become stuck in your recovery is continually obsessing about the affair, about what your partner did and how you have been hurt. You may become trapped in your mind, in your preoccupation with the betrayal. Your thoughts may race out of control, spinning around the same issue, the affair, causing you to feel incapable of focusing your attention on anything else. You may protest the injustice of the betrayal and affirm your own innocence. Of course, the obsessing covers over a huge reservoir of pain. It can feel like a relief. However, it may also express a righteous anger that prevents you from stepping back and looking clearly at yourself and the whole situation. In such a state of mind, you can see the trees, but not the forest.

I have observed that individuals who react by persistent obsessing tend to keep their emotions at a distance. They often do not recognize their feelings or what they want in life. Instead, they live under the sway of many authoritarian rules they learned growing up. They live under the tyranny of many "shoulds" about how their lives ought to be. They also gravitate toward familiar roles and repetitive behaviors. However, in the process, they become distant from their own experience and do not trust it. Furthermore, they cannot quiet their minds enough to make a thoughtful and wise decision about their lives. They now feel lost because all the rules have changed with the discovery of the affair. Because they are so out of touch with their own feelings and desires, they are disabled in the decision-making process. The danger is that they will persist in deliberating without coming to a conclusion about what is in their best interests. In my clinical experience, such a pattern of being trapped in the mind, unable to decide, is more common with men.

As an illustration: Alex brought his wife, Elaine, to marital therapy because he suspected she was having an affair but could not prove it. He had intercepted some emails she received from a man she claimed she met through a girlfriend. Elaine admitted that they had become friends but denied any sexual involvement. Alex did not believe her because of the romantic tone of the messages. He could not stop thinking about her being with another man. He obsessed about it constantly. Alex, a successful advertising executive, thought his life was in perfect order until he read those emails. Now he was so preoccupied with what he believed was his wife's infidelity that he could not sleep at night or concentrate at work. Alex was a dedicated

Catholic and did not believe in divorce. He refused to think about leaving Elaine but did not know how he would keep from going crazy with his suspicious thoughts.

3. Frozen in a self-defeating pattern of relating

The self-defeating patterns of relating discussed above can get you stuck in the following ways:

a. The dependent: ruled by fear

b. The aggressive: ruled by anger

c. The emotionally detached: ruled by mistrust

a. The dependent: ruled by fear

Those who are dependent and cling to love are often ruled by fear. Continuing to see themselves as weak and helpless, they do not trust themselves to make decisions. Consequently, they assume a passive stance toward life and their relationships. When they consider separating from their unfaithful partners, they are overcome with anxiety and self-doubt. How will I ever survive on my own? Will people accept me if I am divorced? What will people think of me? Because they do not recognize their personal authority, they look to others to help them decide. When their friends offer conflicting advice, they are thrown into confusion. I notice in therapy that these dependent patients want me to give them advice and guidance and are disappointed, even angry at times, when I do not. Instead, I invite them to trust themselves.

Take the example of Elizabeth. She had been married for forty years when she discovered love letters written by her childhood friend to her husband, Tom. It took all of Elizabeth's courage to confront Tom. In response, he mocked her for being so suspicious and insisted it was only a friendship. When Elizabeth came into therapy with me, she was not sure what to think about her husband's supposed friendship. I encouraged her to listen to herself and trust her own perceptions and judgments. She confronted Tom about the secrecy of his friendship and came to believe he was being unfaithful to their marriage vows, despite his protests to the contrary. She began to explore their life together and acknowledged that Tom continually complained about their sexual relations and had had many "friendships" with other women throughout the years. When she thought about divorcing him, she was paralyzed with fear. She was a devout Catholic and believed she would be an outcast, wearing a scarlet letter D for divorced. She was terrified that none of her married friends would ever socialize with her if she were divorced.

b. The aggressive: ruled by anger

Second, those who are aggressive and fight for control in their relationships also have difficulty making wise decisions. Their continuing anger remains a screen that prevents them from recognizing their true feelings, which is an essential ingredient of wise decision making. When they discover their partner's infidelity, their hurt and rage are expressed through a relentless obsessing about the injustice of the affair. They may retaliate with their own affairs or cling to a self-righteous position. Because of their fear of appearing weak, they do not seek the advice of others, unlike those who are dependent. However, they are so caught up in their anger that they cannot calm themselves enough to recognize the pain and self-doubt that drive their behavior. They do not quiet their minds and emotions enough to consider thoughtfully their true desires and goals in life and what is in their best interests. Often, they are ambivalent and cannot make up their minds, complaining, "I can't live with or without my partner." Instead of making a wise decision, they take action, often in an aggressive, attacking manner.

Jack and Marianne had known each other for almost thirty years, but only half of the time did they live together. From the beginning, their relationship was on again, off again. They dated after high school for three years, fought constantly, and separated numerous times. They established a fragile peace when they finally became engaged and proceeded with the marriage. Reflecting on their marriage, Marianne said, "We have always lived in the extremes in our relationship. We either loved or hated each other. We were either completely together or completely apart." Jack had an affair after they had been married for ten years. Marianne divorced him soon after discovering the infidelity. They were separated for seven years, dated others, but could not stand being apart. So they remarried and felt some contentment until Jack had another affair. When the affair ended after much battling, Marianne decided to stay married because she and Jack owned a business together. She admitted, "I think I learned to survive by putting all my energy into the business."

c. The emotionally detached: ruled by mistrust

Those who detach and flee from intimacy in relationships have enormous difficulty making decisions. Because they appear so independent, aloof, and self-assured, it seems that decisions come easily to them. That may be the case in business or money matters, where they can be cool and calculating. They have no difficulty intellectually weighing options. However, decisions regarding emotional concerns are another matter. These individuals survive by pretending to be above it all because deep down they do not trust themselves. They avoid intimacy with others, but also with themselves. They are disabled in making wise decisions of the heart because they lack an intimate knowledge of their feelings and true desires, which can be the only secure base for deciding about committed relationships. When they discover their partner's affair, they attempt to disconnect from their own emotional reactions. They may withdraw more into their own worlds and avoid making any heartfelt decision regarding the relationship. It is not unusual that these detached individuals give a tacit consent to their partner continuing the affair to fulfill their partner's emotional needs, which they have ignored. They turn a blind eye to a "marital arrangement," as long as it does not interfere with their world.

As the case of John illustrates, there is a price to pay for the suppression of feelings. John was recently retired when he came to me for therapy. He had suffered from an anxiety disorder since childhood and had drunk heavily for years to cope. When he decided to become sober, he became aware of many uncomfortable feelings he had suppressed. He complained of problems sleeping and occasional nightmares about his wife being with another man. He told me that his wife had been unfaithful thirty years before. His friends had advised him at the time to divorce her, but he decided to stay married. He had believed that he was at peace with his decision. However, after his sobriety, he became aware of how much rage he felt about her infidelity. He also acknowledged a deep regret because he did not forcefully confront her about the affair many years before. John berated himself as a weakling for being so passive and never learned to assert himself in any relationships.

IMPACT ON THE CHILDREN: SOME QUESTIONS

An important consideration in making the decision to stay or leave the relationship is the impact on the children. The following are some frequently asked questions:

What is the effect of infidelity on our children?

Your children can also be traumatized by the discovery of your partner's infidelity, and the effects can be long lasting. Patients have told me stories about when they were children of accompanying a parent for meetings with their sex partners and being told to keep it secret from their other parent. In therapy, they reported much anger, confusion, and fear. They were angry at their unfaithful parent for pressuring them to collude in the lie, and guilty about participating in the cover-up. If they were young, they were confused about what was happening and often developed confused notions about sex, deception, and forbidden activity. They were exposed to something that was too overwhelming for them. They also received mixed messages about sexuality, fidelity, and marriage. Because of their exposure to betrayal, they began to mistrust themselves and others, not sure of what was true and reliable. Research indicates that there is a generational influence regarding infidelity: children of unfaithful parents tend to be unfaithful in their marriages or choose unfaithful spouses.

Should I tell our children about the affair?

There are two schools of thought on this issue. One group of experts believes that the children should not be told because of the danger of alienating the children from the unfaithful parent. They argue that children need to think well of their parents and keep a connection with both of them. Revealing an affair puts the unfaithful parent in a bad light and influences the child to take sides in their parents' conflicts. Parents need to be sensitive about overwhelming their children with too much information before they are ready to receive it. Parents also need to be careful about influencing their children to side with them in their conflicts by dramatizing their pain and the bad behavior of their spouse. Finally, they argue, parents have a right to privacy and need to maintain the boundary between their marriage to each other and their relationship with their children.

Another group of experts recommends that parents tell their children in an age-appropriate manner about the affair. They argue that the children are already aware of the unavoidable tension in the home because of conflicts over the affair. Children are like sponges that soak up the emotions in the home, often without understanding them or their source. Furthermore, the children may learn about the affair from overhearing conversations or being told by someone else. It is better that they learn from the parents. Affairs thrive in silence and deception. These professionals suggest that keeping the affair secret colludes with the conspiracy of silence that maintained the betrayal. Since children already know something wrong is happening in the home, a sensitive, age-appropriate explanation can help relieve some tension. Children's greatest fear is that their parents will divorce, and they will be abandoned. If they pursue the path of honesty, parents can begin to address their children's fears as soon as possible.

I recommend that you tell your children about the affair with three provisos: at a suitable time, in an age-appropriate manner, and without getting into details. For example, you might tell your ten-year-old son: "Your daddy and I have not been getting along for a while. You know how sometimes friends have disagreements. We have been disagreeing about a friendship your daddy has with another woman, and we are trying to work it out. That's not something you have to worry about. That's our problem, and we're working on it. We'll always take care of you."

Ideally, both you and your partner together should explain what is happening in an age-appropriate way and help your children work through their feelings. It may also be helpful to reveal the affair with the assistance of a therapist, possibly in a family session. Admittedly, there are many dangers in this honest approach. You must be extremely careful not to present the information in a self-serving way, portraying yourself as the innocent victim and your spouse as the guilty persecutor. It is essential that you exercise care not to alienate the children from the unfaithful parent through blame. You must also be extremely careful not to overwhelm your children with information that is beyond their capacity to assimilate. As parents, you need to trust your judgment about the best way to present this sensitive information and help them through their reactions.

IF I DECIDE TO DIVORCE, WHAT IS THE IMPACT ON MY CHILDREN?

Certainly, your children will experience significant distress. They must make many adjustments over which they have no control or understanding. They may have to move, change schools, spend less time with you, and have less money. Their familiar life and routine will be disrupted. Furthermore, they fear losing a parent. Nevertheless, as difficult as the adjustment is to divorce, lasting harm is not inevitable. Children are resilient, resourceful, and capable of adjusting well with your help, support at school, and counseling. Research indicates that the most harmful aspect of divorce is not the separation from the parents, but the intensity of the conflict between the separating parents. Children feel caught in the middle of the emotional tug-of-war and believe they must take sides. Such an experience of intense conflict, during which their needs are often ignored, teaches them about the dangers of intimacy, which can become a lasting legacy.

HOW CAN I MINIMIZE THE NEGATIVE IMPACT OF OUR DIVORCE ON OUR CHILDREN?

Recognizing that the disruption of divorce is difficult on everyone—yourself, your partner, and your children—there are things you can do to help during this transition time:

1. Avoid fighting in the presence of your children. The conflict will only increase their anxiety. Certainly, you will have disagreements with your partner, but keep them as private as possible.

2. Assure your children that they are not responsible for the problems in your marriage. Younger children normally think of themselves as the center of the universe, creating an illusion of control over their environment to compensate for feelings of helplessness. They may believe that you are divorcing because of something they did.

3. Frequently assure your children that both you and your partner love them and will never abandon them, even if you live apart. Children need to maintain an emotional bond with both parents. It is important that you and your spouse assure them with both words and actions.

4. Resist the impulse to blame your spouse for the divorce or elicit your children as allies. Children experience an impossible bind if they believe they must take sides in your dispute.

5. Do not burden your children with too much responsibility. Let them continue to be children. During the transition you may feel overwhelmed and need more help from them. Be careful not to overburden them.

6. Do not lean on your children for emotional support. That will overburden them emotionally and divide their loyalties. Seek your support from family, friends, and therapy.

7. Do not let your children manipulate you. You may feel guilty for causing them pain and want to make up for it by overindulging them. Your children need to know that you are still the authority in the family, even if you are feeling distress.

A DECISION TO STAY AND REBUILD: BILL'S STORY

After the initial shock of discovering his wife's affair wore off, Bill, a police officer, was enraged. He was a man who prided himself at keeping a tight rein on his feelings and was surprised by the intensity of his emotional reaction. His first impulse was to confront "the other man," who was married and a fellow officer. The man was frightened of Bill, apologized profusely, and assured him that he never had any intention of leaving his wife. Bill was also surprised by how anxious he felt at the prospect of losing his wife of twenty-five years. For the first time in their marriage, he sat down to talk honestly with Sarah. He heard how lonely, neglected, and controlled she felt for many years. He told her how betrayed he felt and frightened of losing her.

Bill and Sarah came together for therapy. During the sessions we discussed their mutual dissatisfaction in the marriage. Sarah felt alone and bored and sought affection from someone else. She hated Bill's drinking, his tight control of the finances, and his marriage to his job. She believed she had lost her voice in the marriage. Bill believed he had always provided well for his family, admitting that he was conscientious and conservative about their finances. He hated what he considered Sarah's nagging, financial irresponsibility, and demands for attention. After a few sessions, I suggested that both begin individual therapy to explore their personal issues further.

During the individual sessions with Bill, it became clear that he had rushed to a decision to remain with Sarah. He suppressed much of the anger he felt about her betrayal. Instead, he was preoccupied with his fear of losing her. He could not imagine himself living alone as a divorced man. I invited him to acknowledge all that he was feeling, the rage, fear, guilt, and sadness. We also began to explore the way he and Sarah had interacted throughout their marriage, how she begged for attention and he withdrew into his work and preoccupation with money. We also examined his drinking, and he decided that he had a problem, like his parents, and needed to stop. We explored his need to be in such tight control of himself, his feelings, and his surroundings, and its impact on himself and his relationships. For the first time in his life, Bill began to take an honest look at himself and pay attention to his own feelings and desires. He was also able to have some empathy for what Sarah felt in their relationship.

After several months of meeting separately, Bill and Sarah came for couple's therapy. Sarah listened to Bill's expressions of hurt and anger regarding the affair, and she sincerely expressed remorse. She broke up with the other man but admitted that she was still feeling some grief over the loss of that relationship. She also expressed fear about whether they could rebuild their marriage. Bill told Sarah honestly about his struggle to trust her again but also acknowledged his need to be more open with her. After much soul-searching, he told her that he wanted to work on the marriage with her. And Sarah agreed. Both made a commitment to begin again and continue to work on the issues that kept them disconnected.

Bill was able to make a wise choice for the marriage only after he faced his feelings and obtained some understanding of what Sarah's affair meant in the context of their relationship. He was not stuck in angry blame or in a victim role. Instead, he developed some empathy for himself and for Sarah's struggles in the marriage. He also avoided blaming himself but acknowledged his contribution to their marital problems. He was able to stop, think, and honestly consider what he wanted in his life and whether Sarah would be included in his dreams.

There are no shortcuts to a wise decision regarding the relationship in this "action" stage of change. The following are some areas that need to be considered in the decision-making process:

1. For reconciliation to occur, you must have assurance that the affair is over and that your partner intends to make a commitment to the relationship. One important way of demonstrating commitment is her willingness to be involved in therapy to work on both her personal and relational issues.

2. This may seem obvious, but you need to ask yourself if you really love your partner. Some relationships begin as mismatches, and the couple never really connect emotionally. Or the relationship is based on an unhealthy neediness rather than a genuine

emotional attachment. The affair may then be a symptom of a disconnected relationship, waiting to be recognized.

3. Did your partner express genuine remorse for the infidelity? You need to know that he understands the pain he caused you, accepts the responsibility for his behavior, and is willing to make amends. If he continues to blame you for his affair, it is a clear sign that he is avoiding personal responsibility and may be unfaithful again.

4. Do you believe your partner is trustworthy and that he has learned from his mistake? Is he willing to confront the painful issues that led to his unfaithful behavior? Again, his willingness to engage in therapy is a sign of his sincerity. If he has a sexual addiction or has had serial affairs, his commitment to treatment is essential for recovery.

5. Are you willing to invest yourself in therapy to address your personal and relational issues? If not, you are setting yourself up for being betrayed again by your present partner or someone else.

6. Are you committed to rebuilding your relationship with this person? That means, are you willing to face your continuing insecurity and mistrust?

7. What is the impact of your decision on your children? This issue was discussed in the section above.

A DECISION TO SEPARATE: JENNIFER'S STORY

Jennifer always saw Bruce as the love of her life and never imagined they would divorce. Through therapy, she began to realize how little she thought of herself and how much she had idealized Bruce. But now she was overwhelmingly disillusioned by his deceit and betrayal. She was paralyzed with fear, asking herself, "How will my daughter and I survive?" Jennifer continued to obsess about the affair for a long time and was frustrated by Bruce's defensiveness about it. She felt stuck, not believing she could live with him or without him. How could she ever trust him again? How could she ever feel secure with him?

Jennifer felt hopeful when Bruce began therapy. They had several sessions together, and Bruce spoke more openly about his feelings than he ever had in their relationship. He claimed he had the affair with his secretary to comfort himself from the pressures of his job. He enjoyed her attention and complained that he was feeling emotionally and sexually neglected by Jennifer because she was so focused on caring for their daughter.

Jennifer, who was always so reserved, found the courage to express directly to Bruce the hurt, anger, and disappointment she felt. She complained of many lonely evenings without him and of her insecurity about his flirting with other women. She too missed having sex with him and knowing that she was still desirable to him.

Jennifer's hopes for reconciliation began to fade when Bruce missed therapy sessions and gradually withdrew. He protested, "I don't want to air my dirty laundry with a stranger." Jennifer begged that Bruce spend more time with her so that they could talk and work out their problems. However, he balked and insisted that he could not neglect his job if they were to survive financially. His pattern of late-night work resumed, and Bruce ignored Jennifer's requests that he call. Despite his adamant denials, Jennifer suspected that he continued to see his secretary. Jennifer was again feeling desperately alone, but still clinging to hope for the marriage.

Instead of giving up in defeat, Jennifer devoted herself to therapy and her own recovery. She felt paralyzed by indecision. On the one hand, she was feeling miserable, suspicious, and insecure with Bruce. On the other hand, she was terrified of moving out on her own. During the sessions, we focused on her lack of self-confidence and inability to trust herself to make a good decision about her future. She carefully weighed the pros and cons of continuing the marriage and finally gained the courage to ask Bruce for a divorce. She felt relieved to finally make a decision, but also great sadness at the loss of her dream marriage. She exclaimed, "Even though my marriage is dead, I am very much alive."

When you have made the decision to end your relationship, you have certainly reached a milestone. The decision has required a great deal of courage and soul-searching. Perhaps you felt confident because you faced your fears, listened to yourself, and took decisive action. Nevertheless, you are aware that the challenge to build a new life has just begun. The old pattern of relating with dependence, aggression, or detachment may surface again and again in your relationships. You may be discovering through your recovery that old habits do not die easily. Replacing them with new, more effective behaviors requires much insight and effort. Consequently, it will be beneficial for you to continue working on your recovery with the insights you have gained. Furthermore, you may experience flashbacks as you take the risk of becoming involved in new relationships. One woman reported intense anxiety while dating because she feared her new boyfriend cheating on her. Another woman told me she had recurrent nightmares of her new husband transforming into her previous unfaithful husband. I assure you that your taking decisive action will be an important building block for your further work at recovery.

Those who have been unfaithful also have to make a decision regarding their relationship: whether to stay or leave. Of course, for any relationship to work, both parties must want to be in the relationship and be committed to it. In making a wise decision, the unfaithful person also needs to face her fears about intimacy. She may discover she is ruled by fear, anger, or mistrust, which paralyzes her decision making. She may discover that she was unfaithful as a way of avoiding an intimate connection. If she chooses to separate, like Bruce, she will confront the many ways she disconnects in relating to others or face another failure in the next relationship, with or without her affair partner. If she chooses to reconcile, like Sarah, she will need to convince her betrayed partner of her sincere remorse, trustworthiness, willingness to change, and desire to rebuild their relationship. Even if she wants reconciliation, her wounded partner may still choose to move on without her.

SOME AIDS TO DECISION MAKING

I have observed in many of my patients that one of the greatest obstacles to their making a decision is their sensitivity to loss. I remind them that a loss, as painful as it is, is inevitable, no matter what they decide. If they choose one path, they give up everything they could find on the other path. The acceptance of limitation, the giving up of the wish to have it all, is one of life's painful lessons. The following suggestions will help you find clarity and move forward with whatever you decide.

1. Individual therapy to discover your inner compass

Individual therapy can be beneficial as you contemplate what needs to change in your life and decide what you want to do. Because you have been traumatized, lied to, and discouraged from trusting yourself, making a wise decision about your future can be especially difficult. I work with patients to help them remove any obstacles to listening to themselves and learn to trust their own perceptions and judgments. Many feel they have lost their inner compass. Consequently, they need to learn, possibly for the first time, to pay close attention to themselves. That means listening with a nonjudgmental attitude to their feelings, thoughts, and desires. It also means acknowledging their intuitions and perceptions about themselves and the significant people in their lives, and making the effort to discern their truthfulness. Finally, their decision making involves recognizing and accepting their values, desires, needs, and judgments about what is important to them. I then invite my patients to examine closely their relationship and sort out for themselves the benefits and costs of staying with their partner versus leaving. I remind them that a new life is possible, if they are willing to reach out for it.

2. Keeping your journal to sharpen your inner focus

Keeping up with your journal can be helpful in this personal discernment process. Think carefully about your relationship with your partner. Review in your mind the history of your life together, paying close attention to what attracted you to him and the faults you discovered in him and yourself. Remember both the happy and distressful times.

Try to be as honest as possible with yourself. If you choose to stay with your partner to rebuild your relationship, you will be recommitting yourself to him as he is, not as you wish him to be. Now, in your journal, select two pages and draw a line down the middle of each. At the top of one page write, "reasons for staying together," and on the second page, "reasons for leaving." On one half of each page, write in detail all the benefits of staying or leaving. For example, some benefits of staying might be financial security, a stable home for the children, a realistic hope of rebuilding the relationship. Some benefits for leaving might be the possibility of forming a healthy relationship with someone else, freedom from abuse and mistrust, starting a new life. On the other half, write the costs and risks. For example, the cost of staying might be living with insecurity about his faithfulness, always being suspicious or angry, poor modeling for the children. The risks in leaving might be financial hardship, having to work and care for the children, being alone. It is often helpful to see your thoughts in black and white to clarify your own thinking and deciding.

3. A personal exercise: discernment of spirits

An exercise to help you make a wise decision was proposed many years ago by Ignatius Loyola, the founder of the Jesuit religious order. To assist his followers in deepening their spiritual life, he wrote *The Spiritual Exercises*.[3] In his teachings, Ignatius expressed several beliefs that are the foundation of his practice: (1) that God is intimately involved in each of our lives, (2) that doing God's will is the only path to salvation and personal happiness, (3) that we can know God's will for us if we hunger to discover it and are interiorly free to embrace it, and (4) that we can use our reason to know what God wants of us. Ignatius adds a word of practical advice. He recommended that we not make a major life decision until we are ready. If we are experiencing significant turmoil, we are not interiorly free enough to make a wise decision and should wait until we have achieved a measure of inner peace.

As you have been making your journey through recovery, you have worked at quieting the emotional storm and understanding your own thoughts, feelings, and behaviors so that you are free enough to listen carefully to your deepest desires. In the Christian tradition,

God reveals His will for us through those desires that reflect who we really are, beneath the facade. We are children of God, reaching out to our Father in love. The following is an exercise in decision making to discern the true spirit of our desires and their correspondence with God's will.

1. Place yourself in the prayerful presence of God.

2. Ask God for enlightenment that you may see clearly what He wants for you, how you can best serve Him.

3. Reflect on the alternatives you wrote about in your journal: whether to stay together or leave. Consider carefully the benefits and costs of each choice, the advantages and disadvantages of each for you.

4. If clarity does not emerge after this initial consideration, think more deeply about what decision is more consistent with the movement of your own life history.

5. Make a tentative decision and pray about it, asking God for confirmation. A sustained sense of inner peace will normally follow a wise decision, although there still may be anxiety attached to implementing the decision.

6. If you do not achieve a sense of inner peace, repeat the process at a later date.

4. Joining a support group

There are many self-help groups within the community and sponsored by churches that can be of immense assistance at the various stages of your recovery. These groups are so valuable because you learn that you are not alone in your suffering, that others can offer you support and advice, and that there is hope for recovery. You can learn about the various groups in your area on the Internet and in the phonebook. For example, in my area, a typical metropolitan region, there are several support groups available. One group, called Betrayal, is a newly formed support group for women whose relationships have ended in betrayal. Divorce Anonymous meets regularly to offer a twelve-step approach, similar to Alcoholics Anonymous, for those working through the pain of divorce. Churches offer support groups for divorced, separated, widowed, or single persons. Bethany groups are sponsored by the Catholic Church, while Helpmates is offered through a Lutheran Church in my area. At these groups, presentations on personal growth and relationships, Bible discussions, and group sharing are typically offered. Furthermore, communities and churches sponsor groups for singles who are interested in meeting others through social activities. At whatever stage you find yourself in recovery, there are opportunities for companionship on your journey. You may be surprised how many others you find share the same trauma of being betrayed.

5. Praying from the heart for the Spirit's gifts of wisdom, counsel, and fortitude

Go to your quiet place to relax and pray. The basic attitude in prayer is one of listening to God speaking to our hearts, rather than our speaking about ourselves. We need to listen first before we speak in prayerful dialogue. Begin by asking God, however you conceive of Him, to open your mind and heart to hear His word of love to you. After a while, express your sense of fear, confusion, and helplessness regarding the important decision you are making. Allow yourself to experience your sense of being lost and afraid. Then ask God to share His wisdom, that you may see clearly the path that lies before you, and His counsel, that you may exercise right judgment in choosing a way. You may be so paralyzed by fear and by mistrust of your insight and judgment that you do not feel free to decide about your future. Pray also for the gift of fortitude, which is the courage to move beyond your fears. Fortitude is similar to the *paramitas* of joyful energy and resolute determination to follow the path of enlightenment. Before concluding your prayer, allow yourself to feel confidence that the uncertainty will eventually clear, and you will find a path and the courage to follow it.

Only when you have sufficiently calmed your emotions and gained some insight into what went wrong in the relationship will you be in a position to make a wise decision about whether to stay in the relationship with your unfaithful partner. That will require an understanding of how you and your partner interacted with each other and the patterns of interacting you learned from childhood. Because you may have learned to distrust yourself because of experiences within your family and with your partner, making a wise decision may be difficult. You will need to face your fears, acknowledge your blind spots, and pay close attention to your feelings, desires, and values to make a wise decision. However, grappling honestly with your confusion and fears can become an opportunity to exercise and develop the virtues of wisdom, counsel, and fortitude. After making the decision, you can then focus your energy on rebuilding your life, with or without your partner, with the self-knowledge and self-confidence you have gained. The next step in recovery will involve regaining trust and learning to forgive yourself and your partner.

SOME DOS AND DON'TS FOR RECOVERY

1. Pay close attention to your wishes and desires. What do you hope for from your partner, yourself, your relationship? What are your goals in life? Where do you see yourself ten years from now?

2. Trust your intuitions and perceptions. Do you lack confidence in your sense of reality? What keeps you from trusting yourself? Did you see yourself as a perceptive, intuitive person before the affair? Do you see yourself differently now?

3. Discern your own values, what is important to you. What do you value most: honesty, integrity, comfort, stability? What motivates you in your day-to-day life? Do you see yourself as an inner value–driven person or someone controlled by circumstances and others' expectations?

4. Don't be handcuffed by guilt. Do you blame yourself for the affair? Do you tend to judge yourself harshly? How has guilt held you back

in your life? Do you feel bound by others' expectations of you? Do you feel responsible for others' disappointment in you?

5. Feel free to explore all possibilities. Do you feel too frightened to think seriously about all your options? Are you ruled by fear, anger, or mistrust, which interferes with your explorations? Do you trust your imagination, which illuminates options?

6. Trust your judgment about what is in your best interest. Are you afraid to take risks? Are you overconcerned about what others will think about your decisions? What interferes with your trusting yourself: fear, anger, ignorance?

7. Have confidence in your ability to live out your decision. Do you look to the future with excitement or dread? Do you tend to imagine the best or the worst outcomes? Do you see yourself as a survivor or a defeated person?

8. Cultivate the virtue of courage to pursue your own dreams. Are you paralyzed by fear about the unknown future? Do you feel the energy and determination to move on with your life? Does anything hold you back?

NINE

STAGE 5: EMBRACING SELF-FORGIVENESS
Freeing Yourself to Love Again

If you haven't forgiven yourself something,
how can you forgive others?

—DOLORES HUERTA

The next, and most difficult, step in recovery is toward forgiveness. Forgiveness begins with yourself. You may be surprised, or even outraged, at the suggestion that you need forgiveness, protesting, "What did I do wrong? It was my partner who betrayed me." That is a natural reaction. However, those who have been traumatized often blame themselves, imagining they could have done something to prevent the catastrophe. They turn their anger against themselves. Similarly, you may blame yourself for not being a good enough partner, for not seeing signs of problems in the relationship, or even for contributing to the problems. Furthermore, you may not like the angry, depressed, insecure, anxious person you may have become since discovering the affair. Rebuilding your life after the affair will require a letting go of the hurts of the past. It will require forgiving yourself.

The journey toward forgiveness entails a grieving process that unfolds in stages. At this stage you may feel a profound depression, an overwhelming sense of loss. The sadness might sap your energy, making you pull back from life. You are well aware of all that you have lost because of your partner's unfaithful behavior. Likely, you have lost trust in your partner, yourself, and the predictability of your world. You have lost the security of your home, the relationship, and your way of life. Your beliefs about the permanency and reliability of love may also have been shattered. Perhaps, most painfully, you blame yourself for the failure of the relationship, which deepens your depressed mood. The danger at this point in recovery is from two sides. You may avoid the painful and profound sense of loss, covering it up with some addictive behavior. Or you may indulge your self-pity, identify with your pain and sense of helplessness, and remain in the victim role. Such a trap can only be escaped through embracing the pain with the confidence that it will not consume you and learning to be patient and gentle with yourself.

JENNIFER'S STORY CONTINUED

After the divorce, Jennifer preferred not seeing Bruce. She was so angry with him, and the mere sight of him triggered overwhelming feelings of betrayal. However, they had a daughter together, Chrissy. She knew Bruce had a right to see his daughter, although she did not think he deserved it. She also knew in her heart that her daughter needed to have a connection with her father.

When Bruce came to pick up their daughter, Jennifer was irritable and impatient with him. She could hardly believe how she had idealized Bruce and overlooked his faults. Now his weaknesses were painfully evident, as a husband and father. Jennifer now realized how much Bruce was drinking and often questioned him about what he did in the presence of their daughter. Did he ever drink and drive with her? Did he ever leave her alone? Jennifer was feeling more and more insecure about leaving Chrissy with him and began watching more closely, prepared to take legal action if necessary.

During therapy, Jennifer realized how much she had suppressed her dissatisfaction and anger with Bruce for neglecting her. She acknowledged, "Growing up I learned to stuff my feelings, especially my anger. My father had a terrible temper, and I didn't want to become like him. My sisters and I were punished severely whenever we spoke up, so I learned to keep quiet." She assumed the same quiet, long-suffering demeanor with Bruce in their marriage. She saw herself like a turtle who withdrew into her shell when faced with conflict. Now she could hardly contain her anger at him. At times she was frightened by the intensity of it.

Jennifer had the courage to examine closely her anger and what triggered it. She confessed, "I never realized what a judgmental person I was. I always entertained in my head expectations about how people should act but never spoke them directly." She had been more secretly critical of Bruce and his behavior than she admitted to herself. She also realized that she shined that critical searchlight on herself as well, judging herself mercilessly. Jennifer was always irritated that her father, who claimed to never make a mistake, had a program that he imposed on all the family members. Jennifer believed she could never live up to her father's expectations, his program of perfection for her. Jennifer was embarrassed when she realized how much she identified with her father in his unreasonable demands.

Jennifer also confessed how angry she had been with herself about the infidelity. She berated herself, "How could I have been so blind to the affair? How could I have been so naively trusting?" She prided herself on being an honest, trustworthy person, yet she allowed herself to live a lie, giving unconditional loyalty to a man who did not deserve it. Jennifer wondered about how little she thought of herself to allow herself to be abused as she was. She pleaded, "Please tell me what's wrong with me." Jennifer even thought of the divorce as a personal failure. It violated her dream of a lifelong commitment to maintain a family. She felt untold guilt for the harm she was inflicting on her daughter because of the divorce.

As difficult as it was for Jennifer to face her personal demons, she was amazed at the peace it brought her. She had always been an anxious and insecure person, judging herself and others by harsh standards. But she was learning to give herself a break and was more relaxed with herself.

BILL'S STORY CONTINUED

Bill pleaded with Sarah not to leave him. She agreed, and they began therapy together. Bill never saw himself as an emotional person. He was usually cool, calm, and rational. Those qualities helped him in his work as a police officer. But now he struggled with unfamiliar feelings of rage and fear. His anger urged him to push her away, punish her, and divorce her, but his fear made him decide to fight for the marriage. He hoped that in the battle he would rekindle the love he felt for her somewhere deep inside.

In the therapy sessions, I asked both of them to talk about their feelings for each other. It was a new experience for Bill. However, with my help over time, he was able to put into words the hurt, pain, fear, and anger he felt toward Sarah. What helped him most was that Sarah did not try to defend herself but listened and acknowledged the harm she caused him. She showed a heartfelt remorse. She also expressed her objections to his drinking and time away from home partying. Sarah was honest enough to tell Bill she was grieving the loss of attention from the other man and was afraid that Bill would never change, would never show her the love, respect, and affection she longed for. With much effort to restrain himself, Bill listened. Bill was equally honest in telling her his struggle to trust her again. He asked her repeatedly, "How can I be sure you will not lie and cheat again? How can I ever trust you?"

Because both were committed to the marriage, they worked together on the issues that kept them apart for many years. Bill's anger was slowly replaced with a sense of sadness over the many years of unhappiness they both endured. He had withdrawn into his own world to avoid repeating his parent's tumultuous marriage of constant fighting. However, what resulted was a lifeless union. Admittedly, there was little conflict, but there was also no life or passion. Bill began to feel guilt for his detaching from the marriage and ignoring Sarah and their son. He was an absent husband and father. He also admitted that he had developed a drinking problem, joined AA, and made a commitment to recovery.

As Bill struggled to recognize and accept his feelings through therapy, he developed a sense of compassion for himself and for Sarah. He had always been an uptight person who had to be in control, but now he was learning to let go and relax. Instead of secretly blaming himself for driving Sarah away, he was learning to reach out to her with kindness.

Whether you choose to leave or stay with your partner, you will need to forgive yourself. What do I mean by self-forgiveness? Self-forgiveness signifies an attitude of complete acceptance of yourself, including your faults, failures, and weaknesses. Instead of directing anger at yourself for your failings, you strive to embrace them with gentleness. Self-forgiveness entails having empathy for your wounded self and letting go of the urge to condemn yourself. What self-forgiveness does not mean is that you accept all the blame for the conflicts in the relationship or condone your partner's unfaithful behavior.

AN INNER BATTLE, A HOLY WAR

If you pay close attention and take an honest look at yourself, you may well observe that you are waging a war on two fronts. You fight with your partner who has hurt and betrayed you, trying to heal the wound in the relationship, establish intimacy, and rebuild trust. You also battle within yourself, a conflict between powerful and conflicting thoughts and feelings. The struggle with self-blame, internalizing the anger you feel about the betrayal, highlights the internal battle. You may experience this internal battle as a conflict between good and evil, between what you regard as positive thoughts, feelings, and memories and negative ones. Since the affair, it may seem the forces of evil, of negativity, have gained strength. You may be preoccupied with feelings of anger, hurt, shame, and despair. You might have thoughts of revenge, failure, helplessness, and hopelessness, attacked by bitter memories of betrayal.

There is a legend from the Muslim tradition that when the warriors of Mohammed returned from battle, the Prophet told them, "You have returned from the lesser struggle to the greater struggle." They asked him, "What is the greater struggle?" He responded, "The struggle against one's self, which is between the two sides of your body."[1] The Prophet was referring to the ongoing inner struggle, or holy war (jihad), against the negative desires of anger, lust, anxiety, depression, boredom, regret, self-pity, and forgetfulness of God's presence. This inner battle echoes the torment of St. Paul, who laments, "I cannot even understand my own actions. I do not do what I want to do but what I hate. . . . I know that no good dwells in me, that is, in my flesh; the desire to do right is there, but not the power. What happens is that I do, not the good I will to do, but the evil I do not intend. . . . What a wretched man I am!" (Romans 7:15–19, 24). Similarly, the Buddha observed, "Though one defeats a million men in battle, one who overcomes the self alone is in fact the highest victor."[2]

How will you ever defeat these oppressive enemies of your inner tranquility? The secret revealed through recovery is that the battle against these negative thoughts, feelings, and memories can never be won by fighting or suppressing them. A lasting peace will only be achieved by making them your friends. Self-forgiveness means coming to peaceful terms with what disturbs you and making what you have regarded as your enemy your friend. That seemingly impossible task is the heart of recovery, which takes time and is accomplished through courageously and honestly facing your demons, coming to recognize their illusory power, and releasing their energy to renew your life. While the trauma of the affair obviously unleashes a torrent of pain, it also surprisingly releases energy for healing. The paradox you experience is that new life will come only through embracing the pain of what you hate in yourself. Your suffering is your path to growth.

Anthony de Mello recounts a story about accepting imperfections. A man who took great pride in his lawn was distressed because his grass was invaded by a huge crop of dandelions. As an accomplished gardener, he tried every method he knew to get rid of them. But they still plagued him. Finally, at his wit's end, he wrote the Department of Agriculture. He enumerated all the things he tried and closed his letter with the desperate plea, "What can I do now?" After a while, the reply came, "We suggest you learn to love them."[3]

WHAT TO FORGIVE IN YOURSELF

What do you think you need to forgive in yourself? Many who have been traumatized typically are consumed by rage for a long time. Most likely, you are furious at your partner for her betrayal. That is understandable. However, what does not make sense is the common tendency to turn that anger also against yourself, turning a critical eye toward yourself, magnifying your faults. As irrational as it may seem, you may begin to blame yourself for the affair. Actually, the self-blame is a subtle way of creating the illusion of control. You feel insecure and out of control because of what your partner did. As an unconscious strategy to regain your balance, you imagine you have some control over her behavior by blaming yourself. You might imagine that if you had acted differently, the betrayal would not have occurred. For those who have suffered a trauma and are terrified of being victimized again, self-blame is easier to tolerate than feeling powerless.

I have heard my patients make numerous self-accusations in the face of their partner's affair. The following are some typical reactions:

"Why didn't I see the signs of the affair?"
"What was wrong with me?"
"My anger is so out of control."
"Why can't I get over the affair?"
"I am such a failure because my marriage failed."
"I had my faults in our relationship."

"How could I be so stupid that I did not see the signs of the affair?"

One obvious reason you likely did not readily pick up on the signs of the affair is that your partner worked hard to keep it secret. He tried to cover his tracks to avoid detection and was well practiced in deceit. Affairs thrive in secrecy. Some unfaithful partners become so overwhelmed with guilt that unconsciously they want to be discovered. Often the trusting partner learns about the affair when his guilt makes him careless. Another factor, discussed earlier, that may affect your unawareness of the affair is your own unconscious need not to know. You did not want to know something so overwhelmingly hurtful. Without realizing it, to protect yourself you put on blinders. Furthermore, if you had allowed yourself to know about the affair, it would have precipitated an overwhelming crisis for you to make a frightening decision about the relationship. Unconsciously, you wanted to avoid such a decision and maintain a false sense of security in ignorance.

"What was wrong with me that my partner found someone else more attractive?"

You may discover a tendency to make yourself responsible for the infidelity by focusing on your own perceived defects, rather than your partner's deficiency. However, it was not what was lacking in you that caused your partner to wander but what was lacking in him, particularly his own insensitivity, insecurity, and lack of commitment. Perhaps your partner was unhappy in the relationship and did not like some of your behaviors. You may honestly admit that you had your own faults, since no one is perfect. Nevertheless, he had the option of addressing those problems directly, rather than indirectly by pursuing a relationship with someone else. The affair represents his unhealthy way of disconnecting from you, rather than honestly facing himself.

"When I discovered the affair, I was so enraged that it scared me."

You may feel guilt because of the intensity of your anger and desire for revenge. You may even be surprised at the extent of your fury, something you had never experienced before. That can be frightening. However, the intensity of your anger reveals the depth of the hurt you experienced. It is only natural that you feel a great deal of anger at the betrayal. Your anger is an appropriate response to inappropriate behavior, to the seriousness of the offense against you and the relationship. Nevertheless, you may feel guilt about how you expressed anger in retaliation. One man told me how he beat his wife severely when he discovered her affair. A woman related how she piled up her unfaithful husband's clothes and burned them. Others reported feeling guilty for turning their children against their unfaithful parent. There is no need to feel guilty for being angry, which is only a natural reaction. However, you may need to seek forgiveness for the destructive ways you expressed your rage.

"I was so embarrassed when I fell apart after learning about his affair. I can't understand why I can't get over it. I thought I was stronger than that."

You may be disappointed by the magnitude of your distress and how long it is lasting. If you are surprised by your reaction, you may be underestimating how traumatic the betrayal was. Your world was turned upside down. An infidelity strikes at the heart of your relationship, shattering any assumptions you had about trust and commitment. You may also be intolerant of any weaknesses exposed in your reaction, maintaining an unrealistic image of yourself as a superperson. Your humanness is revealed in the face of the traumatic discovery, and you may not like what you see. Furthermore, as mentioned previously, you may become impatient with your struggles through recovery. It may be harder and take longer to find peace than you ever imagined.

"My marriage has failed. I am such a failure."

Certainly, your dreams of a happy life together have been dispelled by the infidelity. The person you trusted most, your life companion, has failed you. You are left to rebuild your life through the wreckage of the relationship. But does the failure of your partner or of your dream about marriage make you a personal failure? Even if you realize that you made a mistake in marrying this person, does that make you a mistake? Through this painful experience, you may learn how much you found your identity in your relationship, how much you drew your life meaning from another. When the relationship ends you believe your life is over. You feel lost. Believing you are such a miserable person, perhaps you further think that no one will ever love you and that now you are condemned to live alone.

Those belonging to religious traditions with a strong belief in the sanctity of marriage and disapproval of divorce are particularly vulnerable to feeling like guilty failures if they choose to divorce. They may judge themselves moral outcasts because of what they have been taught. For example, one Catholic woman, who had been married for over forty years and endured her husband's multiple affairs, agonized over her decision for divorce. Even after she deliberated about the need for divorce to protect herself from the ongoing infidelities, she was wracked with guilt. She lamented, "I knew I married him for better or worse and was willing to sacrifice myself to make the marriage work. But his last affair, which he refused to end, was the last straw." She remarked that she considered herself a "moral leper" because of the divorce. She imagined that her church and all her Catholic friends would look down on her.

"I had my faults in the relationship that may have led to the affair."

As a result of your self-examination of how you related with your partner, you may acknowledge some regretful behavior. You were not always the kind of partner you wanted to be, contributing in some measure to the dissatisfaction you both experienced. For example, if you realize that you were overdependent in the relationship, you may have some regrets about blindly trusting, fearing to speak up, tolerating abusive behavior, lacking in self-confidence, having unrealistic expectations about love, or refusing to take responsibility and control of your life. If you see yourself involved in a power struggle with your partner, you may feel some guilt about your temper outbursts, vengeful behavior, lack of empathy, reluctance to express tender feelings, or refusal to compromise. Finally, if you see yourself relating in an emotionally detached manner, you may regret your absence from the home, overinvolvement with work or children, obsession with control, demands for perfection, or lack of emotional intimacy.

BARRIERS TO FORGIVING YOURSELF

Accepting yourself unconditionally can be a daunting task because so much is demanded of you. First, humility is required to recognize both your strengths and weaknesses, to see yourself as you really are, not as you would like to be. Second, you'll need courage to accept what you discover about yourself, both your virtues and your faults. Finally, patience is needed for the long journey into the night and the struggle for inner healing. I have observed that my patients avoid forgiving themselves in predictable ways, according to their personality patterns. You may recognize yourself in these portrayals of casting blame in different directions.

1. The overdependent tend to blame themselves.

2. Those who fight for control in relationships tend to blame others.

3. The emotionally detached believe they are above blaming.

1. The dependent self-blamers

Those who are dependent and tend to cling to others in relationships lack the courage necessary to accept themselves. They view themselves as deficient human beings and lean on others for support, protection, and encouragement. They tend to idealize their partners, until their world is shattered by the disillusionment of the discovered infidelity. Instead of honestly acknowledging their anger at the betrayal, they tend to bury these uncomfortable feelings. They direct that anger toward themselves and ruminate about how they have failed as partners. These individuals lack the courage to see clearly their own strengths, which would impel them to take responsibility and control of their own lives. Instead, they hide within a sense of powerlessness. They prefer to be dependent on their partner, rather than themselves, lacking the courage to venture on their own. They are terrified of living on their own, lacking confidence in their ability to survive. They cannot forgive themselves because they are so preoccupied with what is lacking in themselves. In effect, their sense of inadequacy gives them an identity.

Louise is an example. She was married to Frank for nearly thirty years. She developed lupus shortly after they were married. As the years passed, her condition worsened, and she became more crippled and eventually required a wheelchair. Needless to say, their sex life suffered because of her physical limitations and pain. Her husband was an impatient and selfish man who never denied himself anything he wanted. Throughout their marriage, he had numerous affairs "to satisfy his needs." Louise accepted the ongoing humiliation of his affairs and lamented, "It's really my fault because I am an invalid. I don't think I could survive without him." Eventually, Frank divorced her, leaving her to fend for herself.

2. The aggressive blamers

Those who are aggressive and fight for control in relationships lack the patience necessary to tolerate and work through imperfections in themselves and others. Because deep down they feel insecure and powerless, they need to maintain a facade of independence and invulnerability. They avoid getting too close to people for fear of being exposed and exploited. Their anger keeps others at a safe distance. When they discover their partner's infidelity, their mistrust of others is confirmed. They often retaliate, causing an endless spiral of attack-counterattack. They lack the patience necessary for the give-and-take of compromise. Instead, they remain in the grip of intense anger and blame their partner for their problems. Their preoccupation with blame interferes with their taking an honest moral inventory, acknowledging their faults, and forgiving themselves. Gentleness is not in their vocabulary because it connotes weakness to them.

As an example, Sharon, a hard-driving businesswoman, discovered her husband Lou was having an affair with his coworker at the factory where he was employed. She confronted him, but Lou insisted he just had a close friendship with the woman. He stubbornly maintained his innocence, while she was convinced of his guilt. They argued incessantly about the relationship. Sharon withdrew into the guest room and refused to talk with Lou for weeks on end. She proclaimed, "I'll never divorce that man and give him the satisfaction of driving me away." They continued to maintain the cold war for many years, living parallel lives. Sharon was so frozen in her anger and bitterness that she could not acknowledge her hurt and release the poison inside her.

3. The detached nonblamers

Those who are emotionally detached lack the humility to see themselves clearly. They maintain a facade of self-sufficient pride, proclaiming by their attitudes and behavior, "I don't need anyone." They choose to live on the surface of life, never venturing to explore their inner thoughts, feelings, and desires. However, beneath the prideful exterior is an insecure person. They fear being emotionally close to others and to themselves. Instead of relying on their inner intuitions to guide their lives, they conform to roles and rules that give them a sense of security. When they discover their partner's infidelity, they react with a cool indifference that hides an insecure, unworthy sense of self. They live life as if they are above blame, without acknowledging the intensity of the hurt and anger they really feel. They refuse to blame themselves or others and have the ability to rationalize away any faults. Their lack of humility is revealed in their pretense that they are above ordinary human frailties and the struggle of life. They avoid the work of forgiveness by pretending that there is nothing to forgive.

To illustrate, Raymond, a computer geek, stumbled upon romantic emails his wife, Linda, received. Raymond was in shock and needed time to think about what the correspondence meant. After a week, he summoned the courage to talk with Linda about it. She admitted that she felt neglected in their marriage and enjoyed the attention she received from men she communicated with in chat rooms. When Raymond pushed her further, she admitted that she had a sexual rendezvous with one of the men. She claimed it was a one-time meeting but said she could not give up talking with him on the Internet. Raymond was angry but refused to argue with Linda because she was so determined. Instead, he threw himself into his work and said, "I'll just try to forget about it until she gets over her fling."

HOW TO EMBRACE SELF-FORGIVENESS

In her book entitled *When Things Fall Apart*, Pema Chodron, a renowned spiritual teacher, recounted that her first genuine spiritual experience occurred when her husband announced that he was having an affair and wanted a divorce. She was stunned and saw her world falling apart. She claimed she became involved with her spiritual quest because she was so angry with her husband. The catastrophe of betrayal, according to her, saved her life. Because she could not rely on the clinging dependency that had ruled her life, she faced her lonely sense of responsibility for the first time in her life. She was challenged to stay with her shakiness and learn to relax in the midst of chaos. She learned to let go of what had created a false sense of security in her life and to value her day-to-day experience. She learned to let go of her anger, which allowed her to relax with herself.[4]

Forgiving yourself, letting go of the anger at yourself, is a process that takes time. It is not a one-time decision. Rather, an unconditional acceptance of yourself, with all of your hurts, failings, weaknesses, shame, and guilt, is the result of an ongoing healing process. It requires effort to prepare the ground for this genuine self-acceptance, a healthy self-love, to emerge. You can expect there will be times when you feel at peace with yourself, but other times when you experience impatience, shame, and even self-loathing.

Remember the Gospel injunction: "Love thy neighbor as thyself" (Luke 10:27). The key word is "as." The command is to love others, not more or less than ourselves, but in the same measure. Genuine love entails a balance of loving ourselves and others. A failure to love ourselves will interfere with our ability to give generously to others. Our self-hatred will inevitably overflow in our relationships with others. In the end, we will treat others as we treat ourselves. Similarly, the Buddha, who preached compassion for all living beings, advocated the importance of self-care: "Do not neglect your own need for another's, no matter how great; having discerned your own need, do what is really useful."[5] If we can come to a genuine self-acceptance, befriending ourselves, we will be able to love and accept others. That is precisely why forgiving ourselves is so important. Not only does it bring us peace, but it opens us to love others.

As you struggle to forgive yourself and your partner, it is helpful to bear in mind that forgiveness is the perfection, the highest form, of love. Such an ideal is not easily attained, requiring much purposeful effort. In the Sermon on the Mount, Jesus taught, "My command to you is: love your enemies, pray for your persecutors. . . . If you love those who love you, what merit is there in that? . . . In a word, you must be made perfect as your heavenly Father is perfect" (Matthew 5:44–48). We participate in the perfection of divine love when we forgive from the heart. At this point in recovery, you may be aware in your self-blame of how much you have become your own worst enemy. You may realize you are engaged in an inner battle that can end peacefully only through self-forgiveness.

SOME AIDS FOR RECOVERY

The following suggestions can help in the healing process:

1. Taking steps toward inner healing

Guilt, which is a sense that you have failed to live up to your standards, can be a tenacious emotion that interferes with your inner healing. It can gain a stranglehold on your life, squeezing out peace and contentment, and smothering you with self-hatred and the wish to be punished. If you maintain a desire for revenge, and especially if you retaliate against your partner, you will likely suffer pangs of guilt. Even if you try to rationalize your harmful behavior, saying to yourself, "He deserves it for the way he treated me," the guilt will not disappear. It may just go underground and influence your thoughts, feelings, and behaviors in unrecognized ways. Furthermore, it is obvious that if you continue to blame yourself, criticize yourself mercilessly for your failings, you will interfere with your own happiness.

Inner healing is facilitated through a four-step process, which is common to many religious traditions and to Alcoholics Anonymous. I recommend that you take your time and not rush through the steps of this process. It may take months to complete, but I assure you the effort will be well rewarded.

The first step is to make an honest personal examination of your life. You began this recovery process by looking honestly at how you interacted with your unfaithful partner. Now, using your journal, write down the behaviors you regretted during your relationship. For example, your self-examination may reveal that you were too trusting and not honest with your feelings, thoughts, and desires. Perhaps you regret the ways you displayed your anger and retaliated. Maybe you feel some guilt about how self-absorbed you were and how neglectful you were of your partner's feelings and needs. Take your time and try to make the list of harmful behaviors as complete as possible. Using some of the previous exercises, allow yourself to be aware of any memories for which you feel guilt. Guilt and shame want to remain hidden. However, in darkness they gain power. Exposure to the light of awareness lessens their impact on your life.

The second step to inner healing involves the confessing of your faults to another. Confession is a powerful antidote to guilt and shame. When you confess your failings to another, you are exposing what you dread to the light of day. If you choose someone with whom you feel safe and secure, such as a spouse, close friend, priest, or therapist, their acceptance is experienced as a profound relief. You show them the worst side of yourself, fearful of their rejection, and experience their affectionate embrace instead. You realize that you are your harshest critic, not others. Confessing to another also helps you to avoid self-deception because your trusted confidante can give you honest feedback. We know ourselves at a deeper level through the mirroring responses of those closest to us. Finally, by taking the risk to confess to another, you verbalize a commitment to change your life and invite the other person to hold you accountable. It strengthens your resolve to correct your faults. Your refusal to keep your faults secret helps break their spell on you.

The third step to release yourself from the grip of guilt, and to develop a loving attitude toward yourself, is to make specific reparations for the harm you have caused others. Such activity also rebuilds trusting relationships. I recommend that you write in your journal specific actions you can take to reverse the damage caused by your behavior. For example, I suggest that you write a personal letter to your unfaithful partner sincerely apologizing for specific wrongs you have done in your relationship, the anger, neglect, dishonesty. The letter is important for you to put into words what you feel guilty for in a concrete way. You can decide later whether to send that letter or discuss it with your partner in therapy. Undoubtedly, you have become aware of ways you have hurt your children, perhaps unintentionally, by your preoccupation with the infidelity or by your habitual patterns of interacting with others. You can make a commitment to treat them differently, in a more loving and honest manner. For example, you can make up for lost time with them by planning activities and committing specific times to spend together.

The final step flows naturally from a genuine sense of remorse for the harm you have done. Realizing the impact of your behavior on others, especially those you love, impels you to avoid causing hurt again.

It is not sheer force of will, pushing yourself to be better, imposing a higher standard, that leads to healthy behavior change, but a recognition of your own goodness. You realize that you are better than what you have been doing. You are not happy with yourself because of what you have done and come to the awareness that your actions violate who you really are. Instead, you are determined to be your best self, which is a basically good person. Your resolution to change flows from your acceptance of yourself in your natural goodness, which you express in your actions. Healthy change reflects your accurate self-awareness.

2. A personal exercise: extending loving-kindness

A traditional Eastern practice to uproot fear, anger, and guilt is called *metta*, or loving-kindness. The practice, which releases the power of love and forgiveness, can be addressed to yourself so that you can develop an attitude of unconditional friendliness toward yourself. It helps you to replace the fear, anger, and guilt with love and compassion. Positive and negative emotions cannot coexist in you at the same time. The following exercise is a deceptively powerful one that has been used for twenty-five hundred years. The exercise is simple but requires much practice and dedication to produce results. It is based on the belief that we shape our lives by the way we think. By changing the way we think about ourselves, we transform our inner attitudes and outer behavior. For this exercise, sit comfortably and follow your breath until you are relaxed. Shut out all distracting thoughts. If any arise, gently put them aside and refocus on your breathing. Once you are relaxed, think about your life situation for a moment and allow yourself to feel the pain and turmoil. Then select and focus your attention on phrases that embody meaningful wishes for yourself. For example, say to yourself, "May I be happy; may I find peace; may I be healed; may I be loving; may I be kind," and so on. Repeat three or four phrases slowly and thoughtfully for a period of time, perhaps ten minutes. Coordinate the repetition of the phrases with your breathing. Allow the words to sink into your mind. Simply relax, repeat the phrases, and observe whatever experiences or emotions arise.

You can then extend wishes for loving-kindness to others in your life. Begin by thinking about a loved one, a parent, child, or friend.

Think about their lives and their sorrows. When you sense that their pain has become yours, reach out to them in love. Extend the same or similar wishes to that person. Repeat the phrases slowly and with feeling. Allow yourself to draw close to that person. Finally, after a period of time, but only when you feel ready, think about your unfaithful partner. If possible, identify with his suffering, which you both share. Begin to repeat the phrases, wishing him happiness, peace, freedom, and healing. Say the phrases quietly to yourself, in concert with your breathing, allowing yourself to feel compassion for him.

3. Continued therapy toward rebuilding your life

Therapy can be an immeasurable aid in ongoing recovery toward self-acceptance. If you decide to reconcile with your partner, I recommend that you participate in marital therapy together to address the ways that you disconnected from each other. Building trust and honest communication will be the primary challenges in the face of the betrayal you experienced. If you choose to separate from your partner, your personal therapy can help overcome the ongoing trauma of betrayal and build a new life for yourself. It is helpful to discuss with your therapist what you learned about yourself in your examination of conscience and how you can repair the damage. Your focus during therapy in this phase of recovery is to become aware of and move beyond the self-defeating behaviors that have caused you so much pain.

4. Praying from the heart for the Spirit's gifts of piety, kindness, gentleness, and patience

Ask for a heart open to His blessings. During this prayer time, it is important that you follow the promptings of your heart and set aside your analyzing mind. Just allow yourself to experience deeply God's presence without your usual self-monitoring and incessant self-scrutiny. Now feel deeply your sense of loss because of the betrayal, the darkness in your heart. Let the self-blame, with all the self-critical thoughts and feelings of self-contempt, rise and fall away. In the midst of this darkness, pray for God's light. Specifically, pray for the Spirit's gift of piety, which is reverence for God who resides within you. In the midst of self-blame, it is easy to lose sight of the fundamental truth about who you are: a child of God. You are more precious in God's eyes than any of your faults and failings. Pray also for the fruits of the Spirit, especially for kindness, gentleness, and patience with yourself. These gifts are similar to the *paramitas* of patience and generosity. For a period of time, allow yourself to experience the blessing of God's kindness, gentleness, and patience, even though you may not believe that you deserve these gifts. Pray that you may maintain these attitudes toward yourself in your daily life. Remember that you cannot genuinely love God or others unless you love yourself. Conclude by praising God for the wonders of His gifts.

The fifth stage of recovery begins with a recognition of your need to forgive yourself, to fully accept yourself. An honest self-examination often reveals how much you blame yourself, rightly or wrongly, for the failure of your relationship. You imagine you could have prevented the betrayal if you had been more aware or a more worthy partner. You may even delude yourself into thinking the affair was your fault. This self-critical delusion comes at an enormous price. When you internalize the anger at being betrayed, you risk becoming depressed and may fall into despair. However, a wise personal discernment can lead you to make a realistic assessment of your responsibility and faults and take corrective action, which leads to inner healing. With courage and gentleness toward yourself, you can avoid the trap of self-blame. With patience, you surrender the blame of your partner. With humility, you acknowledge your strengths and weaknesses, freeing you to love again. In the process of self-examination, you discover that honestly confronting your faults can become the occasion to develop the virtues of humility, kindness, patience, gentleness, and generosity toward yourself. It also prepares you to extend forgiveness toward your unfaithful partner.

SOME DOS AND DON'TS FOR RECOVERY

1. Don't obsess about the affair and how you were victimized. Do you tend to dwell on the past? Are you prone to self-pity? Is it difficult for you to live in the present moment?

2. Don't get stuck in self-blame. Is it difficult for you to express your anger directly, to assert yourself in a constructive way? Instead, do you internalize your anger, holding it in? Do you tend to beat yourself up?

3. Take an honest look at yourself. Do you keep yourself too busy to stop and take a good look at yourself? Are you afraid of what you might discover? Do you lack self-esteem?

4. Humbly admit your faults. Are you a proud person, concerned about how you appear to others? Do you crave the approval of others? Do you always need to be right and have difficulty admitting mistakes?

5. Be gentle with yourself. Are you impatient with your faults, even minor ones? Are you a perfectionist, maintaining excessively high standards for yourself and others? Do others consider you intolerant?

6. Try to correct your faults. What do you see as your principle vice: fear, anger, envy, laziness, greed, pride, deceit, arrogance? What virtues do you need to develop to counteract your weaknesses?

7. Make amends for the harm you have done to others. How do you harm others most: by striking out in anger, by clinging, by ignoring? How can you act against these tendencies to repair damage in relationships? Are you confident in your ability to change your behavior?

8. Focus on rebuilding your life. What areas in your life need most attention? Do you tend to be overdependent on others, combative, or disengaged from others? Do you need to reestablish trust with your partner?

9. Cultivate the virtue of reverence for yourself and others. Do you see yourself and others as precious in God's eyes or a valuable addition to the world? Do you tend to focus on fault-finding? Do you indulge in self-hatred and maintain a negative image of yourself?

TEN

STAGE 6:
FORGIVING YOUR
UNFAITHFUL PARTNER
A Healing Journey

The weak can never forgive.
Forgiveness is the attribute of the strong.
—MAHATMA GHANDI

The final, and perhaps lifelong, stage of recovery involves forgiving your unfaithful partner. Those who have been traumatized are normally filled with rage at their offender. When you consider the harm she has caused you and your family, you may wonder if you ever want to, or ever can, forgive her. You might think to yourself, "I do not owe her forgiveness." That's true. Your forgiveness is a free gift. There is no obligation to show mercy. You may also wonder if you can ever get over the hurt and anger enough to say with sincerity that you forgive the wrong she has done. "It takes a saint to turn the other cheek," you reason. It certainly takes courage and humility to let go of anger and the desire for revenge and to replace it with kindness. But it is possible, with time, effort, and prayer.

Just as those who are dying protest in anger that death is being imposed on them against their will, those who have been betrayed are outraged at what is taken from them. It is only natural to feel anger, to protest the injustice suffered. It is normal to close yourself off behind a wall of anger for protection. However, if that wall of anger becomes a permanent structure in your life, it will imprison you. Your world will shrink, and you will suffocate. At some point, for your recovery to proceed, you need to let go of your anger. It is for your own sake. If you refuse to forgive either yourself or your partner, you will remain in the grip of your anger and hurt. The anger will eventually consume you, seep out in ways beyond your control, and result in continued unhappiness. The desire to punish your partner will rebound as a loss of inner peace. The anger will also color your view of the world, making it difficult to trust others, because you will be ever alert to being betrayed again.

Paradoxically, entering the fiery furnace of your anger provides an opportunity to purify your love. Let me explain. The opposite of love is not hatred, but indifference, the avoidance of intimacy. Both anger and love are passions directed toward those we care about. Intimacy is always a risk, approached with fear and trepidation, because when we care about another we open ourselves to the inevitability of being hurt. We allow ourselves to become vulnerable to another. Because we are unique individuals, misunderstandings, disappointments, and separations happen often in every intimate relationship. Infidelity provides a near ultimate test of love. At that moment of betrayal, our vulnerability is exposed. Our lover has become our enemy, and we naturally react with anger to nurse the wound. By embracing the rage we feel at the betrayal, any superficial consolations we received from the relationship are destroyed. The ensuing struggle to forgive and love again produces a different quality of love, a more mature and wiser love. As Jesus repeatedly taught his disciples and demonstrated by his life and death, the highest form of love is the love of our enemy, of those who have harmed us. The price of such a love is a dying to ourselves, a generous giving of ourselves for the good of another, without expectation of return.

JENNIFER'S STORY CONTINUED

When Jennifer learned Bruce moved in with his secretary, she was enraged. Before moving out, he was never completely honest with her about the affair and never apologized, so she entertained a sliver of doubt. However, his move confirmed the truth. Jennifer thought she was getting over the affair and beginning to move on with her life, but she relived the trauma of betrayal with the latest news.

In her therapy, Jennifer came to the conclusion that she needed to let go of the hurt and anger she felt toward Bruce. She complained, "I was feeling stuck. All I could do was think about what he had done. I realized I was giving him too much power over my life." After much agonizing, she made the decision to forgive him. She hoped all her negative feelings would disappear, but she was wrong. She felt sad, hurt, and irritable whenever he came to pick up their daughter. Sometimes at night, though less frequently, she had nightmares about him with the other woman. Whenever she thought about what had been taken from her, her security and comfortable life, she had moments of sadness, anger, and regret.

Jennifer had been raised Catholic but attended services only on holidays. After the divorce, when she felt so hopeless, she returned to the Church. She joined a prayer group and prayed regularly for healing. In the group she voiced her struggles to forgive Bruce and rededicated herself to giving up her grudge against him. She realized also how much she blamed herself for his infidelity, imagining that if she had been a better wife he would have been a faithful husband. She acknowledged her need to forgive herself.

For two years after the divorce, Jennifer did not date anyone. She felt too insecure about herself and her judgment about men. Because she was such an attractive woman, men showed interest in her. When Todd asked her out, she accepted, with much fear and trepidation. She liked him and expected just to keep a friendship with him. But she found herself caring about him and looking forward to spending time with him. These desires frightened her. She exclaimed, "The last thing I wanted to do was to get involved with anyone, but I couldn't help falling in love with him."

During therapy, Jennifer talked about her growing attachment to Todd and her fears. One incident caused her a severe panic. Todd was going away for the weekend with some friends. Jennifer cried, "All I could think about was that he was going to be unfaithful and eventually leave me, as Bruce did." She confessed to nightmares of Todd becoming Bruce, waking up in a cold sweat. With encouragement, she was able to stop and consider her perceptions of Todd, his attractive qualities, and his difference from other men in her life. She also took the risk of talking to him about her fears. He listened with understanding and admitted his own struggles with intimacy, and they felt closer. Jennifer observed, "The more confident I feel in my relationship with Todd, the easier it is to let go of my anger toward Bruce."

BILL'S STORY CONTINUED

After Sarah gave up her relationship with the other man and agreed to work on their marriage, Bill was hopeful that everything could return to normal fairly quickly. After the initial shock of the discovery of the affair and the outburst of fear and anger, he returned to his usual calm demeanor. In therapy, he was encouraged to probe beneath his placid facade and express his thoughts and feelings. Sarah pleaded with him to talk because she had felt neglected for so many years. Even though he denied feeling any distress, Bill's actions told another story. He kept checking up on Sarah's whereabouts and monitored her phone calls. He continued to withdraw into his work and hobbies. He lacked sexual interest. When I pointed out these behaviors, he initially denied feeling anxious or angry or obsessing about the affair, but eventually admitted his inner struggle.

Bill claimed that he had forgiven Sarah and just wanted to move on with their life together. He acknowledged his difficulty knowing and expressing his true feelings because he had never been encouraged to pay attention to them. But after many weeks working in therapy, Bill began to unthaw. He told Sarah how much he was hurt and angered by her betrayal and flight from responsibility in their marriage. Sarah listened with empathy at the pain she had caused. Without offering any excuse, she attempted to let Bill know the loneliness she felt in the marriage that led to the affair and her fear of speaking up to him. She offered a heartfelt apology and a promise to work on their relationship, assuring him that she wanted to rediscover the love she had for him at the beginning of their marriage. Sarah's sincere remorse helped Bill to release his buried anger.

Bill made some confessions of his own, admitting, "I know how much I have hurt Sarah by being so absent and controlling. I had no idea of the impact on her and our son." Sarah expressed skepticism about Bill's ability to change, and he admitted that he had been emotionally stuck his whole life. He told her of his fear of her being unfaithful again. They began taking some emotional risks together. Bill invited her out on weekly dates, and they spent the time talking about themselves and their hopes and dreams. He spent less time at work and refused overtime. They began reconnecting sexually. They both sat down together for the first time to work out their family budget, and Sarah took the risk of saying what she really wanted. Over time, Bill obsessed less and less about the affair and gave up checking on Sarah's activities.

After many months in therapy together, Bill exclaimed, "I feel like I'm beginning to trust Sarah for the first time in my life. I never really trusted anyone before." He observed that his anger, which was expressed by withdrawing, was slowly fading. Although he had occasional flashbacks about the affair, he felt happier and more alive than ever before in his life.

Whether you leave or remain in the relationship with your unfaithful partner, your inner peace will depend upon your ability to forgive. In the dictionary, forgiveness is defined as "the act of ceasing to feel resentment against an offender." The need for and value of forgiveness are proclaimed by all the major religious traditions. In the Christian Scriptures, Jesus teaches: "You have heard the commandment, 'You shall love your countryman but hate your enemy.' My command to you is: love your enemies, pray for your persecutors" (Matthew 6:43–44). The Muslim holy book, the Koran, addresses God as the Most Merciful, the Most Compassionate, the Most Forgiving and instructs believers: "Show forgiveness, enjoin what is good, and turn away from the foolish" (7:199). Buddhist teachers relate that enlightenment comes from living with wisdom and compassion. They also teach the need to love better, rather than worry about how much we are loved.

You may protest, "That kind of forgiveness is an impossible ideal, attained only by saints. Why even try?" That is true, if you think of forgiveness only as a goal, rather than as a journey. Forgiveness is a lifelong journey that begins with an initial decision to give up the claim for retribution. It progresses with many fits and starts through a gradual releasing of your anger and hurt, developing a renewed understanding of yourself and your partner, and resolving to rebuild trust in yourself and others. A forgiving attitude emerges as the result of the ongoing effort to achieve an unconditional acceptance of yourself and to build intimate relationships. At some point, as you work at your own recovery, you wake up surprised that you no longer hold a grudge against the one who harmed you. You do not make forgiveness happen by sheer will power but discover its peaceful presence. You have prepared the ground with your efforts toward recovery and are amazed when the long-awaited fruit suddenly buds forth. Kindness and gentleness replace the harsh anger.

BARRIERS TO FORGIVING

It is not easy to take even the first step on the journey of forgiveness. I have observed that my patients hesitate to embrace forgiveness for several reasons, which I shall explain below. First, they entertain mistaken beliefs about forgiveness; second, they are preoccupied with their pain of being victimized; or third, they fear facing the pain and accepting the demands for a genuine forgiveness, either rushing to or refusing to forgive.

Anthony de Mello relates a humorous story about half-hearted forgiveness. "Why do you keep talking about my past mistakes?" said the husband. "I thought you had forgiven and forgotten." The wife replied, "I have, indeed, forgiven and forgotten. But I want to make sure you don't forget that I have forgiven and forgotten."[1]

Mistaken Beliefs about Forgiveness

1. Forgiveness is a sign of weakness

2. Forgiveness implies condoning the wrongdoing

3. The offender deserves forgiveness

4. Forgiveness involves forgetting the harm done

5. Forgiveness implies reconciling with the offender

6. There is a moral obligation to forgive

1. Forgiveness is a sign of weakness

"If I forgive my unfaithful partner, I will be showing weakness and become vulnerable to being hurt again." You may see forgiving as a sign of weakness because you are giving up the anger that makes you feel powerful. Your anger is an armor that you put on to protect yourself from further harm. It deters others from taking advantage of you. It is a shield against a hostile world. How frightening it would be to take off that armor and expose yourself.

In reality, it takes tremendous courage to risk forgiveness. It is a sign of strength, rather than weakness. Let me explain. Your anger is a temporary respite while you heal from the trauma and nurse your wounds. It is necessary that you protect yourself with a healthy, adaptive anger when you are feeling so fragile. However, as you recover from your wounds by facing the pain without falling apart, you begin to grow in self-confidence. Your partner no longer has the power to harm you as he did before. Consequently, you no longer need to hide in fear behind the protective wall of anger. Your forgiveness announces that you have reached a point of security that you are less vulnerable than before.

2. Forgiveness implies condoning the wrongdoing

"If I forgive my partner, I will be condoning what he did and saying that it was okay." You may believe that forgiveness means condoning intolerable behavior, giving the offender permission to harm you again. It may appear that you are minimizing the hurt and damage caused by her offense.

It is important to understand that forgiving your partner does not mean that you condone what she has done. Her infidelity is intolerable, and you need to express clearly to her the pain it has caused you. You forgive a person, not her deed. Just as many religious traditions teach, you love the sinner but hate the sin. In the process of coming to forgiveness, you learn to separate the person from her behavior. Initially, because you are so overwhelmed by the trauma, that separation may seem impossible. However, while learning about your partner and yourself, you may develop some empathy for her as a person who acted unfaithfully out of her own misery. Your forgiveness expresses your conviction that she is better than her destructive behavior. Such confidence in her as a person may eventually move her toward her own recovery.

3. The offender deserves forgiveness

"Because of the terrible harm he caused, he does not deserve to be forgiven." You may believe in an eye-for-an-eye and a tooth-for-a-tooth justice. You reason that justice demands that he suffer in the same measure that he has caused you to suffer, in order to restore some imagined balance in the universe. You may further reason that he needs to be punished in order to feel right again, that his guilt cries out for it. Your anger will be the instrument of his punishment.

Whether or not your unfaithful partner deserves forgiveness is not really the issue. Who can demand forgiveness from another? Your forgiveness is a gift, freely given. However, you deserve the fruits of forgiveness. You are the primary beneficiary of your decision to forgive. As we discussed earlier, holding on to your anger causes you both emotional and physical damage. However, it harms you more than your partner, who proceeds with his life. Nurturing anger is like consuming rat poison and expecting the rat to die. Your forgiveness releases you from the grip of anger and frees you to love with an open heart. It releases you from preoccupation with your pain so you can rebuild your life.

4. Forgiveness involves forgetting the harm done

"If I forgive her, I must forget what she has done to me." You can easily identify with the Jewish people who were traumatized by the German Holocaust. They refuse to forget the atrocities done to their people. They build memorials of the Holocaust, which proclaim their dedication to the victims, and protest, "Never again!" Likewise, you never want to forget the trauma of infidelity so that you will never be victimized again. To forgive and forget would mean a dangerous lowering of your vigilance.

Forgiveness does not mean forgetting what has happened. That would be impossible. Because you have been traumatized, you may always have some scars and feel a sense of loss. Admittedly, over time the intensity of the feelings and the memories will fade, but they will not disappear altogether. Because of the severity of the wound, you can expect to have moments of anger and hurt and even flashbacks. Some of my patients who have forgiven their partners have reported nightmares many years after the affair ended. You may be disappointed in yourself because of unexpected moments of anger and suspicion after you have forgiven your partner. That is normal and expected for what you have experienced.

5. Forgiveness implies reconciling with the offender

"If I forgive him, I must reconcile with him." You may believe that genuine forgiveness leads to reconciliation, to ongoing contact with the person who betrayed you. Or you may think that if you choose not to remain in the relationship you are refusing to forgive him. In your mind forgiveness implies a return to your previous relationship, which has caused you so much pain.

Both assumptions are untrue. The decision whether to reconcile is separate from the decision for forgiveness. Forgiveness means releasing the resentment you feel toward the person who harmed you. You can choose to forgive, whether you stay with or leave your partner. The decision for or against reconciliation involves a careful consideration of what you believe is in your own best interest, whether to rebuild your life with or without your partner. As discussed previously, this decision involves a careful assessment of your desires and needs, your partner's trustworthiness, and your willingness to work together to rebuild the relationship.

6. There is a moral obligation to forgive

"I must be a terrible person because I can't forgive my unfaithful partner." You may blame yourself because of your refusal or struggle to forgive your partner. You judge yourself by the traditional religious mandate to love your enemy. That may seem like an impossible ideal as you grapple with the profound pain of betrayal. Your self-blame for not forgiving only adds to your misery and interferes with your recovery.

There is no obligation for you to forgive your partner. That is a free gift, which you can choose to give or not give. Genuine forgiveness can only overflow from the heart, not from a sense of duty. As you proceed through your own recovery, you may discover a need to forgive your partner for your own sake. You begin to think seriously about the personal cost of anger and what kind of person you want to be, whether a hateful person or a loving person. However, a forgiving attitude will occur only when and if you are ready, and in your own time. In the best of circumstances, a genuine forgiveness takes time and emerges gradually as the wound of infidelity heals.

Caught in the Victim Role

The second barrier to forgiving is feeling caught in the victim role. When you first discovered your partner's infidelity, you undoubtedly felt victimized. Your partner committed a serious crime against you and the relationship. She betrayed your trust. It was only normal that you were preoccupied with the pain and outrage you felt and obsessed about her betrayal. The sense of helplessness may have been overwhelming. Perhaps you asked yourself, "How could she have done this to me? What did I ever do to deserve this?" Over time, and with diligent work on your own recovery, the hurt, anger, and depression will recede. However, you may be surprised at the persistence of these feelings and the thought that you are an innocent and helpless victim, while she is a guilty and powerful persecutor.

Those who have a long history from childhood of being abused often persist in viewing themselves as helpless victims in relationships. From an early age they learned to submit to mistreatment in order to keep connected to important people in their lives. They form addictive "betrayal bonds" with their loved ones. They feel a profound sense of shame and unworthiness, clinging to relationships that are readily seen as destructive by everyone but themselves. They live in denial of the harmful nature of their relationship. When they discover, and allow themselves to acknowledge, their partner's infidelity, they experience the accumulated pain of all the previous betrayals in their lives. Amazingly, they believe they deserve abuse. These wounded individuals feel paralyzed to make a decision to leave the abusive relationship. The word "forgiveness" is not in their vocabulary, because they never overcome their sense of being wounded.

Christina, a thirty-year-old woman, is an example. She grew up in an Albanian family where her father ruled with an iron fist. He was an imposing man who insisted that his wife and daughters wait on him. Christina was terrified of her father who often beat her and her sisters if they did not respond quickly enough to his demands. Her parents arranged Christina's marriage to an Albanian man, who was a distant relative. Although she hardly knew her husband when they married, she felt relief to escape her father's prison. Shortly after the wedding, however, Christina was dismayed to discover her new husband's jealousy and cruelty. He often went out drinking with his friends and demanded that Christina remain home. He beat her whenever she questioned him, and he pursued friendships with other women. Christina felt trapped and feared for her life. She came to therapy when her husband was arrested for domestic violence after a neighbor called the police. She complained, "I feel like a beaten person, too miserable to stay and too terrified to leave."

If you find yourself ruminating about how you have been victimized, you may be having difficulty releasing the anger toward your partner. Without realizing it, you have become a prisoner of the past and begun organizing your life around your wound. You may see yourself in very narrow terms as "the betrayed person." The more energy you invest in thinking about what happened to you, the less you have for living the present and rebuilding your life. When you nurse the anger and hurt to protect yourself, you build walls around yourself that do not let in light and joy. Your world shrinks. Darkness envelops you. You exclude the openness that a forgiving attitude can provide.

Seeing yourself as a victim provides you with some short-term benefits, which you may believe are necessary initially to recover from the trauma. First, your anger and indignation may help you feel powerful and superior when deep down you feel powerless and defeated.

It gives a temporary boost to your fragile self-esteem. It also allows you to feel powerful in inducing guilt and punishing your wayward partner. Second, viewing yourself as a victim enables you to see yourself as innocent, undeserving of harm. Those close to you may then offer sympathy and support when they see how you have been hurt. Finally, your victim status allows you to express your anger and feel justified. You may be so enraged that you feel as if you will burst. What are you to do with all that anger? Instead of directing it at yourself, you take dead aim at your unfaithful partner.

Before healing can take place, you need to feel deeply your hurt and anger, to embrace it with gentleness. However, allowing it to solidify in shaping your self-image as a victim will only increase your sense of helplessness in the long run. Only forgiveness, the giving up of the grudge, will give you a sense of lasting freedom.

Ways of Avoiding a Heartfelt Forgiveness: Rushing and Refusing

A third barrier to forgiving is a fearful avoidance of it. I have noticed in my traumatized patients two patterns of avoiding an authentic forgiving attitude. Some rush to forgiveness, while others refuse it. Those who rush to forgiveness say, "I will overlook your behavior so we can move on quickly with our relationship." They do not allow themselves to feel the depth of their pain, anger, shame, and sadness at the betrayal. Instead, they quickly embrace a forgiving attitude to escape their discomfort. It's as if they pretend that nothing serious has happened. An atom bomb has exploded in their home, but they ignore the rubble and fallout. Furthermore, in their rush to forgiveness, they avoid the work and uncertainty of trying to understand what happened. Why did the affair occur in the first place? What does it say about me, my partner, and our relationship? These obvious questions are avoided. Finally, the struggle to make a wise decision about whether to stay in or leave the relationship is avoided. Through their quick forgiveness, they cling to the security of the status quo because they want harmony at all costs.

Three groups tend to rush to forgiveness:

1. Those with strong religious convictions often forgive quickly without grieving the loss of their familiar relationship. They believe

in the sanctity of marriage and refuse to consider divorce. They also embrace the ideal of forgiveness they have been taught since childhood. Religious obedience sustains them through the uncertainty of their lives. In this moment of relationship crisis after discovering an affair, they seek security in their faith, forgive quickly, and ignore their feelings and doubts.

2. Those who are dependent and cling to others in their relationships fear conflict and being on their own. Forgiveness provides them with a speedy return to harmony, on which their sense of personal security depends. They avoid facing their anger and asserting themselves.

3. For those who tend to detach from their emotions, forgiving their partner enables them to remain in control of their emotions and maintain their facade of calmness and freedom.

The second pattern of avoiding authentic forgiveness is in refusing it. Those who refuse to forgive say to themselves, "I'm so angry I will never forgive him for what he has done." Since forgiveness means a giving up of anger, they adamantly refuse. For them, refusing to forgive is a way of affirming the validity of their feelings and of punishing their partner for his wrongdoing. They feel strong and powerful by hanging on to their grudge. In the process, they avoid facing the terrible hurt and sadness that underlie their rage. Finding a refuge in blaming their partner, they avoid taking an honest look at themselves and exploring their role in the failure of their relationship. They take pride in their sense of righteousness. They may decide to remain in the relationship and continue to punish their partner, or they may leave, proclaiming themselves the innocent victim.

Three groups tend to refuse to forgive:

1. Those who have a long history of abusive relationships come to identify with their roles as victims, to which they cling and derive some satisfaction and measure of protection.

2. For those who are aggressive and fight for control in their relationships, forgiveness is a sign of weakness and a surrendering of control. Nurturing anger stimulates them and makes them feel alive.

3. Those who detach emotionally do not openly acknowledge their hurt, or even their anger. They do not even recognize the need to forgive. Instead, they remain stuck in their buried rage and express it indirectly by withdrawing from their partner, both physically and emotionally.

There is a common denominator for both those who rush to forgiveness and those who refuse to forgive. It is fear. These are frightened people who avoid facing the full weight of their feelings, for fear of being overwhelmed. Having been traumatized by their partner's infidelity, they are too emotionally fragile to allow themselves to feel and work through the pain of betrayal. Instead, they avoid facing their pain by taking premature action. They submissively pretend that all is forgiven or defiantly hide behind an angry facade of refusal to forgive. However, despite the outward appearance, they live in fear. This fear has many faces and is expressed differently by the various groups described above:

1. Those caught in the victim role fear being exploited.

2. The religious are afraid of losing their sense of security.

3. The dependent fear losing their love.

4. The aggressive are afraid of losing control of their lives.

5. The emotionally detached fear losing their sense of freedom.

Pema Chodron recounts a story about the illusory nature of fear. Once upon a time, there was a young warrior who had little experience in the ways of the world. Her teacher instructed her to do battle with fear, but she balked. She claimed fear was too powerful a foe. Nevertheless, her teacher dismissed her objection and gave her instructions for battle. When the day of battle arrived, the young warrior stood face to face with fear. She felt extremely small and weak, while fear appeared gigantic and powerful. Both held their weapons in readiness. As instructed, the young warrior walked up to fear, prostrated herself, and asked, "May I have permission to fight you?" Fear responded, "Thank you for showing me so much respect." Then the warrior said, "How can I defeat you?" Fear replied, "My weapons are talking loud and fast and getting close and threatening. Then you become unnerved and do whatever I say. But if you do not do what I tell you, I have no power over you. You can listen to me, respect me, but do not have to do what I say." In that way, the young warrior learned to defeat fear.[2]

MARKS OF AUTHENTIC FORGIVENESS

Simply defined, forgiveness is the act of ceasing to have resentment against the offender, replacing it with kindness. However, forgiveness is a complex act, psychologically. The following are some marks of authentic forgiveness:

1. Forgiveness involves the whole person

2. It begins with a decision to forgive

3. Forgiveness honestly acknowledges the hurt and the harm

4. It is aided by empathy, the understanding of yourself and the offender

5. Forgiveness takes time and is ongoing

6. It is a process of releasing the anger and pain of the past

7. Forgiveness occurs as your wounds heal

8. It results in freedom to love again

1. Forgiveness involves the whole person

Forgiveness does not mean just saying the words, "I forgive you." It is a response to an offense that involves the whole person, requiring a change of heart toward the offender, no simple matter. It engages the will, emotions, and mind. Forgiveness begins with a decision to commit yourself to a process of giving up your anger toward your unfaithful partner. That decision is made again and again as you face squarely the pain of loss and betrayal. Your emotions are also fully engaged because you cannot forgive unless you acknowledge to yourself and others the pain you feel. Finally, through forgiveness you seek to understand yourself and your partner in a new light. Eventually, you will come to the realization that you are fellow sufferers in need of compassion.

2. Forgiveness begins with a decision to forgive

Forgiveness does not just happen. It is consciously chosen, an act of the will. You begin by deciding in your heart that you want to forgive your partner, even though everything within you resists showing mercy. That decision is saying, "I want to move on with my life and not let the suffering over what happened hold me back." No one can coerce you into making that decision. You decide only when you are ready, when you feel inwardly moved to surrender your anger. However, the decision is just a beginning, not an end point. It expresses a willingness to become fully engaged in your own healing process. Furthermore, the decision is not once and for all. Instead, you will recommit yourself repeatedly, often in the face of many personal obstacles, to the journey toward recovery and release of your anger.

3. Forgiveness honestly acknowledges the hurt and the harm

You cannot sidestep feeling the pain of being betrayed. You may be tempted to bury the hurt by rushing toward a quick forgiveness without acknowledging the harm done. Or you may hide the pain, strike out in rage instead, and refuse to forgive. Or you may wallow in the pain by clinging to the victim role. The middle course between suppressing and indulging your feelings leads to inner healing and genuine forgiveness. It is the way of gently holding your pain. Unless you acknowledge to yourself and your partner the full emotional impact of the betrayal, you can forgive only superficially. I tell my patients, "If you ignore your feelings, they will not disappear. Instead, they will come back to haunt you, influencing your mood and behavior in indirect ways outside your awareness." What is denied increases in power. The repressed feeling often returns with a vengeance. Forgiveness as a conscious act requires a full awareness of the hurt and the harm experienced by the offense.

4. Forgiveness is aided by empathy, the understanding of yourself and the offender

As explained previously, an important step in recovery is understanding why the affair occurred and what was transpiring between you and your partner. An honest look reveals the unhappiness you were both experiencing, which often went unacknowledged. There's an old saying, to understand all is to forgive all: Through understanding the roots of your partner's and your own behavior in suffering, you can develop empathy, which prepares the ground for forgiveness. Through empathic understanding, you can gain a new perspective on yourself, your partner, and your relationship. You begin to challenge unrealistic assumptions you hold about yourself and relationships. Such a clear vision enables you to rebuild your lives on a firmer, more realistic foundation.

5. Forgiveness takes time and is ongoing

Many mistakenly believe that forgiveness is a one-time decision. Nothing could be further from the truth. Rather, forgiveness is an ongoing, adventurous journey. The initial, ever-renewed decision to forgive starts you on a path toward a full acceptance of yourself and your partner, but not his destructive behavior. Forgiveness gives you direction, as on a compass, and does not settle in a particular location. You cannot complacently say, "I have completely forgiven my partner; there's nothing more to do." Instead, it is more accurate to say, "I want to forgive him and I am letting go of my anger as it raises its ugly head." You cannot even accurately say you are halfway to your goal because you cannot imagine from the here-and-now what a full and unconditional acceptance, without anger or regret, looks like. You can only engage wholeheartedly in the journey, which ultimately leads to your own inner healing.

6. Forgiveness is a process of releasing the anger and pain of the past

The betrayal is the center of your life for a period of time. That is normal. Initially, you may need to hold on to your anger for a sense of safety. Your world has been wrecked, and you feel adrift on dangerous waters. Who can you trust? You certainly cannot rely on your partner, and you learned your perceptions and judgments about the relationship were faulty. You may not trust yourself. Letting go of anger is like freeing yourself from Chinese handcuffs, which are bamboo tubes that grip the fingers. The more you struggle by pulling, the stronger the grip of these restraints. It is only by relaxing, by giving up the struggle, that you escape the grip of the grudge against your partner. As you work on your recovery, you learn to relax with yourself and your pain. In the process, you can develop compassion and trust in yourself. No longer do you need the armor of anger to feel safe. Instead, you can find strength in an inner peace, which no one can take away.

7. Forgiveness occurs as your wounds heal

As the lyrics of the song express it, "You can't hurry love." You also cannot rush healing or forgiveness. Many patients have told me they wish they could "fast-forward" their recovery from their wounds. However, healing takes time and patience as you courageously expose your emotional wounds to the light of day. Your anger and refusal to forgive hide the pain. But as you face your suffering with an open mind and heart, something remarkable happens. The pain no longer dominates your life as it did before. The injury does not hold center stage. There is room for other concerns. What happened in the past commands less of your attention, so you can fully engage yourself in the present. You no longer identify with the victim role you embraced to cope with the betrayal. With a renewed self-confidence from courageously facing your pain, you gain a sense of freedom to begin a new life.

8. Forgiveness results in freedom to love again

As you release your anger and embrace the pain, there is an almost miraculous release of life-giving energy. Holding a grudge keeps you locked within yourself. You feel miserable, isolated, preoccupied with revenge. However, when you embrace your pain, you develop a sense of compassion for yourself, which impels you to feel compassion for all those who are suffering, even for the one who has harmed you so grievously. In the process, you cultivate a tender heart that enables you to open yourself in love to others. Through recovery, the poison of anger is transformed into the medicine of compassion.

While obviously forgiveness is more satisfying when the offender displays true remorse, I do not think that forgiveness must be earned by the offending party. I believe that genuine forgiveness is a free gift that emerges from the inner healing of the person who has been harmed, whether or not the offender apologizes. You continue working on your own recovery, whether or not your unfaithful partner is remorseful. However, I believe it is important that your partner show genuine remorse as a condition for reconciling with her. You can still forgive her without a heartfelt apology, but I do not recommend that you reconcile, rebuild your life together, unless she apologizes. Unless she acknowledges the pain she has caused, takes full responsibility for her behavior, strives to understand the reasons for her infidelity, and works to make amends, you will not be assured that the unfaithful behavior will not happen again. A full honesty is needed to rebuild intimacy and trust. Your unfaithful partner must earn your trust, not your forgiveness, by a full engagement in her own recovery.

Making a sincere, heartfelt apology can be a difficult task for the offender. Just as the hurt partner can avoid genuine forgiveness by rushing or refusing it, the offending person can avoid the demands of a genuine apology. On the one hand, the unfaithful person may rush to apologize because he does not want to feel the full impact of the pain he caused or make the effort to understand his own harmful behavior. He does not want to feel the depth of his guilt, which is activated by listening to his partner's pain and anger, demands for details and explanations, and threats to retaliate. Furthermore, he may be fearful of his partner leaving and try to appease her, so things can quickly return to normal. Consequently, he avoids the struggle and uncertainty of deciding what he wants in the relationship and what needs to change to restore trust and intimacy.

On the other hand, the offending person may refuse to forgive because he is not sorry for what he has done. For him the relationship is over, and the affair is a way of exiting. He may find refuge in blaming his partner for his unhappiness and think of himself as justified for his behavior. Out of a false sense of pride, he refuses to take an honest look at himself, admit his faults, and accept responsibility for his actions. Finally, apologizing may, for him, be a sign of weakness and a surrendering of control in the relationship. Either the rush or the refusal to forgive reveals personal deficiencies that need to be addressed before reconciliation and the rebuilding of the relationship can proceed.

SOME AIDS FOR RECOVERY

By striving for love and forgiveness, you are allowing for springtime life to flourish. The spirit of the earth accompanies your spirit in the growth of new life after the barrenness of winter. The following are some tools that can prepare the ground for the flowering of forgiveness.

1. Journaling about your struggles to forgive

Dedication to keeping your daily journal can help you immeasurably to keep connected with yourself. The daily discipline encourages you to stop, attend to your experience, observe yourself, and reflect on your life. Write about what you discover about yourself through your meditations. Pay close attention to your struggle to forgive your partner. What are your mistaken assumptions about forgiveness? What hurt is most difficult to forgive? What are you most angry about? What are the costs to you for holding on to your anger with your unfaithful partner? What are the benefits of releasing the anger? Also pay close attention to your deep desire, perhaps obscured, to forgive your partner and move on with your life. Write honestly and spontaneously about the thoughts and feelings that emerge as you consider forgiving your partner.

2. Continuing counseling to rebuild your life

Therapy takes a different direction, depending on your decision to remain with or leave your partner. If you choose to stay together, I recommend that you and your partner meet together with the therapist to work at rebuilding trust and intimacy in your relationship. An important step in healing is for you to express what you learned about your struggles to forgive through your personal reflections and journaling. If your partner listens without being defensive, accepts full responsibility for his behavior, and expresses sincere remorse, your forgiveness will flow more easily. If he remains defensive and makes excuses for himself, you may reconsider the wisdom of continuing the relationship. Your partner's honesty is essential to reestablishing trust and emotional closeness. Your willingness to forgive and release your anger is also required.

If you choose to separate from your partner, the focus of therapy is on rebuilding your own life, regaining confidence in yourself. I recommend that you share with your therapist your pain, struggles, and desire for forgiveness. It is important that you not suppress your hurt and anger because these emotions will only fester if you do not acknowledge them. In your personal therapy, you also need to address the ways you have disconnected in your relationships. You want to avoid repeating the same painful dance with another partner.

3. Joining a prayer group

If your spiritual beliefs provide you a source of comfort, joining with others in prayer can increase your sense of consolation. A powerful source of strength and healing can be found in your local church community. Many churches sponsor both small and large prayer groups where members gather to pray for themselves and others. For example, in the Catholic Church, as well as in many Protestant communities, Pentecostal prayer groups meet to invoke the presence of the Holy Spirit in their lives. Members gather to praise God, sing, interpret God's word in their lives, and petition for blessings. They also pray for healing, both physical and spiritual, and some recount extraordinary miracles. Many prayer group members have reported how joining the group renewed their faith and helped them overcome many sorrows in their lives. Additionally, many Protestant churches sponsor Bible study groups in which the participants read and reflect on the meaning of various passages and books of the Sacred Scriptures. Often a leader guides the group, provides teachings, and encourages the members to discover the personal meaning of the Scriptures in their lives. Obviously, such faith-based groups can offer immeasurable support for you as you struggle to follow the Gospel injunction to forgive your partner and yourself. There is much personal sharing in these groups, and you will be surprised by how many share your suffering and your struggles to forgive from your heart. Nondenominational groups, such as Renaissance and Unity churches, also offer a variety of meditation groups and instruction sessions on life issues that can be helpful.

4. A personal exercise: a healing walk with Jesus

The following is a healing of memories meditation that may be difficult or overwhelming for you because it requires you to experience deeply the painful memories of betrayal. I recommend that you approach this exercise with caution, using it only when you feel ready. Begin by relaxing in a quiet place. Consciously place yourself in God's presence, however you conceive of Him, and recall His love for you and desire to heal you. Pray that you may be open to any painful memories that arise and to His healing presence in your life. Now think about your relationship with your unfaithful partner. Allow yourself to remember some of the painful incidents with your partner, for example, the discovery of the affair with all of your reactions of stunned disbelief, rage, and deep sorrow. Allow yourself to embrace all the distressful thoughts and feelings at the time. Relive the moment, despite your natural resistance to recall it. Then, as far as you are able, express your forgiveness to your unfaithful partner.

Next, relive that painful moment again, but this time, imagine that Jesus is standing by your side. Even if Christianity isn't the religion you subscribe to, you can still imagine Jesus and his presence. Imagine what Jesus would say to you and your partner at that moment, how he would extend his love and compassion. Imagine Jesus embracing your partner in forgiveness and then holding you in his arms, reassuring you of his love and protection. Finally, thank Jesus for his love and healing, for not leaving you alone in your suffering. Thank him for giving you a forgiving heart, like his. You can repeat this meditation many times as painful memories arise. Each time, re-approach the scene with Jesus at your side, praying that you can have the mind and heart of Christ.

5. Praying from the heart for the Spirit's gift of love

Return to your quiet place of prayer and relax in God's presence. Take a few moments to feel refreshed and relaxed in the knowledge of God's unconditional love for you. When you feel sufficiently calmed, recall the bitter pain of betrayal. Allow yourself to feel the full weight of your hurt, rage, sadness, and fear. Acknowledge your fury at your partner and your inner struggle to forgive him. Allow yourself to feel the pain without being completely consumed by it. You are infinitely more than your thoughts and feelings of hurt and hatred. Next, pray with all your heart for the gift of love, the greatest of God's blessings. Love is such a wondrous gift because it is a participation in God's Life. It is also a complex and rich gift that encompasses all the virtues. As St. Paul reminds us, love is patient, kind, not jealous, never rude, never self-seeking, not prone to anger, with no limit to its forbearance, its trust, its hope, and its power to endure (I Corinthians 13:4–7). Christian love corresponds with the *paramitas* of generosity and loving-kindness, which the Buddhist tradition considers the universal antidote to suffering. Experience in your heart the power of loving-kindness, and let that love overflow in all your relationships, particularly toward the one who has harmed you most. End your period of prayer with an expression of gratitude for God's most intimate communication of love. After your prayer time, it is valuable to take a few moments and review what you experienced in prayer. What promptings of the Spirit did you perceive? What was your mood? Where were your mind and heart drawn? What was enjoyable? Moving? Uncomfortable? Where was God working? How did you respond?

The whole process of recovery from the trauma of betrayal can be described as a gradual release of pain and anger, replacing them with kindness, to begin your life anew. As the wound heals, you discover that you are able to forgive your partner and move on with your life, a wiser and more compassionate person. Forgiveness is a journey that begins with a decision to forgive, involves a working through of anger, and results in a renewed understanding of yourself and your partner. Through the pain, you gain a larger, more compassionate perspective on life and renew your faith in life itself. You cultivate the virtues that give meaning to your life. It can be a perilous journey, requiring immense courage to face the profound pain of betrayal and to risk beginning a new life, with or without your partner. It is a journey that moves toward freedom to love again. But the way you love, having passed through the fire of betrayal and recovery, is a deeper, wiser, more mature love.

SOME DOS AND DON'TS FOR RECOVERY

1. Do not bury your hurt and anger. Are you afraid of your feelings, especially pain and anger? How do you react when hurt or angry? What pattern do you observe in the way you manage or disengage from your uncomfortable feelings?

2. Do not strike out at your partner in anger. Is your anger toward your unfaithful partner lingering? Do you have thoughts of revenge? Who is harmed most by your anger? What physical and emotional consequences do you see in yourself when you either suppress or indulge your anger?

3. Allow yourself to grieve the losses in your relationship. What is the most painful loss for you in your partner's betrayal? What do you miss most in your relationship with that person? Have you lost confidence in yourself, in your ability to perceive reality and to survive?

4. Acknowledge your personal struggle with forgiveness. Do you want to forgive your partner? Where do you feel stuck in forgiving your partner? What are your mistaken beliefs about forgiveness? How do you envision genuine forgiveness?

5. If you feel comfortable doing so, invite your partner to hear your pain and express remorse. Are you ready to speak honestly from your heart to your partner? Do you believe he is ready to listen and respond honestly? Are you afraid to take the risk? What will it take for you to be ready and to know that your partner is ready?

6. Be patient with yourself in the journey toward forgiveness. Are you in a rush to get over the pain and move on with your life? Does your impatience help or hinder you in your recovery? How can you learn gentleness with yourself?

7. Trust in the power of forgiveness to renew your life. Do you believe that forgiving your partner is really in your best interest? Do you feel more powerful in withholding forgiveness? Do you believe forgiving will liberate you?

8. Have confidence in your ability to grow through this crisis. Are you more aware of the danger or the opportunity presented with this crisis? Can you imagine a new, better life emerging through your recovery? How do you envision your future?

9. Cultivate love and compassion in all your relationships. If you can love the one who harmed you most, do you believe you are freed to love everyone? What keeps you from being a loving and compassionate person? Where do you hold yourself back in relationships?

EPILOGUE

A BROKEN HEART BECOMES AN OPEN HEART

I know God will not give me anything I can't handle.
I just wish that He didn't trust me so much.

—MOTHER TERESA

My patients never cease to edify me, to revive my hope in the strength and courage of the human spirit. People come to me in the depths of despair, having endured unimaginable losses and humiliations, but seek my help because they have hope. They hope to escape the darkness of their lives and believe it is possible. Some have been caught in the web of addictions, filled with self-hatred, and abandoned by everyone close to them. Others have suffered the ravages of mental illness and borne the burden of its shame. And still others, whose stories are recounted in these pages, have endured the trauma of being betrayed by the one with whom they dreamed of having a never-ending life together. These traumatized individuals have displayed a remarkable courage in facing the collapse of their dreams, embracing their deep sadness, and exploring difficult truths about their partner, themselves, and their relationship. Their hearts were broken, but through their courageous recovery, learned to love again, in a deeper way.

JENNIFER'S CONTINUING STORY

Let us return to Jennifer's story. She experienced alternating waves of self-confidence and self-doubt for a long time after her divorce. She felt empowered when she faced her fears of being on her own and made the difficult decision to leave Bruce. For several months, she kept herself busy rearranging her house, her schedule, and her life. But the worm of self-doubt emerged when she thought about dating again. She felt so unsure of herself, wondering if anyone would really love her or if she could trust another man.

Jennifer met Todd, a successful businessman, through a friend. They took an immediate liking to each other. However, Jennifer was cautious and tried to keep her distance. But Todd was an honest, sincere, and straightforward man, unlike Bruce or anyone else in her family. He was honest with her and encouraged her to express her feelings, especially if she disagreed with him. He persisted in communicating openly, despite Jennifer's hesitancy. She said, "It's so scary to tell him what I think and feel because while growing up disagreements always led to arguments. Todd keeps asking me to trust him. It's hard to really believe that he is different from the other men in my life."

Despite herself and her mistrust of men, Jennifer began falling in love with Todd. Her family complained that she was less available to them in her new life with Todd. Whenever her family called, Jennifer had always been available and catered to their needs. She sensed their resentment when she refused invitations or did not rearrange her schedule to suit them. Jennifer enjoyed her growing self-confidence, despite the disapproval it provoked from her family. When Todd proposed to her after a year of dating, she was initially paralyzed with fear, imagining everything that could go wrong in their relationship. Her family expressed their reservations and withheld their blessing. Todd was patient and told Jennifer to take whatever time she needed to decide. Finally, after much soul-searching and acknowledging that it was only her fear that blocked her path to happiness, she agreed to marry him.

After several years, when Jennifer was happily remarried and had a son, she came to see me. She was a different person and seemed to glow with a radiant peace. She confessed, "I never imagined how long it would take me to really forgive Bruce. I always felt some resentment every time I saw him when he dropped Chrissy off, and we never really sat down to talk. Suddenly, one day I noticed that I no longer felt any anger. I didn't have any more nightmares of Todd becoming Bruce or have flashbacks of our bad times together. In fact, I could even enjoy some fond memories of our marriage." She related that this remarkable change came about after she sat down one day and had a long talk with Bruce. He apologized for the way he had treated her throughout the marriage and admitted that he was too immature to settle down at the time. Jennifer felt empathy for the lost young man that Bruce was when they were married. For the first time in her life, she felt secure enough to be herself with Todd.

BILL'S CONTINUING STORY

While reconciling with Sarah, Bill became aware of how much mistrust ruled his life. That natural quality of suspiciousness helped him as a police officer but interfered with his personal relationships. Although he told Sarah he wanted to forgive her and rebuild their marriage, he was nagged by thoughts of the affair. He admitted to me frankly, "If the affair was just about sex, that would be bad enough. What disturbs me more is that Sarah felt emotionally connected to her lover." When he saw Sarah sad, he imagined that she was thinking about her lover and preferred to be with him, rather than in the marriage. Bill took the risk of asking Sarah about the feelings he noticed. She was honest about her grief over the affair but affirmed her desire to rekindle the love in their marriage. Also, for the first time in their marriage, Bill made the time to sit and talk with Sarah about their life together, their hopes, dreams, and fears. He was dedicated to his recovery program, attended AA regularly, and remained sober. Instead of losing himself in staying busy and socializing with his fellow officers, he was stopping to look at himself and his life. When mistrust reared its ugly head, Bill acknowledged his discomfort and talked with his wife about it.

As the years passed, Bill and Sarah gained a closeness they had never before experienced in their marriage. They became friends and lovers, spending more and more time together and enjoying each other's company. They developed hobbies and interests, which they pursued together and apart from each other. Bill's mistrust faded as he felt more secure in his love for Sarah. As he approached retirement, he looked forward to spending his days with Sarah, an adjustment he never imagined being able to tolerate in the past. Their lives were filled with renewed hope for the future.

THE FAR SIDE OF GRIEF

The trauma of infidelity results in a loss that initiates a process of grief. The journey toward forgiveness, like grief, unfolds in overlapping stages of denial, anger, depression, and bargaining against the demands of personal change. The final stage is acceptance of the loss, which is really a forgiving attitude. The far side of this journey is a place of peace, gentleness, joy, and self-confidence in which we come to a complete acceptance of the lost dream of love. As the loss is accepted, the pain and anger at betrayal are released. Three things happen on this journey, which is really a pilgrimage of the soul. In accepting the loss, you learn to let go, open up, and move on, as Jennifer's and Bill's stories illustrate so well.

1. Letting go of the past and its pain

First, acceptance involves letting go of the past and its pain. Those who have suffered interpersonal trauma feel like victims and struggle to let go of the pain, for fear of being hurt again. When you love, and open your heart to another, you make yourself vulnerable and risk being hurt. You allow yourself to care about another, to feel her pain, and to be affected by her. The alternative is to endure the pain of isolation. When you love, you risk having your heart broken. If you love deeply, you inescapably bear the scars of many misunderstandings and disappointments. Acceptance means embracing the risks of love and not allowing yourself to be burdened by the hurts from the past, even if the pain is from betrayal. You have confidence in your ability to survive. Going beyond the fear of being crippled by the pain of betrayal frees you to love wholeheartedly in the present. In the process of letting go, you learn patience, gentleness, and equanimity.

2. Opening up your heart to love

Second, acceptance implies opening up your heart to the newness and freshness of a loving relationship. Those who have been traumatized hide behind a wall of fear and anger to protect themselves from further pain. Typically, they withdraw in fear and direct their rage against their unfaithful partner, seeking revenge. They turn the anger against themselves in self-blame. Furthermore, they project their anger onto their world, which they then perceive as hostile and dangerous. With acceptance, instead of closing yourself off, you can develop an attitude of unconditional friendliness toward yourself, accepting even the hated and disowned parts of yourself. That acceptance overflows into compassion for others, even those who have harmed you most. By embracing your own pain, you are able to connect with the suffering of others and learn a new way of loving. Your broken heart becomes a heart open to love. In opening your heart, you grow in generosity, peace, joy, and loving-kindness.

3. Moving on with hope

Finally, acceptance involves moving on with your life with an attitude of hope. Those who have been traumatized feel powerless and defeated, caught in a web of deceit and betrayal. Through recovery you come to understand yourself in a new light, becoming aware of the self-defeating behaviors that keep you stuck in unhappy relationships. You discover the ways you disconnect by clinging to love, fighting for control, or detaching emotionally. Learning the truth about yourself sets you free to escape these habitual behavior patterns. Your hope resides in empowering yourself, in taking full responsibility for your life, instead of blaming others for who you are. Whether you leave the relationship like Jennifer or remain to rebuild it like Bill, you sense the freedom to create your life according to your own desires and designs. Moving on, you cultivate the virtues of courage, wisdom, and knowledge.

In short, the acceptance beyond grief blossoms into a life of faith, hope, and love. You have faith you can survive the pain, you hope you can rebuild your life, and you love with an open heart. By mourning everything you lost through the betrayal, you discover your indestructible inner self that reaches out to others. You learn to appreciate the wisdom of Rumi, the Sufi mystic and poet, who exclaims, "Don't grieve. Anything you lose comes round in another form."[1]

CAN THE TRAUMA BECOME A BLESSING?

Several of my patients have come to recognize the trauma of infidelity as a disguised blessing, a challenge to awaken themselves. For those who call it a blessing soon after discovering the affair, it may seem like a hollow rationalization to ease the pain. But for those who have grappled with all their distressful thoughts and feelings in recovery, it is a hard-won truth, an affirmation of hope beyond the pain. Tragically, many are crushed by the betrayal, and their wounds never heal; they are consumed by their rage and pain. However, others have been empowered by the crisis and used it as an opportunity for personal growth, for cultivating virtues.

Becoming empowered by a crisis has the ring of psychological truth. We are born helpless, vulnerable, and dependent on our environment for survival. When our needs are not adequately met by our caregivers, our instinct for survival impels us to adapt ourselves for personal protection. We develop a hard shell of defenses to protect our soft, tender selves. As time goes on and we encounter more threats to our well-being, these defenses become even more rigid. We learn to cling to others for safety, fight for control of our environment, or withdraw into our own worlds. As we relate to others, these habitual behavioral patterns interfere with our strivings for intimacy, frequently causing us to disconnect from ourselves and others. Often, it takes a crisis to overturn our sense of complacency, to break through the hard shell of protective, yet self-defeating, behaviors. In the midst of a crisis, we feel like we are breaking down, but it is really just our defenses failing. In reality, we are broken open, allowing feelings at the core of our being to break through. Energy, which had been bound up for self-protection, is released to re-create our lives in a way that conforms to our true nature.

214

The Chinese symbol for crisis means both danger and opportunity. It suggests that we must face danger, not avoid it, to grow. You are certainly aware of the danger precipitated by the discovered infidelity because you are thrust from your apparently secure and familiar life into an unknown world, an unknown future. In the midst of your personal turmoil, you may not have been so aware of the opportunity imbedded in the crisis. However, as you journey toward inner healing, a new and unexpectedly rich life will emerge.

The blessed nature of crisis is affirmed by the spiritual traditions, both Eastern and Western, that proclaim the power and wisdom of paradox. In the Christian tradition, Jesus the Christ tells his followers, much to their dismay, that "the Son of Man had to suffer much, be rejected . . . be put to death, and rise three days later" (Mark 8:31). Jesus elaborates the consequences for his disciples: "If a man wishes to come after me, he must deny his very self, take up his cross, and follow in my steps. Whoever would preserve his life will lose it, but whoever loses his life for my sake and the gospel's will preserve it" (Mark 8:34). Furthermore, he observes that all creation shouts out the mystery of rebirth, teaching, "Unless the grain of wheat falls to the earth and dies, it remains just a grain of wheat. But if it dies, it produces much fruit" (John 12:24). Jesus clearly states that we must embrace suffering and death to find new life. When the illusions of your relationship revealed by the infidelity die, you gain a new life.

Gautama Siddhartha, the Buddha, left the comfort of his palace and encountered the suffering of the sick, dying, and aged. This experience of suffering impelled him to take a spiritual journey that awakened him to the path to peace. Formulated as the four noble truths, he taught that suffering is inevitable, caused by desperate clinging to what is pleasurable and hating what is unpleasant, and relieved by surrendering to Life. He observed that we increase our suffering by our mental attitudes toward life and the illusions we live by. Paradoxically, we become free when we are open to the normal suffering of life, embrace it, and seek to understand it. Like Jesus, he taught that true contentment comes at a price, by embracing the inescapable suffering of life and developing compassion for all beings.

The Native Americans look around and observe that all creation is in a state of constant change. As the stream flows, never the same at any place or any moment, so change embraces all of life. Night follows day, and one season follows another. Plants grow in their season, are harvested, and lie fallow to grow again and feed other living creatures. Animals prey upon each other and provide nourishment for the human race. Human beings are born from the earth, live their lives, and die to return to the earth and the spirit world. Not only is change evident, but everything is connected to everything else, and the change occurs in observable patterns. The Native American shamans teach that the ways of nature reveal the ways of man. An ancient proverb affirms: With all things and in all things, we are related. As everything dies in its proper time, it provides the material for new life.

Finally, the Chinese sages teach that nature is cyclical and life is dynamic, similar to the view of the Native Americans. Life is composed of complementary opposites: yin and yang. Yang is active, dynamic, and assertive, while yin is quiet, yielding, and receptive. Wholeness, contentment, and wisdom come from attuning our lives to the cyclical patterns of nature. Embracing its paradoxes, the union of opposites, releases life-giving energy. To appreciate joy, we must experience sorrow; to know health, we must be familiar with sickness; to enjoy life, we must be acquainted with death. The Taoist poetically invites the celebration of life's paradoxes when he writes:

No-thing remains itself.
Each prepares the path for its opposite.

To be ready for wholeness,
First be fragmented.
To be ready for rightness,
First be wronged.
To be ready for fullness, first be empty.
To be ready for renewal, first be worn out.
To be ready for success, first fail.
To be ready for doubt, first be certain.[2]

One of the most precious jewels in the Christian treasury of wisdom is the Beatitudes. In his Sermon on the Mount (Matthew 5–7), Jesus taught his disciples how they must live in order for God to reign in their hearts. In the few poetic and paradoxical verses of the Beatitudes (Matthew 5:3–12), he describes eight qualities that constitute the path to true happiness. He teaches that those are most blessed and closest to the Kingdom of God who are poor in spirit, sorrowing, lowly, hungry and thirsty for holiness, merciful, single-hearted, peacemakers, and persecuted. What is surprising about this listing of blessed qualities is that half of them involve suffering. Jesus states clearly that those who can expect a great reward in heaven are the poor, sorrowing, lowly, and persecuted. How can it be such a great blessing to suffer in these ways?

Consistent with what Jesus taught throughout the Gospels, the Beatitudes proclaim the necessity of suffering to gain new life. There is a danger for the human spirit to become complacent, stagnant, and self-absorbed if we only experience comfort, pleasure, and the satisfaction of all our desires. If we never suffer, we will never experience the deeper longings of our heart for blessings that only God can give. Suffering has a way of breaking through the hard shell of our defenses and opening our hearts to a fuller life, if it is embraced with hope.

There is a progression in the blessed qualities.[3] The Beatitudes begin with praise of poverty of spirit, sorrowing, and lowliness as a prelude to developing higher virtues. Jesus suggests, as do the Eastern wisdom teachers, that the experience of inner emptiness and poverty prepares the ground for the blossoming of other virtues. Suffering creates a longing for holiness (wholeness), which is then expressed in mercy and forgiveness. A single-hearted pursuit of goodness follows, which is displayed in the ever-widening circle of love. The blessed become peacemakers, seeking to bring peace and reconciliation in all their relationships. The Beatitudes end with a sobering reminder that the pursuit of peace will inevitably be accompanied by suffering and persecution. In a similar fashion, Buddha reminded his followers that suffering is inevitable, but it can be relieved by giving up self-centered desires and seeking the happiness of all.

The following is a story from Anthony de Mello's collection of traditional wisdom stories, which expresses the blessing of suffering from an Eastern wisdom perspective.

"Calamities can bring growth and enlightenment," said the Master. And he explained it thus: "Each day a bird would shelter in the withered branches of a tree that stood in the middle of a vast deserted plain. One day a whirlwind uprooted the tree, forcing the poor bird to fly a hundred miles in search of shelter—till it finally came to a forest of fruit-laden trees." And he concluded: "If the withered tree had survived, nothing would have induced the bird to give up its security and fly."[4]

Recovery from the trauma of infidelity brings you to a new place in your life, a place never before envisioned. As the saying goes, you can never return home. Similarly, after suffering the hardship of betrayal, embracing its pain, and mourning your losses, you can never return to your old familiar ways of living. Through recovery, you have gained a hard-fought wisdom about yourself and cultivated the gifts of the Spirit. You have faced your demons, discovered their illusory power, and transformed their energy for the good. Having faced your fear of death, especially the death of your relationship and old self-defeating ways of relating, you know how to celebrate life. You can be grateful for all that is and cherish laughter in the face of life's tragedies. Your world, which had become hostile because of the infidelity, is now a friendly place in which to make new friends and find new love.

EIGHT EXERCISES TO DEEPEN RECOVERY

The most important decision we make
is whether we live in a friendly or hostile universe.
—ALBERT EINSTEIN

The following are some additional personal exercises that may help you in your recovery. These exercises may help you manage and learn from your feelings, know yourself, and aid in the struggle for forgiveness. These practices may also aid in the recovery of those who have been unfaithful.

1. ANGER: NURTURING YOUR INNER CHILD

Thich Nhat Hanh, a Vietnamese Buddhist monk exiled to France, taught an approach to coping with anger. He suggested that our anger is like a "howling baby," suffering and crying. An infant cries when it is in distress. Some need is not being met, and the infant, unable to verbalize the need, cries out for attention and care. A loving parent does not ignore the cries or become impatient with them. Instead, the parent has compassion for the child and tries to understand why he is crying. Is he hungry, wet, tired, or in pain? What is causing the suffering? What needs to be done to relieve it?

Our anger is a wounded child crying out for attention and care. We are a nurturing mother for our baby, our anger. We can become an impatient, neglectful, or punishing parent toward our anger, and only increase our suffering. Or we can embrace our anger with tenderness and listen to the wounded child within. We can try to understand the suffering that underlies our anger. Why are we crying out in anger? What is the pain we are experiencing? Are we feeling frightened, sad, ashamed, or helpless? Anger is a complex emotion, and it is not easy to disentangle the knot of feelings involved in it. However, unless we understand the suffering that underlies our anger and its causes, we will not escape our misery. We may believe that others cause our anger, but the reality is that the seed of anger lies within us. We need to explore what inner wound is expressed through our angry reaction.

Thich Nhat Hanh suggests a deep relaxation exercise for embracing and healing anger. To counter the tension of anger, it is helpful to cultivate a relaxed body and mind. The best position for this exercise is lying on your back in a quiet place. Next, focus your attention on a part of your body, such as your heart. Follow your breath, being aware of your heart as you breathe in and smiling as you breathe out. Have a sense of love and tenderness toward yourself. Then begin scanning your body with a beam of mindfulness, as if with a searchlight. While breathing deeply from your abdomen, scan your body slowly from your head to your feet, being aware of each of the areas. Say to yourself, "Breathing in, I calm my whole body, breathing out, I feel peace." You can sense your muscle tension, which holds your anger, disappear as you maintain your attention on your breath and body. Spend twenty to thirty minutes with this exercise, showing yourself love.[1]

2. MENTAL NOTING

Children are increasingly being diagnosed with attention deficit disorder and prescribed medication to help them focus their attention. However, we live in a culture that encourages us to keep busy, productive, entertained, and distracted. In short, we live in a society that suffers from attention deficit disorder. The price we pay for being so distracted is that we rarely stop, look, and listen enough to understand ourselves and our reactions. Joseph Goldstein, a spiritual teacher, describes a technique of "mental noting" to help strengthen personal awareness in the midst of our chaotic lives. This meditation exercise is simple and powerful, with practice. Sit comfortably in a quiet place, with your back erect and eyes closed. Relax and focus on your breathing. Follow your breath and shut out any other distractions. If you are distracted, gently bring your attention back to your breathing. After a few minutes, when you feel calm, allow your attention to follow any physical sensations, thoughts, images, or emotions that spontaneously arise. Just observe these phenomena that pass through your awareness without dwelling on them or making a judgment about them. Just observe them. Now take a mental note of what you are observing by labeling the objects arising in your experience. Gently, "like a whisper in the mind," identify and label what you observe. For example, when thoughts arise, note "thinking." When you notice physical sensations, label them "tension" or "pressure." When feelings or images emerge, note "feeling" or "image." The technique of mental noting helps to keep you undistracted and to highlight your own mental processes. You will begin to observe the recurring thoughts, feelings, and spontaneous judgments you attach to what passes through your mind.[2] What is revealed in this meditation exercise can be the stuff for personal reflection and analysis in your therapy and journaling.

3. MEDITATING ON THE SCRIPTURES

One of the best sources of consolation and self-knowledge for Christians is through praying with the sacred texts of both the Old and New testaments. Christians believe that God personally communicates His wisdom and love through His inspired writings. The Bible is God's love letter addressed to all believers. Through the Scriptures, God speaks personally to those who listen in faith with an open mind and heart. The following is a simple technique for praying with the Scriptures:

1. Choose a short passage from one of the books of the Bible that addresses a current concern. For example, when fearful or worried, read Luke 12:22–31; when sad, read Romans 8:26–39; when feeling guilt, read Psalm 103; when ashamed, read Psalm 8; when angry, read Matthew 5:21–26.

221

2. Sit comfortably in a quiet place. Take a few moments to relax and quiet yourself down. Give all your cares and concerns to the Lord and let Him hold them for you. Be aware of His presence and unconditional love for you. Ask Him to open your mind and heart to His word.

3. Slowly read the chosen Scripture passage and let the words soak into your heart. Believe that the words are God's own words meant specifically for you in your here-and-now situation.

4. Find one or more resting places in the passage, a word or phrase that strikes you. Allow yourself to savor the phrase, repeating it to yourself slowly, and reflecting on it in silence. Remain with the same passage for the whole prayer period.

5. Do not become discouraged if nothing seems to be happening. Sometimes God lets us feel dry and empty to remind us that it is not in our power to communicate with Him and that all consolations come from Him at the time He deems right. It is all part of the healing process.

6. Thank God for His presence during this prayer time.

7. After the period of prayer is over, it may be helpful to reflect over the experience of praying, noticing what the Lord is doing in your experience.

4. REMAINING LIKE A LOG

Another powerful exercise to relieve anger is suggested in the classic Buddhist text, *The Way of the Bodhisattva*. The author, Shantideva, advises,

> *When the urge arises in the mind*
> *To feelings of desire or wrathful hate,*
> *Do not act! Be silent, do not speak!*
> *And like a log of wood be sure to stay.*[3]

In her commentary on this text, Pema Chodron, an American Buddhist monk, describes an exercise she calls "remaining like a log." She advocates the practice of refraining from expressing destructive anger, rather than repressing or indulging it. She observes that the powerful urge to anger builds from a tiny seed and follows a predictable chain reaction. If we bring a calm awareness to the rising anger, we can prevent the explosion. By stopping and observing ourselves as the anger arises, we can let go of the angry thoughts and learn to relax with the underlying energy. Chodron explains that there are four places we can interrupt the urge to anger:

1. At the preverbal level, the anger begins with an initial perception, a sight, sound, thought, or memory, that causes discomfort. Awareness of this initial discomfort and its cause can keep us from fanning the flame with angry thoughts.

2. Next, we can be alert to the angry thoughts that are arising from the discomfort and interrupt them before they gain momentum. Spontaneous thoughts of hurt and revenge emerge.

3. If we overlook these subtle thoughts that accompany our anger, our emotions will escalate. Even at this point it is not too late to stop the avalanche of emotion if we focus attention on our thinking pattern.

4. Finally, there is a moment before the angry thoughts and emotions lead to action. We can learn to stop, think, and observe ourselves at this point before speaking or acting out. We can consider how we want to act. We are not helpless, even in the face of intense emotion that seems overwhelming.[4]

5. SEEING THE GOOD

In the midst of self-blame, it is easy to overlook your basic goodness. Sharon Salzberg suggests an exercise to combat self-critical thoughts. Sit comfortably in a quiet place with your back erect and eyes closed. Relax yourself by following your breath for a few minutes and dispel any distracting thoughts. Especially let go of critical and judgmental thoughts. When you are relaxed, call to mind some kind or good action you performed. Think of a time when you were generous, caring, or loving. Think about what you did, how you felt, and how the other person reacted. Allow yourself to feel the happiness that accompanies the memory. Dwell on the memory and the peaceful feelings for a few minutes. If distracting negative thoughts arise, do not fight them; return gently to the happy memory. Express gratitude to yourself for the opportunity you had to be so kind. If no event comes immediately to mind, focus your attention on some quality you appreciate in yourself, an ability, a strength, or even a desire for happiness.[5] Instead of the natural tendency to focus on what is missing in yourself, this exercise reminds you of the more fundamental truth of your goodness.

An extension of this exercise in self-appreciation is an exercise in seeing the goodness of your unfaithful partner. That may be particularly difficult for you because you have been shaken by his betrayal and are naturally focused on the harm he has caused and all his negative qualities. You may find yourself rebelling at the suggestion of trying to appreciate his goodness. That is a perfectly natural reaction. I recommend that you approach this exercise slowly, only when you are ready. You will be surprised when you take the risk of changing your perspective at how freeing it is. Again, find a quiet place, sit comfortably, and focus on your breathing. When you feel relaxed, think about some quality in your partner that you appreciate. Think about when you first met and what attracted you to him. Think about what led you to make that initial commitment to him in your relationship. Perhaps you appreciated his kindness, sense of humor, generosity, or ambition. If negative thoughts or angry feelings intrude, gently acknowledge them and let them pass. Do not dwell on them. Instead, return your focus to the good quality or memory of your partner. Allow yourself to feel some warmth toward him. If it is particularly difficult to attend to a positive quality in him, think about his desire to be happy, which everyone shares. When all is said and done, we are united in our desire to be happy. Relax for fifteen or twenty minutes in this exercise.

6. MEDITATING ON THE PARABLE OF THE FORGIVING FATHER

An effective way of making the Scriptures come alive is through imaginative visualization. The procedure is simple and straightforward. Select a Scripture passage, read it slowly, and imagine you are there, transported back in time and personally experiencing the event. If you are struggling with forgiving yourself and your partner, meditating on the familiar parable of the forgiving father (commonly called the Parable of the Prodigal Son) in Luke 15:11–32 can be helpful. It is a story of the triumph of life over death and loss. A father had two sons. The younger wanted his inheritance, left home, and squandered his fortune. Meanwhile, the older son remained home, was dutiful, and cared for the land. Imagine yourself as the younger son who loses his fortune and feels desperate and alone. Allow yourself to feel his pain and humiliation. Acknowledging his situation honestly, he comes to his senses, returns home, and begs his father's forgiveness. What joy he feels in unexpectedly being embraced by his father who throws a feast in his honor. Instead of berating him, as he expected, his father welcomes him, exclaiming, "This son of mine was dead and has come back to life. He was lost and is found." Now imagine yourself as the faithful older son who feels resentment at his brother's departure and jealousy at the welcome he receives from their father. Allow yourself to feel his pain and resentment. Listen to his father's loving words to him, "You are with me always, and everything I have is yours." Consider the younger son's embarrassment at being reminded of how much he took his life for granted and did not appreciate what he had. Now imagine yourself as the loving, forgiving father who misses his son terribly, hoping for his safe return. Allow yourself to feel his sadness at his son's absence, his longing for his return, and his pride in his older son. Imagine the overwhelming joy he feels when he sees his son in the distance and his excitement to celebrate the good news that the dead has come back to life, the lost has been found. With whom do you most naturally identify in the story? Who would you most like to be? What experiences do you need to appreciate your life more fully?

7. A FORGIVING LETTER TO OUR PARENTS

Throughout the book, I have encouraged you to keep a journal of your experience. Your daily journal becomes your personal diary about your recovery. You have traveled a long distance in your journey of healing, only to arrive where you have always been but not known it. You have arrived at yourself. You have written about the trauma of being betrayed and your struggles to forgive yourself and your partner. You have expressed your deep longings for happiness and extended compassion to those close to you. Now write about what you have discovered about yourself through the lens of your childhood experience. What was it like growing up? How were you nurtured as a child? How did your parents fail to give you what you needed? How did you respond? What are you most angry about? What did you miss growing up? How have these losses affected you as an adult? Were your parents faithful to each other and to the children? Were you physically or sexually abused? What do you need to forgive? Pay close attention to the spots that hurt and also to your desire for healing.

This may be an extremely difficult exercise for those who were traumatized as children by physical or sexual abuse or profound neglect. Approach this exercise with caution and gentleness with yourself, aware of your reactions. If it is too overwhelmingly painful, do not attempt it, because the exercise may provoke flashbacks. You may be flooded with memories and feelings too overwhelming to manage. The first rule in approaching this exercise, as with all others, is to be gentle with yourself. Undertake the exercise only when you are ready. If the memories of childhood are too painful, it may be helpful to explore them with a competent therapist and not try to work through them on your own.

An effective way of making peace with your childhood, when you are ready, is to write a personal letter to your parents, expressing where you felt wounded and your desire to forgive. It is important to address your parent as the adult you are today, putting into words your deepest feelings. If your parent was unfaithful, you suffered a personal injury, feeling betrayed by this person in whom you put so much trust. You need to express the full impact of the injury to yourself in order to let go of it through forgiveness and move on with your life. In the letter, explain how you felt as a child and how you feel now as an adult. Tell your parent how your life has been affected by the injury and how you have worked to overcome the hurt. Admit any struggles to forgive them and express your desire to forgive. If your parent is alive, you may decide to send the letter to open up communication, although that is not necessary. What is important is that you acknowledge your experience in words, whether or not you send the letter.

I further recommend that you write a second letter to yourself from your offending parent. Imagine what your parent would write to you if he were truly remorseful for the harm he caused you. Make this letter an apology letter from your parent that includes a heartfelt apology, an acceptance of full responsibility for his behavior, an awareness of how he has hurt you, and an explanation, without making any excuses, of what led him to the hurtful behavior. Such a letter invites you to put yourself in the shoes of your parent and feel empathy for him, which can open your heart to forgiveness.

8. A GRATITUDE EXERCISE

Dr. Martin Seligman, a renowned psychologist, has initiated a movement within the field of psychology from an almost exclusive focus on mental illness and its treatment to a focus on personal growth. He calls it positive psychology. In his book *Authentic Happiness*, Dr. Seligman presents, as a result of his extensive research, a formula for happiness: $H = S + C + V$. Happiness is the sum of our genetic set range (S), life circumstances (C), and voluntary variables (V). He contends that each of us has inherited a specific level of happiness or sadness from birth. We are reflections of our parents' level of contentment, based on their personality and temperament. Dr. Seligman indicates that about 50 percent of our potential for life satisfaction is genetically influenced. We Americans, who value having freedom to pursue happiness, believe we can create the circumstances to achieve it. Furthermore, we tend to believe that having money, status, health, success, a good job, and satisfying relationships will produce the contentment we seek. Surprisingly, research shows that favorable circumstances account for only 8–15 percent of a satisfied state of mind. More than a third, 35–40 percent, of our happiness is attributable to the voluntary attitudes we develop about our lives.[6] As Abraham Lincoln observed, "Most folks are about as happy as they make up their minds to be." I frequently remind my patients that they may not be able to change the conditions of their lives, but they are free to determine their attitudes toward those conditions. I also remind them, often contrary to their beliefs, that their joy in life is more dependent on how they think than on what happens to them.

Dr. Seligman recommends a gratitude exercise to increase our general level of happiness. Take five minutes each night to reflect on what you are grateful for in your life. Write down at least five things in your journal. For example, you might feel grateful for waking up each day, having a good conversation with a friend, or enjoying good health. The purpose of the exercise is to shift the focus of your attention to what is positive in your life, rather than being weighed down with negative, self-defeating thoughts. I also suggest that you end the exercise with a prayer of thanksgiving, to remind yourself of the inexhaustible Source of all blessings.

NOTES

INTRODUCTION

1. Shirley Glass, *Not Just Friends* (New York: Free Press, 2003).

2. S. S. Janus and C. L. Janus, *The Janus Report on Sexual Behavior* (New York: Wiley, 1993).

3. Elizabeth Kubler-Ross, *On Death and Dying* (New York: Scribner, 1969).

4. All quotes from the Hebrew and Christian Scriptures are from *The New American Bible*.

5. Phil Lane, Judie Bopp, et al., *The Sacred Tree* (Twin Lakes, WI: Lotus Press, 2004).

6. Word Power, "Quotations by Jalal ad-Din Muhammad Rumi." http://www.wordpower.ws/quotations/rumi-quotes-sufi-mysticism.html.

7. Indries Shah, *The Way of the Sufi* (New York: Dutton, 1970), 224.

CHAPTER ONE

1. Some of the details in this story were previously published by the author in a slightly revised version in *Spirituality and Health* ("Recovery from Infidelity as a Post-Traumatic Stress Disorder," November/December 2004: 19) and the *Journal of Psychosocial Nursing* ("Post-Infidelity Stress Disorder," vol. 43, no. 10, October 2005: 46–54).

2. *Diagnostic and Statistical Manual of Mental Disorders IV* (Washington, DC: American Psychiatric Association, 2000).

3. The concept of post-infidelity stress disorder was previously published by the author in a slightly revised version in *Spirituality and Health* ("Recovery from Infidelity as a Post-Traumatic Stress Disorder," November/December 2004: 19) and the *Journal of Psychosocial Nursing* ("Post-Infidelity Stress Disorder," vol. 43, no. 10, October 2005: 46–54).

4. Eric Erikson, *Identity, Youth, and Crisis* (New York: Norton, 1968), 97.

5. Thomas H. Johnson, ed., Poem 599. *The Poems of Emily Dickinson* (Cambridge, MA: Belknap Press, 1983), 460.

CHAPTER TWO

1. R. Kessler, K. McGonagle, S. Zhao, et al., "Lifetime and 12 Month Prevalence of DSM-III-R Psychiatric Disorders in the United States: Results from the National Comorbidity Study," *Archives of General Psychiatry* no. 51 (1994): 8–19.

2. Glass, 1.

3. Kessler et al.

4. Annette Lawson, *Adultery: An Analysis of Love and Betrayal* (New York: Basic Books, 1988).

CHAPTER THREE

1. *Diagnostic and Statistical Manual of Mental Disorders IV* (Washington, DC: American Psychiatric Association, 2000).

2. Patrick Carnes, *The Betrayal Bond* (Dearfield Beach, FL: Health Communications, 1997).

CHAPTER FOUR

1. Patrick Carnes, "Facing the Shadow" (lecture, Troy, MI, February 26, 2004).

CHAPTER FIVE

1. The source of the research summarized in this section is Bessel A. van der Kolk, "The Body Keeps Score: Approaches to the Psychobiology of Posttraumatic Stress Disorder," *Traumatic Stress* (New York: Guilford Press, 1996), eds. B. van der Kolk, A. McFarlane, and L. Weisaeth, 214–241.

CHAPTER SIX

1. John Bowlby, *Attachment* (London: Penguin, 1969).

2. Mary Ainsworth, M. Blehar, C. Waters, and S. Wall, *Patterns of Attachment: A Psychological Study of the Strange Situation* (Hillsdale, NJ: Erbaum, 1978).

3. Kim Bartholomew and Leonard Horowitz, "Attachment Styles among Young Adults: A Test of a Four-Category Model," *Journal of Personality and Social Psychology* no. 61 (1991): 226–44.

4. Karen Horney, *Our Inner Conflicts* (New York: Norton, 1945).

5. From the collection of stories and sayings by Idries Shah, *The Way of the Sufi* (New York: Dutton, 1970), 63.

CHAPTER SEVEN

1. John Cook, comp., *The Book of Positive Quotations*, 2nd ed. (Minnesota: Fairview, 2007), 65.

2. Emily Brown, *Patterns of Infidelity and Their Treatment*, 2nd ed. (Philadelphia: Brunner Routledge, 2001).

3. Robin Norwood, *Women Who Love Too Much* (Los Angeles: Jeremy Tarcher, 1985).

4. Sigmund Freud, *On Narcissism*, vol. 14, standard ed. (London: Hogarth Press, 1957).

CHAPTER EIGHT

1. Morton Hunt, *The Affair* (New York: World Publishing, 1969).

2. Lawson.

3. *The Spiritual Exercises of St. Ignatius*, trans. Louis Puhl (New York: Random House, 2000).

CHAPTER NINE

1. Alan Godlas, "Sufism: Struggle with One's Nafs," *Sufism's Many Paths*, University of Georgia, http://www.uga.edu/islam/Sufism.html.

2. Thomas Cleary, *Dhammapada: The Sayings of Buddha* (New York: Bantam Books, 1995), 39.

3. Anthony de Mello, *The Song of the Bird* (New York: Doubleday, 1982), 65.

4. Pema Chodron, *When Things Fall Apart* (Boston: Shambhala, 2000), 10.

5. Cleary, 56.

CHAPTER TEN

1. Anthony de Mello, *The Song of the Bird* (New York: Doubleday, 1982), 123.

2. Chodron, 34–35.

EPILOGUE

1. *The Essential Rumi: New Expanded Edition* (San Francisco: HarperSanFrancisco, 2004), 299.

2. *The Tao Te Ching*, trans. Ralph Alan Dale (London: Watkins Publ., 2006), verse 22.

3. Father Ray Sayers, pers. comm.

4. Anthony de Mello, *One Minute Wisdom* (New York: Doubleday, 1985), 202.

APPENDIX

1. Thich Nhat Hanh, *Anger* (New York: Berkley, 2001), 32–35.

2. Joseph Goldstein, *Insight Meditation* (Boston: Shambhala, 2003), 34–38.

3. Shantideva, *The Way of the Bodhisattva*, trans. Padmakara Translation Group (Boston: Shambhala, 1997), verse 48.

4. Pema Chodron, *No Time to Lose* (Boston: Shambhala, 2005), 129–31.

5. Sharon Salzberg, *Loving-Kindness* (Boston: Shambhala, 2002), 29.

6. Martin Seligman, *Authentic Happiness* (New York: Free Press, 2002), 45–61.

SUGGESTED READING

INFIDELITY

Glass, Shirley. *Not Just Friends: Rebuilding Trust and Recovering Your Sanity after Infidelity*. New York: Free Press, 2003.

Lusterman, Don-David. *Infidelity: A Survival Guide*. Oakland: New Harbinger, 1998.

Pittman, Frank. *Private Lies: Infidelity and Betrayal of Intimacy*. New York: Norton, 1989.

Solomon, Steven, and Lorie Teagno. *Intimacy after Infidelity: How to Rebuild and Affair-Proof Your Marriage*. Oakland: New Harbinger, 2006.

Spring, Janis. *After the Affair: Healing the Pain and Rebuilding Trust When a Partner Has Been Unfaithful*. New York: HarperCollins, 1997.

Subotnik, Rona, and Gloria Harris. *Surviving Infidelity: Making Decisions, Recovering from the Pain*. 3rd ed. Avon, MA: Adams Media, 2005.

CODEPENDENCY

Beattie, Melanie. *Codependent No More and Beyond Codependency*. New York: Fine Communications, 2001.

Carnes, Patrick. *The Betrayal Bond: Breaking Free of Exploitative Relationships*. Deerfield Beach, FL: Health Communications, 1997.

Mellody, Pia. *Facing Codependency: What It Is, Where It Comes from, How It Sabotages Our Lives*. New York: HarperCollins, 1989.

Norwood, Robin. *Women Who Love Too Much: When You Keep Wishing and Hoping He'll Change*. Los Angeles: Jeremy Tarcher, 1985.

ANGER

Goleman, Daniel, ed. *Destructive Emotions: How Can We Overcome Them?* New York: Random House, 2003.

Nhat Hanh, Thich. *Anger: Wisdom for Cooling the Flames*. New York: Penguin, 2001.

Tavris, Carol. *Anger: The Misunderstood Emotion*. New York: Simon and Schuster, 1982.

INTIMACY

Gottman, John. *The Relationship Cure*. With J. DeClaire. New York: Crown, 2001.

Gottman, John. *The Seven Principles for Making Marriage Work*. With Nan Silver. New York: Three Rivers, 1999.

Hendrix, Harville. *Getting the Love You Want*. New York: Harper & Row, 1990.

Lerner, Harriet. *The Dance of Intimacy: A Woman's Guide to Courageous Acts of Change in Key Relationships*. New York: HarperCollins, 1989.

Sanford, John. *The Invisible Partners: How the Male and Female in Each of Us Affects Our Relationships*. New York: Paulist Press, 1980.

Viorst, Judith. *Necessary Losses: The Loves, Illusions, Dependencies, and Impossible Expectations That All of Us Have to Give Up in Order to Grow*. New York: Free Press, 1986.

TRAUMA RECOVERY

Herman, Judith. *Trauma and Recovery: The Aftermath of Violence, from Domestic Abuse to Political Terror*. New York: Basic Books, 1992.

Schiraldi, Glenn. *The Post-Traumatic Stress Disorder Sourcebook: A Guide to Healing, Recovery, and Growth*. New York: McGraw-Hill, 2000.

FORGIVENESS

Meninger, William. *The Process of Forgiveness*. New York: Continuum, 1996.

Salzberg, Sharon. *Loving-Kindness: The Revolutionary Art of Happiness*. Boston: Shambhala, 2002.

Spring, Janis. *How Can I Forgive You?* New York: HarperCollins, 2006.

Worthington, Everett L. *Five Steps to Forgiveness*. New York: Crown, 2001.

SPIRITUALITY

Goldstein, Joseph. *Insight Meditation: The Practice of Freedom*. Boston: Shambhala, 2003.

Kabat-Zinn, Jon. *Wherever You Go There You Are: Mindfulness Meditation in Everyday Life*. New York: Hyperion, 1994.

Kornfield, Jack. *A Path with Heart: A Guide through the Perils and Promises of Spiritual Life*. New York: Bantam Books, 1993.

Kornfield, Jack. *The Wise Heart: A Guide to the Universal Teachings of Buddhist Psychology*. New York: Bantam Books, 2008.

Lane, Phil, Judie Bopp, et al. *The Sacred Tree: Reflections on Native American Spirituality*. Twin Lakes, WI: Lotus Press, 2004.

Merton, Thomas. *New Seeds of Contemplation*. New York: New Directions Publ., 1972.

Nhat Hanh, Thich. *Living Buddha, Living Christ*. New York: Riverhead, 1996.

Nhat Hanh, Thich. *The Miracle of Mindfulness: An Introduction to the Practice of Meditation*. Boston: Beacon Press, 1975.

Norris, Kathleen. *Amazing Grace: A Vocabulary of Faith*. New York: Riverhead, 1998.

Nouwen, Henri. *Reaching Out: The Three Movements of the Spiritual Life*. New York: Doubleday, 1975.

Tolle, Eckert. *The Power of Now: A Guide to Spiritual Enlightenment*. Novato, CA: New World Library, 1999.

INDEX